Illustrated Sporting Books

J Herbert Slater

Copyright © BiblioLife, LLC

This book represents a historical reproduction of a work originally published before 1923 that is part of a unique project which provides opportunities for readers, educators and researchers by bringing hard-to-find original publications back into print at reasonable prices. Because this and other works are culturally important, we have made them available as part of our commitment to protecting, preserving and promoting the world's literature. These books are in the "public domain" and were digitized and made available in cooperation with libraries, archives, and open source initiatives around the world dedicated to this important mission.

We believe that when we undertake the difficult task of re-creating these works as attractive, readable and affordable books, we further the goal of sharing these works with a global audience, and preserving a vanishing wealth of human knowledge.

Many historical books were originally published in small fonts, which can make them very difficult to read. Accordingly, in order to improve the reading experience of these books, we have created "enlarged print" versions of our books. Because of font size variation in the original books, some of these may not technically qualify as "large print" books, as that term is generally defined; however, we believe these versions provide an overall improved reading experience for many.

ILLUSTRATED SPORTING BOOKS.

A DESCRIPTIVE SURVEY OF A COLLECTION OF ENGLISH ILLUSTRATED WORKS OF A SPORTING AND RACY CHARACTER,

WITH AN

APPENDIX OF PRINTS RELATING TO SPORTS OF THE FIELD.

By J. HERBERT SLATER.

EDITOR OF "*Book Prices Current,*" *and* "*Sale Prices*"
AUTHOR OF "*The Romance of Book Collecting,*" "*The Library Manual,*" "*Engravings and their Value,*" "*Round and about the Bookstalls,*" etc., etc.

LONDON:
L. UPCOTT GILL, 170, STRAND, W.C.

1899

PRINTED BY
THE "SURBITON TIMES," LIMITED,
SURBITON HILL S.W.

CONTENTS.

	PAGE
Illustrated Sporting Books.	1—140
Additions and Corrections	140—150
Appendix of Prints as under:—	
Ballooning	154
Boxing	156
Bull and Badger Baiting, Dog Fighting, Ratting	158
Coaching, Driving, Riding	159
Cock Fighting	164
Coursing	165
Fishing	165
Hunting	166
Portraits (Sportsmen)	174
Portraits (Race Horses)	177
Racing	182
Shooting (including Sporting Dogs)	187
Various	190

INTRODUCTION.

There are one or two points which I think it necessary to elaborate for the assistance of those who may have occasion to consult this Catalogue of Sporting Books and Prints.

In the first place it will be observed that, with very few exceptions, only English illustrated books are dealt with. The vast majority of sporting books contain illustrations or at least a frontispiece. Those which do not are generally very old, but even the majority of these have been reprinted with illustrations, and consequently come within the scope of the work and are noticed accordingly.

Bibliographers who have dealt with this branch of literature have hitherto adopted one of two methods of arrangement. They either catalogue the works they notice under the names of their authors, or else in order of date. Both these methods seem to me to be more or less unsatisfactory. Quick reference is what is now sought for in books of the kind. In furtherance of this desirable end I have adopted a system of titular arrangement, adding cross references where necessary, and supplying an index of author's names. For instance, Apperley's "Memoirs of the Life of the late John Mytton" is popularly quoted as the 'Life of John Mytton." Though the biography must therefore be looked for under "Memoirs," I have added a cross reference, and many other books are dealt with, when the necessity demands, in precisely the same way, so that with the assistance of the index very little time need be spent in turning to any book that may be required. If a book cannot be found under what the reader believes to be the correct title, reference should be made to the Index, and in any case attention is called to the additions and corrections on page 140, *et seq*. The Prints are arranged under subjects for the reason that many of them have no well-known titles or, at any rate, no titles that are quoted in the same way on all occasions.

It will be observed that not only sporting books, strictly so called, are catalogued, but books of a racy character also. Pierce Egan's "Life in London," the work entitled "Fashion and Folly, or the Buck's Pilgrimage," and many other old time publications of a similar character are thus dealt with. When these books were written the word "Sport" had a much wider application than it has now.

The prices given throughout the volume have nearly all been realised by auction within the last twelve months. In the case of some very scarce and valuable books it has been found necessary to draw upon a much greater period of time, since books of this exclusive kind may not appear more than once or twice in the market for many years. As a rule, however, the quoted values will be found approximately accurate, having regard to the condition and binding mentioned after each entry. It may be observed that in the case of books worth more than about £1, bookseller's prices would necessarily be considerably higher; under that amount they would not seem to vary so much from the auction values quoted. The reason for this will be sufficiently obvious. All the books and prints included in this descriptive survey, which are not quite new and in print, have a distinct tendency to advance in price. They are, year by year, becoming more difficult to meet with, and some of them will, in the near future, be practically unobtainable.

So far as Angling Books are concerned, reference should be made to the extensive library of books of this character formed by the late Mr. Edward Snow, of Boston, U.S.A., which was sold by Messrs. Sotheby, on November 30th, and following day, 1898. The prices realised at this sale were, however, considerably above the average.

J. H. SLATER.

May 1st, 1899.

ILLUSTRATED SPORTING BOOKS.

Above the Snow Line. Mountaineering Sketches between 1870 and 1880, by Clinton Dent, 1885. 8vo. pp. xiv. 327. 4s. (cl.) Published at 7s. 6d.

Academie de l'Espée, L', par Girard Thibault, 1628. Atlas folio, Portrait, 9 plates of armorial bearings and 46 large plates by Bolswaert, Crispin de Passe, and others £15 (cf., sound copy) There is only one edition of this book, and neither the place where it was published nor the name of the printer is mentioned. M Pieters thought that it was printed at Leyden by the Elzevirs.

Academy for Grown Horsemen, An, by "Geoffrey Gambado" (H. W. Bunbury), and **Annals of Horsemanship,** by the same, 1787-91. 2 vols. 4to. The Academy contains 12 plates, and the Annals of Horsemanship 17, all after H. W. Bunbury. £1 12s (old cf.)

Another edition, 1808. 4to Plates as before. £1 1s. (bds., uncut)

Another edition, 1809. 8vo 29 col. pl. by Rowlandson. £1 5s (bds.)

Another edition, 1812 Fol 29 col. pl. £1 5s. (bds.), £2 2s. (mor. ex.)

Another edition, n d 8vo Ackermann 29 col. pl. by Rowlandson and others. £2 10s (orig bds)

An edition of 1822, in 2 vols, roy 4to, is of no importance, and of but little value. The plates are reduced copies.

Account of the Game of Curling, with songs for the Canon-Mills Curling Club, by "A Member of the Duddingston Curling Society" (John Ramsay), 1811. Privately printed and scarce. £1 4s. (cf.)

Another edition, 1882. 8vo. 250 copies printed. 4s. (parchment).

Across Country, by "Wanderer," 1882 8vo. Col. plates, 7s. 6d. (hf. mor.)

Across England in a Dog Cart, by James John Hissey, 1891. 8vo. Illustrated. 8s (orig. cl.)

Adventures in the Air of Great Aeronauts, By W. De Fonvielle, 1877. Cr. 8vo. Illustrations. 3s. 6d. (cl.) Translated from the French by J. S. Keltie.

Adventures of Dr. Comicus, in 12 cantos, By a Modern Syntax. n. d. 8vo. 15 col. pl. £1 5s. (hf. russ.)

Adventures of a Post Captain, By a Naval Officer. 1st ed. 1817. 8vo. with 25 col. pl. by Williams. £4 12s. (orig. bds., uncut) £1 12s. (hf. cf.)

Adventures of Johnny Newcome in the Navy, a Poem in four Cantos, by John Mitford. 1st ed. 1818. 8vo. with 20 full page col. pl. by Williams. £1 16s. (cf ex.)

Second edition, 1819. 8vo. Col. plates as before. £1 5s. (calf).

This work is sometimes quoted as "The Adventures of Johnny Newcome in the Navy," by Alfred Burton, but "Alfred Burton" was merely the *nom de plume* of Captain John Mitford, R N., above named, and the books are one and the same. *See* also "Military Adventures of Johnny Newcome."

Advice to Sportsmen, . . . with Anecdotes of the most renowned Shots of the day, by "Marmaduke Markwell," 1809. 12mo. Plates by Rowlandson. £3 10s. (orig. bds., col. plates). 16s. (cf., plain plates)

Æroplaustic Art, The, or Navigation in the Air by the use of Kites or buoyant Sails, by George Pocock, 1827, 4to. Col. plates. 12s (orig. bds.)

African Hunting, from Natal to the Zambesi, by W. C. Baldwin, 1863. Cr. 8vo. Illustrations by J. Wolf and J. B. Zwecker. 4s. (orig. cl.) This work, though dated 1863 on the title, was first published in 1862.

Third edition, 1894. 8vo. pp. x. 428. 4s. (orig. cl.)

Airy Nothings, or Scraps and Naughts and Odd-cum-Shorts . . . by Olio Rigmaroll. A series of 23 coloured plates by Hunt, 1825. 4to. £5 10s (mor. ex., uncut, fine copy). £2 10s. (original hf. binding).

Alken's Sketches, The Stable, The Road, The Park, The Field. 1st ed. 1854. Oblong fol. A series of six coloured sporting subjects, by Henry Alken. £1 16s. (orig. wrappers)

Almanac of Twelve Sports, by W. Nicholson. Twelve large coloured plates mounted on cardboard, words by Rudyard Kipling. 1898. Folio. £1 13s. (in a Portfolio). 5s. (cl. as issued) 4to

Alpine Ascents and Adventures, by H. S. Wilson, 1878. Cr. 8vo. Illustrations by Edward Whymper. 9s (hf. mor., g.e.) Published at 10s. 6d.

Second edition, 1878. Cr. 8vo. Same illustrations. 3s. (orig. cl.) Published at 10s. 6d.

Alpine Club Journal, The. Edited by H. B. George. Illustrated throughout. Vol. 1. appeared in 1864. 8vo. £5 2s. (vols. i. to iii. uncut), £9 18s (Vols. i. to viii. hf. cf., vols. ix. and x. sewed).

Alpine Guide, The, by John Ball. Part 1, A Guide to the Western Alps. Part 2, The Central Alps. Part 3, The Eastern Alps. 1863-68. 8vo. Col. plates and maps. 10s (cl.) Published at £1 6s. 6d.

Another edition. 3 Parts, 1866-69. 8vo. Maps. 10s. (cl.)
Another edition. Part 2. 1869. 8vo. Maps. 2s. (cl.)
Another edition. 3 Parts, 1873. 8vo. Maps. 10s. (cl.)

Alpine Regions of Switzerland and the Neighbouring Countries, by T. G. Bonney, 1868. 8vo. Illustrations by Edward Whymper. 22s (cl., uncut).

Alps, The, or Sketches of Life and Nature in the Mountains, by H. Berlepsch, translated by Leslie Stephen, 1861. 8vo. 17 tinted plates by Rittmeyer. £1 5s (orig. cl.) Published at 15s.

Alps from End to End, The, by Sir William Martin Conway, 1895. 8vo., with 100 full page illustrations by A. D. McCormick, £1 14s. (L. P., hf. vel.) Published in June at 21s., or on large paper at £4 4s.

Second edition, 1895. 8vo. Same illustrations. 10s. (small paper, orig. cl.) Published in September at 21s.

Alps in 1864, The, by A. W. Moore, 1867. 8vo. Privately printed. Maps. £7 7s. (orig. cl., uncut). The British Museum Library does not contain a copy of this scarce book.

Amateur of Fencing, The, or a Treatise on the Art of Sword-Defence, by Joseph Roland. 1809. 8vo. Etching by Frewer. 12s. (calf).

American Four-in-Hand in Britain, An, by A. Carnegie, 1883. 8vo. Frontispiece. 8s (orig. cl.) Published at 10s. 6d. A popular edition appeared the following year at 1s.

Among the Red Deer. Sketches from Nature in the Forest, by Lt.-Gen. H. H. Crealock, n. d. Folio. Photographs. £2 (hf. mor.) £3 15s (*ibid.*)

Analysis of Horsemanship; teaching the whole Art of Riding in Manège, Military, Hunting, Racing and Travelling System, together with the Method of Breaking Horses, by John Adams. 1st ed. 1799. 8vo. Plates. 6s (cf.)

Another edition, 1805. 3 vols. 8vo. Enlarged. 12s. (bds.)

Analysis of the Hunting Field, by R. S. Surtees, 1846. Oblong 8vo., with col. title, 6 col. pl. and 43 cuts, all by H. Alken. £3 3s. (orig. cl.) £5 (*ibid.*) £7 10s. (*ibid.*) The papers reprinted in this volume appeared in *Bell's Life* during 1845-46

Anatomy of the Horse, by George Stubbs 1st ed 1766 Atlas folio. Plates £2 2s. (hf mor.) Published at £4 4s. The plates are numbered 1 to 15, but some of them having counterparts in outline are counted as 24 in the second edition.

Second edition, 1853. Folio Same plates folded. 10s. (orig. cl.) The impressions in this edition are very inferior.

Anecdotes of Archery, by E. and A. E Hargrove, 1845 8vo Plates. 5s. (orig. cl.) This is the best edition, being revised and much improved by A E Hargrove The first edition appeared in 1792, 12 mo pp 104, with engravings of the Medals of the Yorkshire and Darlington Archers.

Anecdotes of the Turf, the Chase, &c., *see* **Pierce Egan's Anecdotes.**

Anecdotes on the Origin and Antiquity of Horse Racing, 1825. 12mo Front. £1 2s. (calf, g e.) A scarce pamphlet of 57 pp, published by T. Gosden, London.

Angler, The, a Poem in ten Cantos, with proper instructions in the Art, &c., by "Piscator" (T. P. Lathy) 1819. 12mo. Engraved front. 2s. (cf)

Angler and his Friend, The, or Piscatory Colloquies and Fishing Excursions, by J Davy, 1855 12mo. Front. sometimes col by hand 5s (orig. cl.) Published at 6s.

Angler and the Loop Rod, The, by David Webster, 1885 Post 8vo. Illustrations of Flies, and Diagrams. pp xii 340. 3s. (orig. cl.) Published at 7s. 6d.

Angler in Ireland, The, or an Englishman's Ramble through Connaught and Munster, 1834. 2 vols. 8vo. Illustrations. 5s. (bds.) Published at 21s.

Angler in the Lake Districts, The, or Piscatory Colloquies and Fishing Excursions in Westmoreland and Cumberland, by J. Davy, 1857. 12mo. Cuts. 5s. (orig. cl.) Published at 6s 6d.

Angler in Wales, The, or Days and Nights of Sportsmen. by Thomas Medwin, 1834. 2 vols. 8vo. 17 illustrations. 6s. (bds., uncut). Published at £1 4s.

Angler's Assistant, The, or a New and Complete Treatise on the Art of Angling. Plate. n.d. 8vo. W. Mason. £1 1s. (hf. mor.)

Angler's Companion to the Rivers and Lochs of Scotland, The, by T. Stoddart. 1st ed. 1847. 8vo. Map, front. and vignettes. 5s. (cl.)

Another edition, 1853. 8vo. Front. and vignettes. 3s. (cl.)

Third edition, 1864. 8vo. Front. and vignettes. 3s. (cl.)

Angler's Complete Guide to the Rivers and Lakes of England, The, by Robert Blakey. 1st. ed. 1853. 12mo. Illustrations. 3s. 6d. (orig. bds.)

Second edition, 1859. 8vo. Revised and much enlarged. Illustrations. 3s. 6d. (orig. bds.)

Anglers' Evenings: Papers by Members of the Manchester Anglers' Association, 1880-94. Three series in 3 vols. Cr. 8vo. Illustrated by W. G. Baxter and George Sheffield. 12s. (cl., uncut).

Angler's Guide, The, A Complete Treatise on the Art of Angling by T. F. Salter, 1833. Cr. 8vo. Portrait, plan of the Lea, 8 plates, and 88 woodcuts. 3s. (bds.) This is the 8th edition, the last corrected by the author. The following editions appeared previously:

First edition, 1814. 8vo. Three full page illustrations and 152 cuts in text. 7s. (bds.)

Second edition, 1815. 8vo. Front. and cuts. 7s. (bds.)

Third edition, 1815. 8vo. 50 plates and woodcuts.

Fourth edition, 1816. 8vo. Cuts.

Fifth edition, n.d. (1823), Sherwood. 8vo. Two aquatints, map of the River Lea, and cuts.

Sixth edition, 1825. 8vo. Front. and plates.

Seventh edition, 1830. 8vo. 4s. (bds.)

Angler's Magazine, The: or Complete Fisherman, to which is added the Angler's Dictionary, By a Gentleman who has made Angling his study upwards of Twenty Years Dublin, 1760. 8vo. £1 8s. (mor. ex., fine copy.)

Angler's Note Book and Naturalist's Record, The. Illustrated 1880-88. 2 vols. Sq. 8vo. 5s. (the "Green" and "Yellow" Series, cl.)

Angler's Souvenir, The, by 'Paul Fisher" (W. A. Chatto). 1st ed. published by Tilt, 1835. Post 8vo. pp x. 192. Steel plates of fish, flies, angling scenes, &c. by Beckwith & Topham. Each page within woodcut border. 10s (orig. cl.) 16s. (L.P. Sq. 8vo., orig. cl.) Re-issued by Bohn, in 1845 and 1847, 8vo., and by Warne and Co., n.d. (1877), Square 8vo. at 7s. 6d. Engraved title and plates. The last-named edition is not complete, and the plates are much worn.

Angler's Sure Guide, The, (by R. Howlet), 1706. 8vo. Front. and plate of fish. 5s. (cf.)

Angler's Vade Mecum, The, by W. Carroll, 1818. 8vo. 12 pl., containing views of 194 different flies, coloured by hand. 12s. (bds.) Contains pp. viii. 128.

Angler's Vade Mecum, The, or a Compendious yet full Discourse of Angling, &c., by "A Lover of Angling" (James Cheetham), 1st. ed. 1681. 12mo. No illustrations. £4 10s. (cf.)

Second edition, 1689. 12mo. 2 plates. £2 (orig. sheep)

Third edition, 1700. 12mo. No illustrations. 18s. (hf. cf.) One illustrated copy of this edition is known, and probably there are two distinct editions of this date.

Angling, being the first part of a series of familiar letters on Sporting, by Robert Lascelles. 1st ed. n.d. (1815), J. Cornes. 8vo. pp. 123. Three illustrations. Three parts, treating of Angling, Shooting, and Coursing. £2 10s. (cf. ex.)

Second edition, 1818. 8vo. Same plates. £2 10s. (cf. ex.)

Angling Sketches, by Andrew Lang, 1891. 8vo. 3 etchings, by W. G. Burn-Murdock. £1 (L. P., 150 copies only). 6s. (small paper, cl.)

Another edition, 1895. 8vo. pp. xii. 185, with 3 etchings by W. G. Burn-Murdock. Published at 3s. 6d.

Angling Songs, by Thomas Tod Stoddart, with memoir by Anna M. Stoddart, 1889. Post 8vo. 3s. (cl.) Published at 7s. 6d.

Angling Sports, 1823-25. Oblong 4to. Six humorous col. pl., by H. Alken. £9 (sewed)

Angling Sports: in Nine Piscatory Dialogues, by Moses Browne, 1773. 8vo. Front. 5s. (antique bds.) This is the third and best edition. The first edition, entitled "Piscatory Eclogues," appeared anonymously in 1729, and the second in the author's poems ten years later.

Angling Travels in Norway, by Fraser Sandeman, 1895. 8vo. Illustrated with 4 col. plates, 57 full page and other engravings. 5s (orig cl.), 12s (hf vellum, L. P.) 200 copies were printed on large paper.

Annals of Gallantry, or the Conjugal Monitor, by A. Moore, 1814-15. 3 vols. 8vo. Col. plates, by Geo. Cruikshank. £10 10s. (uncut).

Second edition, same date, and same number of volumes and plates, £10 10s. (*ibid.*)

Annals of Horsemanship, by "Geoffrey Gambado" (H. W. Bunbury). 1st edition 1791. 4to., with 17 engravings after H. W. Bunbury. 16s (old cf.) *See* **Academy for Grown Horsemen, An.**

Annals of Newgate, The, or the Malefactor's Register, 1776. 4 vols. 8vo. Plates. £1 10s. (calf, sound copy).

Annals of Sporting, by "Caleb Quizem, Esq.," and his various Correspondents, 1809. 8vo., with col. plates by

Woodward and Rowlandson. £4 (orig. bds., uncut) £2 10s. (cf. ex.)

Annals of Sporting and Fancy Gazette, complete in 13 vols. 8vo. 1822-28. Col. plates by Alken and Cruikshank, and plain plates by Landseer, Herring, and others. £31 (a set, hf. cf. gt.) £26 (hf. mor.) Vols. 12 and 13 are very rarely met with.

Annals of the Road, by Harold Esdaile Malet, with Essays on the Road, by "Nimrod" (C. J. Apperley). 1st edition, 1876. 8vo. 10 coloured plates and 3 woodcuts. £2 10s. (orig. bright red cloth).

The Essays by "Nimrod" first appeared in the form of letters to the *Sporting Magazine*.

Anti-Pugilism, or the Science of Defence, exemplified in short and easy lessons, for the practice of the Broad Sword and Single Stick, by a Highland Officer, 1790. 8vo., with 4 plates by Cruikshank. 16s. (cf ex.)

Approved Treatise of Hawkes and Hawking, An, by Edmund Bert, 1st ed. 1619. Small 4to. Cut on title. A Reprint from the original, with introduction by J. E. Harting, 1891. 4to. pp. vii. 109. Only 100 copies printed. Bert's treatise is the rarest book on Falconry in the English language. Only one copy has occurred for sale during the last 20 years, namely, at the Ashburnham sale held in June, 1897. The title page of this copy was defective and the corner of the last leaf was mended. £4 10s. (cf. gt.)

Archer's Guide, The, by an old Toxophilite, 1st. ed. 1833 F'cap 8vo. Col. folding front. by R. Cruikshank. 5s. (bds.)

Army and Navy Gentleman's Companion, or a New and Complete Treatise on the Theory and Practice of Fencing, by J. McArthur. 1780. 4to. Front. and 18 illustrations by Newton. £1 10s. (cf., uncut).

Second edition, 1784. 4to. Same illustrations. £1 8s. (bds.)

Arrianus on Coursing, *see* **Cynegeticus.**

Art of Angling, The: wherein are discovered many rare secrets very necessary to be known by all that delight in that recreation, by Thomas Barker, 1651. 12mo. £1 18s (cf.)

Another edition, 1653. 12mo. (No author's name given). £2 5s. (cf. ex.)

Another edition, 1820. 12mo. 100 copies printed, as also 3 on toned paper and 1 on vellum. £1 12s. (ordinary paper, as issued)

The edition of 1653 (*supra*) was reprinted at Leeds in 1817.

Art of Angling, by Thomas Best, *see* **Concise Treatise on the Art of Angling.**

Art of Angling, The, and complete system of fly-making and dyeing of colours, by William Blacker, 1842. 12mo. Plates 5s (cl.) This work was re-issued as "Blacker's Catechism of Fly Making," 1843. 16mo., and in 1855 as "Blacker's Art of Fly-making," with engraved title, col. front. and 20 plates of Flies, of which 18 are coloured 8s. (orig. cl.)

Art of Angling, improved in all its parts, especially fly-fishing, The, by Richard and Charles Bowlker, n. d. (*cir*. 1758) 12mo., Worcester, 5s. (cf.) Subsequently issued with a fresh title, "The Art of Angling and Complete Fly-fisher," n.d. (1774), 8vo., Baskerville. A third edition also appeared at Birmingham in 1785, and there are many later editions—among them that of 1833. 8vo., with coloured front. and cuts. 3s. (bds., uncut)

Art of Angling, The, Rock and Sea Fishing . . by Richard Brookes 1st ed. 1740. 12mo., with 133 woodcuts 12s (orig. sheep.) A second edition appeared under the same title in 1743 (10s., orig. sheep.), and a third in 1766, under the title of "The Art of Angling. Now improved with additions, and formed into a dictionary." 10s. (calf). A tenth edition appeared in 1801. 8vo. 3s. (orig. sheep.) and there are many later editions, all of small value.

Art of Angling, The, as practised in Scotland, by Thomas Tod Stoddart. 1st ed. 1835. 12mo. Illustrations. 2s. (cl.)

Second edition, 1836. 12mo. Illustrations. 2s. (cl.)

Art of Archerie, The, shewing how it is most necessary in these times for this Kingdome, both in Peace and War, &c. 1633. 8vo. Frontispiece representing an Archer drawing his bow, presumed to be King Charles, but more probably Gervase Markham. £2 15s. (old cf., sound copy)

Art of Dancing Explained, The, whereby the Manner of Performing the Steps is made easy, by Kellom Tomlinson. 1744. 4to. 37 plates of full length figures, &c. £2 8s. (calf, g e.)

Another and prior edition, 1735. 4to. Plates. £4 4s. (calf).

Art of Deer Stalking, The. Illustrated by a narrative of a few days' sport in the Forest of Atholl, by William Scrope. 1st ed. 1838. 8vo. Illustrations after E. & C. Landseer and the Author. £6 10s. (orig. cl.) £8 (*ibid.*)

Second edition, 1839. Roy. 8vo. Plates. £6 10s. (orig. cl.)

Third edition, 1847. Roy. 8vo. Plates. Published under the title of "Days of Deer Stalking." £1 5s. (orig. green cloth)

New edition, 1897. pp. xviii. 304. Forming Vol. 5 of Sir H. E. Maxwell's "Sportsman's Library."

Art of Defence on Foot with the Broad Sword and Sabre, uniting the Scotch and Austrian Methods. By C. Roworth, of the Royal Westminster Volunteers. 1798. 8vo., with 8 plates by Bantrec. 7s. 6d. (cf.)

Described on the title as "The Second Edition," but in reality the first. In 1804 a work appeared in 8vo. under the same chief title and with the same plates, but engraved by R. K. Porter. This is regarded as a re-issue rather than a new edition.

Art of English Shooting, by George Edie. 1st ed 1760. 8vo. Front 5s (wrappers).

Another edition, 1777. 8vo Front. 5s (cf.)

Other editions of this work are quoted as "A Treatise on English Shooting." None are of any importance.

Art of Fencing, agreeably to the Practice of the most Eminent Masters in Europe, by Guzman Rolando 1820 (?). 8vo. Ackermann. Translated into English from the Spanish, and corrected by J. S. Forsyth.

Another edition. Leigh, 1822. 12mo. 23 col. pl. £1 15s. (orig. bds.)

Art of Fencing, as Practised by Monsieur Valdin, edited by Sulaiman Ibn Yu'Kúb, 1729. 8vo. Portrait. £2 15s. (mor., g e.) A tract of 45 pp. 10s (unbound).

Art of Fencing, The, represented in Proper Figures. Engraved on 24 plates. n.d. Oblong 8vo. J. Bowles. £4 4s (old cf.)

Art of Fencing, The, or the use of the Small Sword, translated by A Mahon from the French of M. L'Abbat, 1734. 8vo. 12 plates, £2 15s. (cf. ex.) £2 (orig. cf) Some copies are dated 1735. These belong, however, to the same edition, and have a new title page.

Art of Fencing, The, wherein the rules and instructions with all the new thrusts and guards which have lately been introduced into the Fencing Schools are in this work, &c., by a pupil of St. Angelo. 1830. Sm 8vo. Folding plate 3s (wrappers). The same folding plate is used in a publication entitled "Easy and Familiar Rules for attaining the art of attack and defence on foot with the broadsword." London, T. Hughes. 8vo 1831. 3s. (cf.)

Art of Hunting, The, by William Twici, huntsman to King Edward II, translated by H Dryden, 1844. 4to. 9 Illustrations Only 25 copies privately printed. £5 (orig. cl.)

The translation is made from "L'Art de Venerie" par Gwyllame Twici, a manuscript formerly in the Library of

Sir Thomas Phillipps, which he caused to be printed at the Middle Hill Press in 1840. 4to

Art of Manual Defence, The, or System of Boxing, perspicuously explained in a series of Lessons by a Pupil both of Humphreys and Mendoza, 1789. 8vo., with 9 plates. £2 2s. (cf. ex. by Rivière)

Art of Riding, The, translated from the Italian of Claudio Corte, by Thomas Bedingfield, 1584. 4to. Woodcuts £2 2s. (cf. ex., g.e.)

Art of Riding newlie Corrected, The, The Order of Dieting Horses and Curing Horses, by Thomas Blundeville, 1597. 4to. Woodcuts £5 5s. (vellum). £3 (*ibid.*)

Other editions appeared in 1580 and 1609. The book is in effect a reprint of " The fower chiefyst offices belongyng to Horsemanshippe " by the same author, but published under a different title. *See* **Fower Chiefest Offices.**

Art of Swimming, illustrated by Forty Proper Copperplate Cuts which represent the different Postures necessary to be used in the Art, by Monsieur Thevenot, 1699. 12mo. 40 plates £1 12s. (hf. calf).

Second edition, 1764. 12mo. 40 plates as before, but reversed and much worn. 12s. (hf cf.)

The title as given above is that of the edition of 1764. The exact title of the first edition is " The Art of Swimming, illustrated by proper figures, with advice for bathing."

Art of Taming Horses, *see* **Instructions for Taming Horses.**

Arte Natandi, De, by Everard Digby, 1587. Sm. 4to. Thos. Dawson, 44 full page woodcuts. None of the leaves are paged, but pp 114. £15 (old cf.) This work, the second exclusively devoted to swimming published in this country, is written in Latin Dialogues. *See* **Short Introduction for to learne to swimme.**

Arte of Defence, *see* **True Arte of Defence.**

Ascent of the Matterhorn, by Edward Whymper. Maps and illustrations. 1880. 8vo £1 5s (orig. cl.) Though dated 1880 on the title, the work was published the previous year. pp. xxii. 325

Ascent to the Summit of Mont Blanc in 1834, by Martin Barry. (1835). 8vo. 2 plates, 10s (cl.)

Another edition, 1836. 8vo. Coloured plates and Panoramic Illustration. 10s. (cl.)

"Ask Mamma"; or The Richest Commoner in England, By the author of "Handley Cross" (R. S. Surtees), 1858. Originally published in 13 monthly parts, red wrappers designed by Leech, afterwards in Demy 8vo. as above. Front. 12 col. pl., and 69 woodcuts all by Leech. £4 10s (orig parts). £2 10s (orig cl.) £1 (hf. cf.)

Another edition, n.d. (but 1888), Bradbury, Agnew and Co., with the col. plates. 8s. (orig. cl.)

Astra Castra: Experiments and Adventures in the Atmosphere, by Christopher Hatton Turnor, 1865. 4to. Illustrations. 12s (orig. cl.) Published at £1 15s

At Home in the Wilderness, by "Wanderer," 1867. Cr. 8vo. Illustrated. 2s (orig. cl.)

Atlas, Fox Hunting, *see* **Fox Hunting Atlas.**

Autumns on the Spey, by A. E. Knox, 1872. Post 8vo., with 4 plates by J. Wolf, and 3 woodcuts in the text. 4s. (orig. cl.) Published at 6s.

Bachelor's Guide to Life in London, The, with its Saloons, Casinos, Clubs, &c. Haymarket, n.d. (1830). Post 8vo., with 10 col. pl. and vignettes. 16s (orig. cl.)

Backwoodsman, The, or Life on the Indian Frontier, by Sir C. Lascelles. 1864. F'cap 8vo. Illustrations of sporting scenes. 4s. (orig. cl.)

Badminton Library of Sports and Pastimes, edited by the Duke of Beaufort, assisted by A. E. T. Watson. Copies of the volumes on small paper can usually be got new (later issues) for 7s 10½d. each (pub 10s. 6d), but as only 250 copies of each were printed on **large paper** the value of these cannot be estimated on the basis of the published price. All the undermentioned books were in hf. mor., uncut., t.e g. 4to. Large Paper. Illustrated The prices realised are corrected to July, 1898.

Archery, by C. J. Longman and Col. H Walrond. 1894. £1 10s.; 18s.

Athletics and Football, by Montague Shearman. 1887. £1 4s

Billiards, by Major W. Broadfoot. 1896. £1 12s. , £1

Boating, by W. B. Woodgate 1888 £1 10s

Boxing, *see* Fencing.

Coursing and Falconry, by Harding Cox and the Hon. Gerald Lascelles. 1892. £1 13s.

Cricket, by A G Steel and the Hon R H. Lyttleton and others. 1888 £2 ; £1 5s.

Cycling, by Viscount Bury and G. L. Hillier. 1887. £1 6s.

Dancing, by Mrs L. Grove and others. 1895. £1 2s.; 16s.

Driving, by the Duke of Beaufort and others 1889. £2 2s

Fencing, by W H. Pollock and others—Boxing, by E. B Mitchell—Wrestling, by W. Armstrong, in 1 vol. 1889 £1 5s.

Fishing, by H. Cholmondeley-Pennell (Salmon and Trout, Pike and other coarse Fish.) 2 vols 1885 £12 10s.

Fishing, by "J. Bickerdyke" and others (Sea Fishing) 1895. £1 10s. £1.

Golf, by H. G Hutchinson, and others 1890 £2 15s.

Hunting, by the Duke of Beaufort and Mowbray Morris, with contributions from others. 1885 £30

Mountaineering, by C. T. Dent. 1892 £2 10s.

Poetry of Sport, The, by H Peek. 1896. £2

Polo, *see* Riding.

Racing and Steeple-Chasing, by the Earl of Suffolk and others. 1886. £2 18s.

Riding, by Capt. R. Weir and others—Polo, by J. Moray Brown, in 1 vol. 1891. £1 15s.

Shooting, by Lord Walsingham and Sir R. Payne-Gallwey (Field and Covert, Moor and Marsh), 2 vols. 1886. £13 10s.; £10.

Shooting, by C. Phillipps-Wolley and others (Big Game), 2 vols. 1894. £5 10s.; £4 15s.

Skating and Figure Skating, by J. M. Heathcote and others. 1892. £1 5s.

Swimming, by A. Sinclair and William Henry. 1893. £1 5s.

Tennis, by J. M. Heathcote — Lawn Tennis, by C. G. Heathcote — Rackets, by E. O. P. Bouverie — Fives, by A. C. Ainger, in 1 vol. 1890. £1 5s.; £1.

Wrestling, *see* Fencing.

Yachting, by Sir E. Sullivan and others. 2 vols. 1894. £3 18s.; £1 10s.

Baily's Magazine of Sports and Pastimes. Commenced in 1860 and still being published. Portraits of Sportsmen. £4 8s. (26 vols. 1860-75, hf. cf.); £8 15s. (40 vols. 1860-83. hf. cf.)

Barker's Delight: or, the Art of Angling, wherein are discovered many rare secrets, &c., by Thomas Barker, 1657. 12mo.

Second edition, 1659. 12mo. £4 10s. (mor. ex., fine copy).

Another edition, 1820. 12mo. 100 copies printed, as also one on vellum and four on toned paper. £1 16s. (ordinary paper).

"Barker's Delight" is not an illustrated book, but is mentioned here as it is reprinted in, and to that extent forms part of, the **Young Sportsman's Miscellany** (*q. v.*)

Bear Hunting in the White Mountains, or, Alaska and British Columbia Revisited, by H. W. Seton Karr. 1891. Sm. 8vo. Map and illustrations by the author. 2s. (cl.) Published at 4s. 6d.

Beauties and Defects in the Figure of the Horse. 1st ed. 1816. Impl. 8vo. 18 col. pl. by H. Alken. £1 9s. (russ.), £1 12s. (hf. cf.), £1 10s. (orig. bds.)

Reprint, 1881. Roy. 8vo. Toovey, with plates. 3s. 6d. (plain plates), 6s. (col. pl., hf. bd.)

Reprint, n.d. Roy. 8vo. Tegg, with plates. 2s. (plain plates)

Benchiana, or Sketches of Life and Character in St. George's Fields. 1st ed. Dolby, 1822. Folding col. front. by R. Cruikshank. £1 12s. (mor., t.e.g.)

Bengal Monthly Sporting Magazine, The, and Bengal Register, conducted by J. H. Stocqueler, 1833-9. 6 vols. 8vo. Numerous col. and other plates, portraits, &c. £2 12s. (hf. cf.) Vol. I. was published at Calcutta in 1833, and then the periodical was conducted as a New Series under the title of "The Bengal Sporting Magazine," this in its turn being incorporated in the **India Sporting Review** (*q. v.*)

Bernese Oberland, The, by Thomas George Bonney, 1874. Folio, with 12 full page col. pl. £1 5s. (orig. cl.)

Best Season on Record, by Edward Pennell Elmhirst, 1884. 8vo. 4 coloured and many plain plates by J. Sturgess. £1 1s. (cloth)

Another edition, 1885. 8vo. Col. plates and cuts. 6s. (orig. cl.)

Bibliotheca Accipitraria, a catalogue of books relating to Falconry, by James Edmund Harting, 1891. 8vo., with col. front. and 25 plates. 14s. (rox.) Published at 31s. 6d.

Billesdon Coplow, a Poem on Fox-hunting, 1811. Oblong 4to. Six hand-coloured plates of hunting scenes, by R. F[rankland.] £1 15s. (orig. wrapper), £7 5s. (mor. ex. very fine copy).

Bits of Turf, by "Priam," 1853. Cr 8vo. Illustrations by McConnell. 2s. 6d. (wrappers).

Blacker's Art (Catechism) of Fly Making, *see* **Art of Angling** and **Complete System,** &c.

Blackguardiana; or a Dictionary of Rogues, Bawds, Pimps, Murderers, &c. No place of publication or date. 8vo., with 18 portraits of remarkable characters. £2 15s. (cf.)

Bokys of Haukyng and Huntyng and also of Cootarmuris (by Juliana Barnes or Berners). 1st ed. St Albans, 1486. Sm. fol. £385 (calf). Reproduced in facsimile, with an introduction by William Blades, 1881. 4to. 15s. (white, old style parchment).

Second edition, 1496. Folio, with wood cuts, printed by Wynkyn de Worde, under the title "Treatyse perteynynge to Hawkynge, Huntynge and Fysshynge with an Angle" £160 (several ll. missing and others inlaid and some in MS.) Reprinted (150 copies only) with an introduction by Joseph Haslewood, 1810. Folio. £4 4s. (hf russ.); and also by Watkins in 1880. 4to. 12s. (cl.)

Another edition, n.d. Wynkyn de Worde. Sm 4to.

Another edition, n.d. Wyllyam Coplande. Sm. 4to. £61 (sound copy).

Another edition, n.d. Wyllyam Coplande for Robert Toye. Sm 4to. £26 (repaired).

Another edition, n.d. Wyllyam Coplande for Rychard Tottell. Sm 4to.

Another edition, n.d. Abraham Vele. Sm. 4to.

Another edition, n.d. Hery Tab. Sm 4to.

Another edition, n d. John Waley. Sm 4to. £62 (good copy).

Another edition, n d. Wyllyam Powell. Sm 4to. £76 (good copy).

Another edition, 1586. 4to. Edward Alde, printed under the title "Hawking, Hunting, Fowling and Fishing, with the True Measures of Blowing." £41 (good and perfect copy).

Another edition, 1596. 4to. Adam Islip. Printed under the same title as the edition of 1586. Value also about the same.

All the above mentioned copies are extremely scarce, and though some of them have quite recently realised the sums mentioned, no implicit reliance can be put on the figures, which naturally vary greatly from time to time, as in the case of all scarce books for which there is an unsatisfied demand.

See also **Gentleman's Academie, The,** and also **Here begynneth a Treatyse of Fysshynge with an Angle.**

Book of Blockheads, The: How and what they Shot, Got, Said, &c., &c. 1863. 4to., with 28 col. pl. by Charles Bennett; 12s. (orig. cl.) £1 4s (cf. ex.) Published at 5s., or with col. pl. at 7s. 6d.

Book of Deer, The, edited for the Spalding Club by John Stuart, 1869. 4to. Facsimile and other plates. Of this work 14 copies were printed on Large Paper. £2 15s. (L.P., hf. rox.)

Book of Duck Decoys, their Construction, Management and History, by Sir Ralph Payne-Gallwey, 1886. 4to. pp. x 214. Illustrated. 15s (cl.) Published at 25s.

Book of Field Sports and Library of Veterinary Knowledge, edited by H. D. Miles, n.d. (1860-4). 4to. Coloured and other plates. 7s. (hf. cf.) Published at £2 15s.

Book of Hawking and Hunting, *see* **Bokys of Haukyng and Huntyng.**

Book of St. Albans, *see* **Bokys of Haukyng, &c.,** also **Gentleman's Academie, The.**

Book of Sports and Mirror of Life, *see* **Pierce Egan's Book of Sports.**

Book of Sports, British and Foreign, devoted to the Pictorial Illustration of the pursuits of the Sportsman in every quarter of the Globe, 1842-3. 2 vols. 4to., with 50 plates by Landseer, Alken and others. 18s. (cl. gt.) Published as a periodical and subsequently in volume form at 32s.

Book of the All-round Angler, The, A Comprehensive Treatise on Angling in both Fresh and Salt Water, by "John Bickerdyke" (C. H. Cook), 1889. 8vo., with 220 engravings. 4s. (cl.), 16s. (L.P., Roxburgh). 201 copies were printed on large paper at 25s.

Book of the Dry Fly, The, by George A. B. Dewar, 1897. 8vo. pp. x 238. Front., col. plates of flies and woodcuts. 8s. (orig. cl.) Published at 15s.

Book of the Grayling, The, by Thomas Evan Pritt. 1888. 4to. Coloured plates. pp. 64. 10s. (as issued). Published at 12s. 6d.

Book of the Horse, The, with hints on Horsemanship, Management, Breeding, &c., by Samuel Sidney. 1st ed. (1873-75). 4to., with col. plates. 8s. (cl.)

Second edition, n.d. (1879-81). Cassell. 4to. 8s. (cl.)

Another edition, n.d. (1884-6) 4to. Cassell. 25 col. and other illustrations. 10s. (orig. cl.)

Another edition. 1892 (-93). 8vo. Cassell. 16s. (cl.)

Book of the Salmon, by "Ephemera" (Edward Fitzgibbon). 1st ed. 1850. 16mo. pp. xvi. 242. 9 col. pl. 14s. (orig. cl.)

Book on Angling, A, being a complete treatise on the Art of Angling in every branch, by Francis Francis. 1st ed. 1867. 8vo., with 15 plates.

Second edition, revised and enlarged. 1867. 8vo. Front. and 16 plates.

Third edition, revised and improved. 1872. 8vo. Front. and 16 plates.

Fourth edition, revised and improved. 1876. 8vo. Front. and 16 plates.

Fifth edition, 1880. Post 8vo. Port. and plates, including some of Flies coloured. 6s. (orig. cl.)

Sixth edition, 1885. 8vo. Port. and plates.

Booke of Engines and Traps to take Polecats, Buzzards, Rats, Mice, &c. **Black letter.** 1600. Woodcuts. £2 5s. (calf).

Booke of Faulconrie or Hawking, The, by Geo. Turberville. 1st ed 1575 4to Christopher Barker. £50 (velvet, with silver ornaments, Ashburnham sale).

Another edition, 1611. 4to. T. Purfoot. Woodcuts £3; (title cropped), £9 (mor , sound copy); £17 (vellum, with the two musical leaves of "The Measures of Blowing," usually wanting from the "Noble Art of Venerie, 1611. Ashburnham sale).

Another edition, 1641 4to. Woodcuts £6 10s. (russ. ex., no title).

Booke of Honor and Armes, wherein is discoursed the Causes of Quarrell, &c , n d (1590) 4to. Woodcut, title, and cuts in the text £8 (cf.) Probably written by Sir W. Segar.

Boxiana; or Sketches of Ancient and Modern Pugilism, by Pierce Egan. 4 vols 1818-24, and a 5th sometimes added, dated 1829. Originally published in parts. Smeeton's Engraved Title Page should be in Vol I. £5 10s. (the 5 vols. hf cf); £1 14s. (vols 1-3, half calf).

Another edition, 1829-30. 5 vols 8vo. Virtue. Value about the same.

Boxing Revived; or the Science of Manual Defence displayed on rational principles, with a description of the principal pugilists, by Thomas Fewtrell, 1790 8vo Portrait of T Johnson 6s. (hf bd)

Breath from the Veldt, A, by John Guille Millais, 1895 4to pp. x 236. Illustrations by the author and Front by Sir J E Millais. £5 (as issued) Published at £3 3s. net., but advanced to £4 4s. in July, 1897.

Brighton and its Coaches, by W C. A Blew, 1894. Roy. 8vo , with 20 illustrations from original water colour drawings, by J and G. Temple. pp xx 354 12s (orig cl) Published at 21s.

British Angler, The, by John Williamson, 1740 12mo. Engraved front 10s. (old cf)

British Angler's Manual, The, by T C Hofland. 1st ed. 1839. 8vo. Plates and cuts. 15s (L P hf. mor.), 6s. (Small paper, orig. cl.)

Another edition, 1841 8vo Revised and enlarged by E. Jesse. 5s (cl)

Another edition, 1848. 8vo. Bohn. 3s. (cl.)

British Dance of Death, n. d. 8vo. Coloured plates by R. Cruikshank and others. £2 4s. (uncut).

British Deer and their Horns, by John Guille Millais, 1897. Impl. 4to. pp. xviii. 224. With 185 Illustrations, mostly by the author, 8 from drawings by Sidney Steel, 2 by E. Roe. . . . A series of unpublished sketches by Sir E. Landseer, &c. £2 18s. (as issued). Published at £4 4s. net.

British Field Sports, by "William Henry Scott" (John Lawrence). 1818 8vo 34 plates after Berenger and cuts by Bewick, including title, often missing. £2 (orig. bds.); £1 17s (russ. ex.)

Another edition 1820. 8vo. Same plates £1 5s. (hf. cf.) *See also* **Delineations of British Field Sports.**

British Field Sports (Orme's), *see* **Orme's Collection of British Field Sports.**

British Game Birds and Wild Fowl, by Beverley R. Morris. 1st ed. 1855. Roy. 4to 60 col. pl. £1 1s (calf).

Another edition, n d 4to. 60 col. pl. 15s (orig cl.)

British Golf Links, by Horace G. Hutchinson, 1897 4to. pp. viii. 331 Some copies were printed on Large Paper (Folio). 12s (as issued, 4to).

British Manly Exercises, *see* **Scientific Swimming.**

British Preserve, The, by Samuel Howitt, n. d. 4to. 36 etchings. 4s. (hf. bd.) Published originally in 9 parts

Second edition, n. d. Roy 8vo. 2s (cf.)

British Proverbs, a series of six plates containing a large number of coloured illustrations, by Henry Alken. 1824. Oblong folio. £7 (bound up in mor. ex., uncut, fine set).

British Sportsman, The, by Samuel Howitt, 1812. Oblong 4to., with 70 col. plates. £1 4s. (calf).

British Sportsman, The, by William Augustus Osbaldiston (1792). 4to., with front. and plates. pp. 664, ii. 7s. (cf.)

Brown's Sporting Tour in India, by William Shapter Hunt, 1865. Oblong folio, with 42 etched plates. 12s. (hf. cf.)

By Hook and by Crook, by Fraser Sandeman, 1892. 8vo. pp. viii. 255. 100 copies printed on L. P. (4to.) £2 8s. (cl., uncut, L.P.)

Cabinet of Comicalities, by T. Spiller, n.d. 8vo. Col. plates by G. Cruikshank. £1 5s. (wrappers).

Camp Fires of the Everglades, The, or Wild Sports in the South, by C. E. Whitehead. 1891. Roy. 8vo. pp. x. 298. Plates on Japan paper and other illustrations. £1 4s. (orig. cl.) Published at £2 2s.

Cavelarice, or the English Horseman, by Gervase Markham, 1615-17. 4to. Eight parts in 1 vol. Engraved title to each book and woodcuts of horses. £8 5s. (cf. ex., fine copy).

First edition, 1607. 4to. Printed for Edward White. Engraved title to each part and cuts. £10 18s. (cf., sound copy).

Celebrated Trials, and Remarkable Cases of Criminal Jurisdiction, 1825. 6 vols. 8vo. Portraits and plates. £2 5s. (cf.) £3 10s. (ibid.)

Chamois Hunting in the Mountains of Bavaria, by Charles Boner. 1st ed., 1853. 8vo., with 6 tinted plates and 6 wood-engravings by T. Horschelt. 25s. (orig. cl.)

Second edition, 1860. 8vo. Plates. 16s. (orig. cl.)

Characteristic Sketches of the Lower Orders, n d. 8vo. S. Leigh 54 col. pl by Rowlandson £3 10s. (hf cf.)

Chase, The, by William Somerville. 1st ed., 1735 4to. Not illustrated £3 10s (orig blue wrappers). Of the numerous illustrated editions which have appeared from time to time, the best is that published in 1802, 8vo, with full page plates after Sartorius and woodcuts by Bewick. 12s. (cf) Bulmer's edition of 1796, 4to, with woodcuts by Bewick, is, however, preferable in many respects, especially when on Large Paper £1 14s., (L P, orig bds.) The third edition, with Bewick's cuts, was published by Bulmer in 1804. Roy. 8vo

Chase of the Wild Red Deer, *see* **Notes on the Chase, &c.**

Chase, the Turf, and the Road, The, by "Nimrod" (C. J. Apperley,) 1837. Demy 8vo Portrait of "Nimrod" by Maclise and 13 full-page plates (uncoloured) by H. Alken. Reprinted from the *Quarterly Review*. £1 5s (orig. cl.) A later edition of 1870 has the plates coloured £1 5s. (orig. cl.)

Another edition, 1898. Roy. 16mo. Illustrations by Alken, portrait by Maclise, and other portraits Published in the "Sportsman's Library" series (q v.) at 15s., or L P. £2 2s.

Chasse du Loup, La, nécessaire à La Maison rustique, par J. Clarmorgan, 1665 4to Cuts of wolf hunting £1 5s. (hf. mor.) The treatise was written for and appears in Charles Estienne's "L'Agriculture et maison rustique," first published at Paris in 1570, 4to, itself a French translation of the same author's "Prædium Rusticum," Paris, 1554, 8vo., and later.

Cheape and Good Husbandry for the well-ordering of all Beasts and Fowles, contayning the whole Art of Riding great Horses . ordering of Hawkes, &c, &c, by Gervase Markham. 1st ed. 1614 Sm 4to £10 (cf) Many later editions of lesser interest and value, including the following :

1615. Sm. 4to.

1631. Sm. 4to. Plan of a Fish Pond. £2 6s. (mor. ex.); £3 *(ibid.)*

1676. Sm. 4to. The 13th edition.

1683 Sm. 4to. £1 10s. (mor. ex.)

Chesterfield Travestie, or School for Modern Manners. 1st ed 1808. 8vo., with 10 col. caricatures by Thomas Rowlandson. £1 8s. (cf. ex., uncut).

Another edition, 1811. 8vo. Col. pl. as before. £1 (orig. bds.)

Chronicles of Crime, The, or the New Newgate Calendar, by Camden Pelham. 1st ed. 2 vols 8vo. 1841. With 52 full page plates by "Phiz." £1 4s. (hf cf.)

Another edition, 1886. 2 vols. 8vo. Reeves. 5s. Published at 12s. 6d.

Another edition, 1887. 2 vols. 8vo. Miles. 5s. Published at 15s

Cleveland Hounds as a Trencher-Fed Pack, The, by A. E Pease, 1887. 8vo. Col. port. of Tom Andrews and plates pp viii 257. 6s. (cl.)

Climbing and Exploration in the Kara Koram Himalayas, by Sir W. M. Conway. 3 vols. 1894. 8vo. 300 illustrations and maps. £1 1s. (uncut, t e.g) Of this work 150 copies were published as an *édition de luxe*, with duplicate proofs of the illustrations on Japan silk tissue.

Climbing Reminiscences of the Dolomites, by Leone Sinigaglia, 1896. 8vo., with 39 plates and a map. £2 10s (text and plates on Japanese vellum paper, only 30 copies were issued in this style at £5 5s. each).

Climbs in the New Zealand Alps, by Edward Arthur Fitzgerald, 1896 Roy. 8vo., with 59 plates by Joseph Pennell and others, and a map in a pocket. 12s. (orig. cl.) Published at £1 11s. 6d. Of this work 60 copies were printed on Japan paper, signed by the authors, at £5 5s each.

Clydesdale Stud Book, The. First volume (the only one published in London) and vols. ii to vii. 1878-85. 8vo. plates. £12 (as published, vol. vi. missing)

A second edition of this stud book was commenced in 1884 at Glasgow. It was revised by the editing committee of the Clydesdale Horse Society.

Coaching Age, The, by Stanley Harris, 1885. 8vo. 16 plates by Sturgess. 18s (orig. cl.)

Coaching Days and Coaching Ways, by William Outram Tristram. 1st ed. 1888. 4to. 214 illustrations by H. Railton and Hugh Thomson. £1 10s. (orig. cl.)

Second edition, 1893. Cr. 8vo. Same illustrations. 6s. (cl. extra, as issued)

Cocker, The. Containing every information to the breeders and amateurs of that noble bird the Game Cock, by W. Sketchley, 1814. 8vo. Contains front. £2 2s (orig. bds., uncut) Often found extra-illustrated.

Cocker, The: A Poem humbly inscribed to the Honourable Society of Sportsmen at Grantham, by Isaac Hallam. Front. 1742. 4to. £6 (mor. ex., good copy) Written in imitation of Virgil's third Georgic.

Cock Fighting, Badger Baiting, Bull Baiting, Bear Baiting, &c. 1823-24. Oblong 4to. Seven col. pl. by H. Alken. £8 15s. (sewed).

Cockney's Shooting Season in Suffolk, A, a series of seven col. plates by Henry Alken. 1822. Folio. £5 15s. (hf. bd.)

Cold Steel: A Practical Treatise on the Sabre, based on the Old English Backsword Play, &c., by Alfred Hutton. 1889. 8vo. Port. and illustrations from old prints. pp. xii 245. 5s (orig. cl.)

Collection of Right Merrie Garlands for North Country Anglers, A, edited by Joseph Crawhall. 1864. 8vo. pp. xv. 312. Facsimile and other cuts. Musical notes. 8s. (hf. mor.)

Collection of Sporting Designs, A, comprising a variety of Entertaining Subjects. 1821-23. Folio, with 50 col. pl. by H. Alken. £8 10s. (hf. bd., g.e.)

Colonel George Hanger to all Sportsmen, *see* **To all Sportsmen.**

Comforts of Bath, The, a series of 12 caricatures by Thomas Rowlandson. 1st issue, Jan. 6th, 1798. £10 10s. (clean).

Another issue, 1859. Oblong 4to. £2 10s. (clean).

Comicus, *see* **Adventures of Dr. Comicus.**

Comparative View of the Form and Character of the English Racer and Saddle Horse during the last and present centuries. 1836. 4to., with 18 plates. £1 (hf. cf., plates on India paper), 12s. (hf. cf., plates on plain paper).

Compendious Treatise on Modern Education, in which the following subjects are discussed: The Nursery, Private Schools, Public Schools, Universities, Gallantry, Duelling, &c. By "The late Joel Mc Cringer, D.D., F.R.S., A.S.S., Rector of the United Parishes of Pigworth, &c." 1802. Oblong fol., with 8 col. pl. by Thomas Rowlandson. Very scarce. From £10 to £12 (bds., as issued)

Compleat Angler, The, or the Contemplative Man's Recreation . . by Izaac Walton. 1st ed., 1653. 12 mo. pp. xvi. 246. Cuts of fish. £415 (original sheep.) The first five editions of this well-known book are much sought after. They run as follows, 1653, 1655, 1661, 1668, and 1676, the last named being in three parts, the first by Walton, the second by Charles Cotton, and the third by Col. Robert Venables. This was the last edition published during Walton's lifetime. A set of perfect copies of these first five editions, in their original bindings (first four sheep., the last calf), brought £800 at the Ashburnham sale, May, 1898. It is worthy of note that in 1847 Dr. Bethune valued a fine and perfect copy of the 1st ed. at £12 12s. More than 100 editions of the Compleat Angler have appeared since 1676, many of them being illustrated. The following are the more important editions :—

1750. 12mo., by Moses Browne. (1st ed.) Cuts of fish and plates. 15s. (hf. cf.) £2 (cf.)

1759. 12mo., by Moses Browne. Front. and 8 plates. 8s. (hf. cf.)

1760. 8vo., by Sir John Hawkins (his 1st ed.) Port., front. and 14 plates. 19s. (cf.), £2 (cf.)

1766. 8vo., by Sir John Hawkins (his 2nd ed.) Port. and 14 plates. 5s (cf. antique).

1772. 8vo., by Moses Browne. Front. and 8 plates. 4s (cf.)

1775. 8vo., by Sir John Hawkins (his 3rd ed.) Port. and 14 plates. 5s. (cf.)

1784. 8vo., by Sir John Hawkins (his 4th ed.) Port. and 14 plates. 5s (cf.)

1792. 8vo., by Sir John Hawkins (his 5th ed.) Port. and 9 plates. 3s. (cf.)

1797. 8vo., by Sir John Hawkins (his 6th ed.) Port. and plates. 3s. (cf.)

1808. 8vo., and also in 4to., by Sir John Hawkins (his 7th ed.) Front. and 14 plates. 18s., (cf. L.P.)

1815. 8vo., by Sir John Hawkins. Bagster's 2nd ed. Port. and 50 plates. 8s. (hf. mor.)

1823. 8vo. Major's 1st ed. Front., 14 copper plates and 77 cuts. Also Large Paper, India plates. 12s. (cf.)

1824. 8vo. Major's 2nd ed. 14 copper plates and 77 cuts. 6s. (cf.)

1825. 18mo. Dove. 2s. 6d (hf. mor.)

1826. 32mo. Pickering's Diamond ed. Ports. and cuts of fish. 5s (mor., gt.)

[1828]. 8vo. William Cole. 2 ports. and cuts of fish. 4s (cf.)

1833. 8vo. James Rennie. Port., engraved plate of music, two views, and cuts. (6s hf. mor.)

1836. 2 vol. Pickering. Two portraits, 8vo. engraved front. by Stothard, and plates. A fine work containing the variations noticeable in the first five editions and extensive notes. £15 10s (cf ex.), £13 (mor ex.), £9 10s (cf ex.)

1839. 8vo. Portraits, plates and woodcuts. £1 1s (orig. bds.)

1844. 8vo. John Major (his 4th ed.) 12 plates and 74 cuts in text. A much better edition than any previously edited by Major. 10s. (orig. cl.)

1851. 8vo. Causton. Front. and 14 plates. 5s. (cl.)

1853. 8vo. by "Ephemera" (Edward Fitzgibbon) Front and 3 plates. 2s (cl.)

1856. 8vo. Bohn. 26 plates and 203 cuts. 7s. (cl.) The "Remainder" was re-issued in 1861 with a fresh title.

1860. 2 vols. 8vo. Nattali. A reprint of Pickering's ed. of 1836, with pedigrees of Ken and Chalkhill. Port and front. £1 5s (cf.)

1861. 8vo. Bohn. *See supra*, 1856. 2s. (cl.)

1883. 8vo. Nimmo. £1 5s (hf. vel., etchings in two states and woodcuts on India paper)

1885. 4to. Major. Portraits, plates, &c. £1 10s (cf. ex.)

1888. 4to. Lea and Dove edition. 2 vols. Edited by R. B. Marston, with 54 photogravures and about 100 woodcuts. Limited to 500 copies. £1 10s. (hf. mor., uncut demy 4to.) £4 (L. P., mor. ex.) This is the 100th edition, Published at £5 5s (demy 4to.), or £10 10s. (roy. 4to., *edition de luxe*)

1893. 2 vols. Impl. 8vo. Bagster. The Tercentenary Edition. Portraits and plates. 350 copies printed. 15s (cl. uncut)

A number of editions and facsimile reprints have appeared since 1893. The prices above quoted must be regarded from a broad comparative view, and may then furnish relative evidence. They vary immensely in practice, being governed principally by the character and quality of the binding.

Compleat Fencing-Master, by W(illiam) H(ope), Gent. 1687. 8vo. 12 folding plates. £6 18s. (old cf.) Published under the title of "The Scots Fencing Master" (q. v.)

Second edition, 1692. 8vo. 12 folding plates. £2 15s (old cf.)

Another edition, 1710. 8vo. Plates. £2 2s. (cf. ex.)

This (according to "La Bibliographie de l'Escrime," par Vigeant) is the first work on Fencing published in the United Kingdom—an erroneous statement. *See* **True Arte of Defence, His Practise, Paradoxe of Defence, Mars his Field,** and **Schoole of the Noble and Worthy Science of Defence,** all of which were previously published in this country.

Compleat Fisherman, The, being a large and particular account, &c., by James Saunders. 1724. 12mo. Front. 5s. (cf.) Reprinted without date (but about 1800) under the title of "The Fisherman or the Art of Angling Made Easy," by "Gumiad Charfy, Esq."

Compleat Gamester, The, by Richard Seymour. Enlarged by C. Johnson. 1754. 12mo. Front. 16s. (cf. ex.) This is a late edition, the 5th having appeared in 1734, 12mo; the 6th in 1739, 12mo; the 7th in 1750, 12 mo., and the 8th in 1754, 12mo.

Compleat Gentleman, The, fashioning him absolute in the most necessary and commendable qualities, &c., by Henry Peacham. 1st edition, 1622. 4to. Engraved title. 16s. (cf.)

Another edition, 1627. 4to. 8s. (cf.)

Another edition, 1661. 4to. Engraved title. 10s. (old cf.) The last edition of a work extensively used by Dr. Johnson in the compilation of his dictionary, all the definitions of terms of blazonry being taken from it.

Compleat History of the Lives and Robberies of the most notorious Highwaymen, Footpads, &c., of both sexes; to which is prefixed the Thieves' new Canting Dictionary, by Alexander Smith. 1719-20. 3 vols. 12mo. Plates. £1 1s. (hf. cf.)

This is the fifth edition. The first (?) edition appeared in 1714. 2 vols. 12mo., and a supplement in 1 vol. 1720. £1 15s. (cf.) Though described on the title as "Second Edition" it is questionable whether there was a prior one.

Compleat Horseman: The, discovering the surest marks of the Beauty, Goodness, Faults and Imperfections of Horses, by Jacques de Solleysell. 1711. 8vo. Folding plates. 12s (cf.)

This is an abridged translation (by Sir William Hope) of Solleysell's "Le Parfait Mareschal," first published in 1664. A prior English edition, translated by the same hand, appeared in 1696, and a later one in 1717. Both these are unabridged, and, therefore, better than the edition of 1711, above mentioned.

Compleat Horse-man, and Expert Farrier, The, by Thomas De La Gray, 1654. 4to. Equestrian portrait after Hollar, £2 15s. (orig. cf.) This is the second edition. The first appeared in 1651, 4to ; the third in 1656, 4to ; and the fourth, with additions, in 1670, 4to. £1 10s (orig. cf.)

Compleat Swimmer, The, or the Art of Swimming, by William Percey, 1658. 12mo. Front. £8 (cf gt John Evelyn's copy with autograph inscription)

A literal translation (though not described as such) of Everard Digby's "De Arte Natandi," first published in 1587. See **Arte Natandi, De.**

Compleatest Angling-Booke that ever was writ · being done oute of ye Hebrew and other Tongues, by a Person of Honor (Joseph Crawhall) *Second edition*, 1881. Small 4to., adorned with sculptures, £6 6s. (mor. ex.)

Complete Angler's Vade Mecum, The, by Capt T. Williamson, 1808. 8vo., pp. xi. 316. 18 engravings of fish and tackle. 5s (bds.) Re-issued with a fresh title page in 1822.

Another edition, 1825. 12mo. 5s. (bds.)

Complete Art of Boxing, The, according to the Modern Method, wherein the whole of that manly accomplishment is rendered so easy and intelligent that any person, &c., &c., by "An Amateur of Eminence." 1788. 8vo. Folding front., Humphreys and Mendoza Sparring. 12s. (cf., uncut).

Complete Farrier, and British Sportsman, The, by Richard Lawrence [1816], 4to. Plates 7s. (orig. cf.)

Another edition, 1833. 4to Plates. 7s. (cf.) Published at 25s.

Complete Fisher, The, *see* **True Art of Angling.**

Complete Sportsman, The, or Country Gentleman's Recreation, containing the whole Art of Breeding and Managing Game Cocks, &c., by Thomas Fairfax. 1st ed. n. d (1760). Printed for J. Cooke. Front. 12s. (orig. sheep.) 5s. (cf.)

Another edition, revised and enlarged, 1795. 12mo. Front. 5s. (cf.)

Concise Treatise on the Art of Angling, A, by Thomas Best. 1st ed. 1787. 12mo. 3s. 6d. (cf.) Many later editions, all of small value. The 10th and 11th incorporate Nobbes' "Treatise on Trolling." 2s. (10th ed. of 1814, orig. sheep.)

Corinthian Parodies, by Tom, Jerry, and Logic, illustrative of Life in London. 1823. 12mo. Folding col. front by J. R. Cruickshank. 12s. (wrappers).

Country Contentments; or, the Husbandman's Recreations, consisting of the Art of Riding, Hunting, Hawking, &c., &c., by Gervase Markham. 1st ed. 1611. 4to. £1 4s. (cf.)

Second edition, 1613. 4to. £1 5s. (cf.)
Sixth edition, 1649. 4to. 5s. (hf. cf.)
Ninth edition, 1660. 4to 5s (hf. cf.)
Eleventh edition, 1675. 4to. 5s. (hf cf.)

Country Sketches, by G. Finch Mason, n.d. (1870?). Oblong folio. 7s. (bds.)

Another ed., 1882. Oblong fol. 4s. (bds.) Published at 10s. 6d.

Cours d'Hippiatrique, ou traité complet de la médecine des chevaux, par Lafosse, 1772. Fol. Port. and 65 pl. £2 (cf. gt., sound copy). The plates are sometimes found coloured, and were so in the copy quoted as having sold by auction for £2.

Courser's Manual or Stud Book, The, by Thomas Goodlake, 1828. Roy. 8vo. Port. and woodcuts. pp. lxxvi. 85. 6s. (boards).

Covent Garden Magazine, The, or Amorous Repository, 1772-3. 2 vols. 8vo. Plates. £13 (calf).

Cracks of the Day, The, edited by "Wildrake" (George Tattersall). 1844. Roy 8vo. Bohn. 65 engravings after Herring, Cooper, Hancock, and others. £3 (cl., uncut), £1 10s (hf. cf.)

The first edition was published by Ackermann in 1841. Roy 8vo. Plates by Alken, Herring, and others. £3 (orig. cl.)

Cream of Leicestershire, The, Eleven Seasons' Skimmings. Notable Runs and Incidents of the Chase, by "Brooksby" (Edward Pennell Elmhirst). 1883. 8vo. pp. xvi. 435, with col. and other illustrations by Sturgess. Portraits and a map. 8s. (orig. red cl.)

Cricket, by William Gilbert Grace. 1st ed. 1891. pp. xii. 512, with illustrations. 3s (cl., uncut). Some copies were printed on Large Paper.

Criminal Recorder, The, being Biographical Sketches of Notorious Public Characters, including Murderers, Traitors, &c. 1804-9. 4 vols. 12mo. Portraits and views. 8s. (calf).

Cruising in the Cascades, a Narrative of Travel, Exploration, Hunting and Fishing, &c., by G. O. Shields, 1889. 8vo. Port. and illustrations. 3s (cl. extra). Published in London at 10s 6d from American sheets with an English title page substituted.

Crumbs from a Sportsman's Table, by Charles Clarke, 1865. 2 vols. 8vo. 6s (cl.), published at 21s.

Included in the "Select Library of Fiction," 1868. 12mo. Published at 2s.

Cuckold's Chronicle, The, being Select Trials for Adultery, Incest, Imbecility, Ravishment, &c., 1793. 2 vols. 8vo. Plates. £12 15s. (mor. ex.); £5 (hf. cf.)

A pamphlet appeared without date (but about 1810) under the almost similar title of "The Cuckold's Chronicle, or the New Bon Ton" Plates. £1 (wrappers).

Cudgel-playing modernised and improved; or the Science of Defence Exemplified, &c., by Capt. Sinclair, 1800. 8vo. "Illustrated with fourteen Positions." 6s. (hf. cf.)

Curling; the Ancient Scottish Game, by James Taylor. 1st ed. 1884. 8vo. Illustrations by Doyle. 5s. (cl.) Published at 10s. 6d.

Second edition, 1887. 8vo. Illustrations by Doyle. 2s. (cl.) Published at 5s.

Cutter, The, in five Lectures upon the Art and Practice of Cutting Friends and Acquaintances and Relations. 1808. 8vo. 6 col. pl. by Atkinson. 12s. (bds., uncut).

Cyclopædia, *see* **Encyclopædia.**

Cynegetica: or Essays on Sporting, . . . by William Blane, 1788. 8vo. Front. and vignettes by Stothard. £1 10s. (cf. ex., uncut). Includes Somerville's Chase.

This book is, in effect, a new edition of "Essays on Hunting," published in 1781. 8vo. *See* **Essays on Hunting.**

Cynegeticon, or the Art of Hunting; translated from the Cynegeticon of Gratius Faliscus, by Christopher Wase, 1654. 8vo. Front. £1 16s. (cf.)

Cynegeticus of the younger Xenophon (Arrianus on Coursing), translated from the Greek, with Annotations, &c., by "A Graduate of Medicine" (W. Dansey) 1831. 8vo. J. Bohn. Contains embellishments from the antique on India paper. 250 copies printed. 16s. (cloth).

Dance of Life, The, a Poem, by William Combe 1st ed., 1817. Roy. 8vo. 26 col. pl. (inclusive of front and title) by Rowlandson. £4 18s. (orig. bds.); £9 5s. (*ibid*, very clean); £3 15s. (cf. extra).

Days and Nights in the Desert, by Parker Gillmore, 1888. 8vo. pp. viii 234. Illustrations. 2s. 6d. (orig. cl.)

Days and Nights of Salmon Fishing in the Tweed, by William Scrope. Tinted plates and cuts after Landseer and others. 1st edition, 1843. Roy. 8vo. £10 10s. (orig. cl.), £11 11s. (*ibid*), £4 10s. (hf. cf. gt.)

Second edition, 1854. Roy. 8vo., with all the plates. £2 10s. (orig. cl.)

Another edition, 1885. 8vo. Glasgow, with the plates. 10s. (cl.)

Days in Clover, by "The Amateur Angler" (Edward Marston). 1892. 12mo. Seven plates. 5s. (L. P. parchment). 150 copies were printed for England on Large Paper.

Day's Journal of a Sponge, by "Peter Pasquin," 1824. Oblong 4to. Six col. etchings. £2 2s. (original wrappers); £7 (mor. ex.; very fine copy).

Days of Deer Stalking in the Forest of Atholl, by Wm. Scrope. 1st ed., 1838. Roy. 8vo. Engravings and lithographs after the Landseers and the author. £7 15s. (hf. mor. gt.); £8 (orig. cl., good copy).

Second edition. Plates as before (with one extra). 1839. 8vo. £5 (orig. cl.); £6 10s. (orig. cl.); £3 10s. (*ibid.*)

Third edition, 1847. 8vo. Two plates by Sir E. Landseer and 12 wood engravings by Chas. Landseer and the author. £1 1s. (hf. mor.), £1 6s. (orig. cl.)

Another edition, 1883. 8vo. Same plates. 10s. (cl.)

Another edition, 1894. 8vo. Illustrated. 5s. (orig. cl.) Published at 12s. 6d.

Another edition, 1897. 8vo., pp. xviii 304, with 10 plates after Sir E. Landseer. Forming Vol. 5 of Sir H. E. Maxwell's "Sportsman's Library." Published at 15s.

Death's Doings, consisting of numerous original compositions in verse and prose by Tom Hood, R. Montgomery, and others. *Second and best edition*, 1827. 2 vols. 8vo., with 30 full p. etchings by Richard Dagley. 10s. (orig. bds.) The *first edition* was published in 1826, with 24 etchings, by Dagley. 8s. (orig. bds.)

Deep Sea Fishing and Fishing Boats: by Edmund W. H. Holdsworth, 1874. 8vo. Illustrations. 8s. (orig. cl.) Published at 21s.

Deer Forests of Scotland, The, by A. Grimble. 1st and only edition, 1896. Large 4to. pp. xxiv. 324. 8 illustrations, by A. Thorburn. £1 8s. (hf. vel. as issued). 500 copies of this book were published at £2 10s. net.

Deer Parks and Paddocks of England, The, by James Whitaker, 1892. 8vo. £1 15s. (orig. cl.)

Deer Stalking, by Sir Robert Frankland, n. d. (1830). Oblong folio. 10 lithographs. Privately printed, 12s. (hf. bd.)

Deer Stalking, by A. Grimble, 1886. 8vo. pp. x. 115. Plates. 8s. (orig. cl.), 21s. (L P., orig. cl.)

Deer Stalking in the Highlands of Scotland, by Lt.-Gen. H. H. Crealock, 1892. Folio. 255 copies printed. 40 full page plates and numerous cuts in the text. pp. xviii. 194. £11 (orig. cl.)

Delineations of British Field Sports, together with the various Methods of Poaching, 1882. Folio, with 24 large lithographic plates by S. Alken. £3 5s. (hf. mor.)

Derby Carnival, The, London's Great Outing. 1869. Oblong 4to. Tinted folding plate and woodcuts by "Phiz." 12s. (orig. wrappers).

Derby Day, The. The Road and the Course 1866 Folio. 8 hand-col. pl. by "Phiz." £5 (cl.)

Description of the River Thames, &c., to which is added a brief description of those fish, with their seasons, spawning times, &c., that are caught in the Thames. (By Robert Binnell). 1758. 8vo. Five plates. £2 (hf. mor.) Roger Griffiths' "An essay to prove that the jurisdiction and conservancy of the River of Thames," &c., 1746, 8vo., is the original of Binnell's work, which is, in fact, a virtual copy with an adapted title page.

Details of a Demirep! or Life and Adventures of the Celebrated Lady Barrymore, *alias* Mary Ann Pierce. . . seasoned with delectable songs, rich morceaux, &c. n.d. 4to. Duncombe. Coloured front. £2 10s. (hf. mor.)

Devil among the Fancy, The, or the Pugilistic Courts in an Uproar. 1822. 8vo. Col. front by J. R. Cruikshank. £2 (cf. gt.)

D'Horsay, or The Follies of the Day, by "A Man of Fashion" (John Mills). 1844. 8vo. Plates. £1 1s (orig. cl.)

Diary of Fifteen Years' Hunting, A, from 1796 to 1811, by John Beard. 1813. 12mo. pp. vii. 292. Woodcuts. £1 18s (orig. bds.)

Diorama Anglais, Le, *see* **Life in London.**

Diary of Colonel Peter Hawker, 1802-53, with an introduction by Sir R. Payne-Gallwey, 1893. 2 vols. 8vo., with 2 portraits of Hawker and 8 full page plates. 6s (orig. cl.) Published at £1 12s.

Dictionary of Slang and Cant Languages, A, by Geo. Andrewes. 1809. Post 8vo. Folding col. front. by Geo. Cruikshank. 16s (wrappers).

Dictionary of Sports, A, or Companion to the Field, the Forest and the River Side, by "Harry Harewood," 1835. Post 8vo. Woodcuts. 5s. (cf.)

Directions for Breeding Game Cocks, &c., 1st ed n. d. (1781). 8vo. Col. folding plate of the Tufton Street Pit, by George Morgan. £2 8s. (orig. wrapper); £4 (ibid.)
  Another edition, 1818. 8vo. Col. front. £2 10s. (mor. ex.)

Discourse of Fish and Fish Ponds, A, [by Roger North.] 1st ed. 1713. 8vo. Small cuts. 10s. (cf. ex.)
  Second edition, 1715. 12mo. 5s. (cf.)
  Third edition, 1773. 4to. 5s. (cf.)

Doctor Comicus, or the Frolics of Fortune, a Comic, Satirical Poem for the Squeamish and the Queer, in 12 Cantos, by a Surgeon, 1828. 8vo. 14 full p. col. pl. in the style of Rowlandson. £1 (hf. cf.); £2 5s. (cf., sound copy).

Doings in London, or Day and Night Scenes of the Frauds, Frolics, Manners and Depravities of the Metropolis, by George Smeeton, 1828. 8vo. 33 plates after R. Cruikshank. £2 (orig. bds., uncut).
  Another edition, 1840. 8vo. £1 1s. (orig. cl.), 6s. (hf. cf.)

Doldenhorn and Weisse Frau, The, by Abraham Roth, 1863. Roy. 8vo. 11 col. pl., 4 other illustrations and a map. 10s. (orig. cl.)

Dolomite Mountains, The, by Josiah Gilbert and G. C. Churchill, 1864. Cr. 8vo., with 2 col. maps, 6 col. pl. and 27 woodcuts by Whymper. 18s. (cl., uncut); £1 5s. (ibid.)

Don Juan, containing his Life in London, or a True Picture of the British Metropolis, by Alfred Thornton, 1st ed. 1821-22. 2 vols. 8vo. 30 humorous coloured plates. £7 7s. (calf gilt, fine copy).
  Another edition, 1825-26. 2 vols. 8vo. £6 15s. (cf., fine copy).

Double Armed Man, The, by the New Invention: shewing some famous exploits atchieved by our Brittish Bowmen, by

"W. N Archer" (William Neade), 1625. Sm. 4to. 18 leaves, 8 full page woodcuts. £12 10s. (mor. ex.)

Down the Road, or Reminiscences of a Gentleman Coachman, by C. T. S. Birch Reynardson, 1st ed. 1875. 8vo. Col. plates by H. Alken. £1 16s. (orig. cl.); £2 5s. (ibid.)
Second edition, 1875. 8vo. Col. plates by H. Alken. 13s. (hf. cf.)

Doctor Comicus, *see* **Adventures of Doctor Comicus.**

Driffield Angler, The, in two parts, containing descriptions of the different kinds of Fresh Water Fish, &c., by Alexander Mackintosh. 1st ed. n d. (1806), Gainsborough. 8vo. pp. xi. 346, with portrait. 4s. (hf. cf.) This work again appeared in 1821 under the title. "The Modern Fisher, or Driffield Angler."

Drive through England, A, by James John Hissey, 1885. 8vo. pp. xiv. 391. Illustrated by the author. 8s. (orig. cl.)

Driving Discoveries, a Series of 7 col. pl. by Henry Alken, 1817. Oblong folio. £7 10s (mor. ex., very fine copy).

Dry Fly Entomology, by Fred M. Halford, 1897. 2 vols. 8vo., with 28 plates, some coloured. 16s (hf. mor.) An *édition-de-luxe* of 100 copies was issued.

Dry Fly Fishing in Theory and Practice, by Fred. M. Halford, 1889. Impl. 8vo. Plates. £2 (mor. g. t., L.P.) 100 copies were printed on Large Paper.

Duell Ease, a Worde with Valiant Spirits shewing the abuse of Duells, by G. F., 1635. Sm. 4to. Engraved title, by Marshall. £2 2s (cf.)

"Eagle's Nest" in the Valley of the Sixt, The, by Alfred Wills. 1st ed., 1860. 2 maps and 12 tinted plates. £1 4s. (orig. cl.)

Second edition, 1860. 2 maps and 12 tinted plates. £1 4s (orig. cl.) This second edition is quoted as "the best."

Eastern Hunters, The, Wild Sports in India, &c., by J. T. Newall, 1866. 8vo. Plates. 6s. (cl. gt.)

Easy and Familiar Rules for attaining, &c., *see* **Art of Fencing.**

Eccentric Excursions, or Literary and Pictorial Sketches of Countenance, Character and Country, &c., 1807. 4to., with 100 humorous coloured plates by G. M. Woodward. £11 (mor. ex., uncut, fine copy).

Eccentric Song Book, The, n. d. 8vo. J. Baily. Col. folding front. by Geo. Cruikshank. £5 (wrappers). This is very scarce, only one or two copies being known.

Ecole de Cavalerie, par Robichon de La Guérinière, *Paris*, 1733. Fol., with Equestrian portraits and plates, mostly after the designs of Parocel. £1 15s (cf.)
Another edition, 1736. 2 vols. 8vo. 7s. (cf.) The best of the octavo editions.
Another edition, 1751. Folio. Same plates, but worn, and therefore inferior. 15s. (cf.)

Ecole des Armes, L', *see* **School of Fencing.**

Eglington Tournament, The, held 30th August, 1839. A series of 21 large col. plates and illuminated initial letters, by Richard Doyle. 1843. Folio. £2 10s (mor. ex., g. e.) A small and unimportant book was published at Glasgow, by Orr and Sons, in 1839, giving a descriptive account of this famous passage of arms. This appears to be the only book specially devoted to the subject in the British Museum Library.

Elementary Course of Gymnastic Exercises, An, and a New and Complete Treatise on the Art of Swimming, by Peter Heinrich Clias, 1825. 8vo., with 9 plates of figures, &c. 6s. (calf.) Published at 10s. 6d.

Elements and Practice of Rigging and Seamanship, 1794. 2 vols. 4to. Moveable and other plates. £1 5s. (calf.)

Encyclopædia of Rural Sports, by D. P. Blaine. 1st ed. 1840. 8vo., with over 600 engravings by Leech, Alken, Landseer and others. 10s. (cf. ex.) Published at £2 10s.

Another edition, 1852. 8vo. by "Ephemera" (Edward Fitzgibbon) and others, with over 600 engravings on wood.

Another edition, 1858. 8vo. Illustrated from drawings by Leech. Published at 42s.

Another edition, 1870. 8vo. Illustrated from drawings by Leech. Published at 21s.

Another edition, 1880. 8vo. Engravings by Leech, Alken and others. 21s. (hf. bd.)

Encyclopædia of Sport, The, edited by the Earl of Suffolk and Berkshire, Hedley Peek and F. G. Aflalo. Complete in two volumes. Vol. I. A to LEO. 1897. Impl. 8vo. With 20 full page photogravures and several hundred illustrations in the text. Published at £1 5s. (buckram, gt.), £1 15s. (hf. mor. by Zaehnsdorf); £3 3s. (Full Levant Mor., by Zaehnsdorf)

English Angler in Florida, The, by Rowland Ward, 1898. 8vo. Illustrations. pp. xii 122.

English Bowman, The; or, Traits on Archery, to which is added the second part of the Bowman's Glory. By T. Roberts, a Member of the Toxophilite Society. 1801. 8vo. pp. 300. Front and engraved dedication. 10s. (cf.) "The Bowman's Glory" here referred to was written by William Wood and published in 1682. 8vo. £1 5s. (cf.) £1 6s. (ibid.)

English Dance of Death, The, by William Combe. 1st ed. 2 vols. Roy. 8vo. 1815-16. With 72 col. pl. by Rowlandson. Originally published in parts with wrappers, afterwards in volume form as above. £35 (orig. parts, fine set), £15 (orig. boards, some plates loose, clean), £3 10s. (hf. mor.), £7 7s. (calf, extra).

English Deer Parks, *see* **Some Account of English Deer Parks.**

English Fencing Master; or the Compleat Tuteroui of the Small Sword [by Henry Blackwell]. 1705. Small 4to., with 5 woodcuts and 24 folding plates. £9 10s. (mor. ex., good copy).

English Sportsman in the Western Prairies, by the Honble. G. C. G. F. Berkeley, 1861. Roy 8vo. Full page plates. 15s. (orig. cl.)

English Spy, The, Portraits of the Illustrious, Eccentric, &c., drawn from the Life, by "Bernard Blackmantle" (W. Westmacott). 1st ed. 2 vols. 1825-26. Coloured plates and woodcuts, by R. Cruikshank. £12 (hf. cf.); £18 (orig. bds.); £27 (hf. mor. ex.)

Epping Hunt, The, by Tom Hood. 1829. 12mo., with 6 full p. illustrations by Geo. Cruikshank. 10s (wrappers). The illustrations are met with separately and sometimes in proof, on India paper. £1 5s (proofs, sm. 4to.)

Equestrian Sketches, by a Walking Gentleman, n. d. Folio. Lithographs of celebrities. £1 12s (hf. mor.)

Erne, The, its Legends and its Fly Fishing, by Henry Garrett Newland. 1851. 8vo. Col. front. and plates. 6s (cl.)

Essay on Archery, An, Describing the Practice of that Art in all Ages and Nations, by Walter Michael Moseley, 1792. 8vo. Front. and 4 plates by Stothard. 10s (old cf., gt.)

Essay on Curling and Artificial Pond Making, by Cairnie, 1833. 8vo. Plates. 10s. (bds.)

Essay on Hunting, An, by "A Country Squire," 1733. 8vo. Front. and vignettes. 25s. (cf.)

Reprint, by Smeaton, 1820. 8vo. Front. and vignettes. 10s (cf.)

A work entitled "Essays on Hunting" (q v), edited by William Blane, was published at Southampton, without date (but 1781). This is founded on the above-named work, portions of which are extracted. A second edition appeared in 1782.

Essay on Shooting, 1789. 8vo. Plates. £1 12s. (hf. mor., uncut).

Second edition, 1791. 8vo. Plates. £1 12s. (hf. mor., uncut).

Essay on the Art of Ingeniously Tormenting, by G. M. Woodward. 1st ed., 1808. 12mo. 5 folding and full page col. caricatures by Rowlandson. £2 (orig. bds., uncut).

Another edition, 1809. 12mo. Plates as before. £1 12s. (bds., uncut).

Essay to prove that the Jurisdiction and Conservancy of the Thames, &c., *see* **Description of the River Thames.**

Essays on Hunting, containing a Philosophical Enquiry into the Nature and Properties of the Scent, &c., edited by William Blane. 1st ed. (1781). 8vo. pp. xxviii 135. 10s. (cf.) Extracted from "An Essay on Hunting, by a Country Squire." A second edition of this book, with "The Method of Hare-hunting practised by the Greeks, By a Sportsman of Berkshire," appeared without date (but 1782 ?) 5s. (cf.) *See* **Cynegetica; Essay on Hunting.**

Evelina, or Female Life in London, being the History of a Young Lady's Introduction to Fashionable Life and the Gay Scenes of the Metropolis, 1822. 8vo. Col. plates by William Heath. A very scarce book, probably £10 (hf. cf. as published).

Evening's Amusement, An, or the Adventures of a Cockney Sportsman, 1846. Roy. 8vo., with 92 full page plates by R. Seymour. 20s (cf.)

Everybody in Town and Everybody out of Town, a series of 12 coloured plates by G. M. Woodward. 1796. 4to. £3 10s (cf ex.)

Every Gentleman's Manual, a Lecture on the Art of Self Defence, by Pierce Egan, 1845. 8vo. Plates and frontispiece of Lord Byron boxing with Jackson. 16s (orig. cl.)

Excursions in Albania, comprising a description of the Wild Boar, Deer and Woodcock Shooting in that Country, by Capt. James John Best. 1842. 12mo. Map and engravings. 4s (cloth) Published at 10s. 6d.

Exercise of Armes for Calivres, Muskettes and Pikes, The, by Jakob de Gheyn, 1607. Folio, with 117 plates. £8 (cf., sound copy).

Another edition, 1619. 4to. £4 15s. (cf., 127 woodcuts, coloured by hand).

Experienced Angler, The, or Angling Improv'd, being a general discourse of Angling, by Col. Robert Venables. 1st ed., 1662. 12mo. pp. xvi 105, with the same cuts as are used in Walton's Angler. £8 5s. (mor., g. e.)

Second edition, 1666 (?) 12mo (?) Said to have been totally destroyed in the Great Fire. No copy is known.

Third edition, much enlarged, 1668. 8vo. £5 15s. (orig. sheep.)

Fourth edition, much enlarged, 1676. 8vo. Cuts as in Walton's Angler, but reversed. £5 (orig. sheep.)

Fifth edition. Front. and copperplate engravings, 1683. 4to. £3 3s (orig. sheep.) A reprint of the first edition, known as "Gosden's Reprint," appeared in 1825 and again in 1827, both in 12mo.

Expert Sword-Man's Companion; or the True Art of Self Defence. To which is annexed the Art of Gunnerie, by Donald McBane, 1728. 12mo. Portrait and 22 cuts. 14s. (cf.)

Exterior of the Horse, by Armand Goubaux and Gustave Barrier, 1892. 8vo. pp. xxvii 916. 380 illustrations. 10s. (orig. cl.) Published at 30s.

Translated from "De l'Extérieur du Cheval," Paris, 1884. 8vo.

Extracts from the Diary of a Huntsman, by Thomas Smith 1st ed., 1838. 8vo. Plates and cuts. £1 15s. (orig. cl.) Published at 21s.

Second edition, 1840. 8vo. 5s. (orig. cl.) Published at 12s. 6d.

Third edition, 1852. 8vo. 2s. (orig. cl.) Published at 5s. 6d.

Fairbairn's Sporting Songster, n.d. 8vo. Col. folding front. 5s. (orig. stiff paper cover).

Fair Diana, by "Wanderer." 1st ed. (1884) 8vo. pp. viii 360, with 22 col. pl. by Georgina Bowers. 8s. (orig. cl.)

Falconer's Favourites, by William Brodrick, a series of coloured plates, with descriptive letter-press, 1865. Folio £3 (orig. cl.)

Falconry in the British Isles, by Francis Henry Salvin and William Brodrick. 1st ed., 1855. 8vo. Col. plates, £4 (orig. cl.), £6 15s (*ibid*)

Second edition, 1873. Imp. 8vo. Revised and enlarged Van Voorst. Col. plates. £6 6s. (orig. cl.), £5 (*ibid*)

Falconry in the Valley of the Indus, by Sir Richard Francis Burton, 1852. 8vo. Tinted plates. 6s. (orig. cl., uncut).

Falconry, or the Falcon's Lure and Cure, *see* **Latham's Faulconry.**

Famous Clyde Yachts, 1880 to 1887. Plates coloured and mounted like drawings. 1888. Folio, £1 15s (as issued).

Famous Golf Links, by Horace G. Hutchinson, Andrew Lang, and others. 1891. 8vo. pp. x 201, with 19 full page illustrations, inclusive of front and 13 woodcuts in the text. 8s (orig. cl.) Published at 6s.

The bulk of the articles which appear in this book were reprinted from the *Saturday Review.*

Famous Horses, with Portraits, Pedigrees, &c., by Theodore Taunton, 1895. 8vo. pp. viii. 396 ; 12s. (cl.) Published at 42s.

Fancy, The, or True Sportsman's Guide, Authentic Memoirs, &c., of Pugilists, by An Operator, 1822. Pub. in 45 parts, wrappers. Ports. and plates. £3 (in parts, clean); £2 2s. (2 vols., bds.); £5 (mor., ex. fine copy).

Fashion and Folly, or the Buck's Pilgrimage, a series of 23 humorous col. plates and descriptive verses, by Heath, 1832. Folio. £9 12s. (mor. ex., uncut, fine series).

These plates form an extra series to "Life in London." Though attributed to Heath, it is probable that they were designed by Robert Cruikshank, whose portrait, as well as that of Pierce Egan, is found in many of the scenes.

Fashion and Folly, or the Buck's Pilgrimage, a collection of 24 humorous col. pl. after H. Alken and others, 1822. 8vo.; £5 (bds.)

Another edition, n.d. (1825). Oblong 8vo. £2 (hf. cf.)

Fashionable Bores, or Coolers in High Life, by "Peter Quiz," 1824. Oblong folio. 12 large col. pl. by D. T. Egerton and engraved title. £2 10s. (orig. pink wrappers); £10 (mor. ex., uncut, very fine copy).

Fencing Familiarised, or a new treatise on the Art of the Scotch broad-sword, shewing the superiority of that weapon when opposed to an enemy armed with a spear, pike, or gun and bayonet, by T. Mathewson. 1805. 8vo., with 34 illustrations. 8s. (cf.)

Fencing Familiarized, or a new treatise on the Art of Sword Play, by J. Olivier. London, 1771. 8vo. Front. and 8 plates by Ovenden. 15s. (cf. gt.)

Another edition, 1780. 8vo. Front. and 8 folding plates. Different from those in the last edition. 7s. (cf.)

Written in French and English under the principal title of "L'Art des Armes simplifié, ou nouveau traité sur la manière de se servir de l'épée."

Festivals, Games and Amusements, Ancient and Modern, by Horace Smith, 1831. 8vo. pp. viii. 382. 3s. (orig cl.)

Another edition, 1831. Cr. 8vo. Plates. 2s (cl.) Number 5 of "The National Library."

Few Ideas, A, being hints to all would-be Meltonians, 1825. Folio. Humorous col. plates by Henry Alken. £5 (pictorial wrappers).

Field Book, The, or Sports and Pastimes of the United Kingdom, compiled from the Best Authorities, by the author of "Wild Sports of the West" (W. H. Maxwell). 1833 8vo. Woodcuts. 3s. (cl.)

Field Sports in the United States and the British Provinces of America, by "Frank Forester" (Henry William Herbert), 1848 2 vols. Post 8vo. 6s (orig. cl.) Published at 21s.

Field Sports of France, *see* **Introduction to the Field Sports of France.**

Field Sports of the North of Europe, by L. Lloyd, 1830 2 vols 8vo. Illustrations £1 10s. (orig. cl)

Another edition, enlarged, 1885. 8vo. pp. 416. 3s. (orig. cl.) Published at 9s.

Finch Mason's Sporting Annual. This periodical first appeared in 1894 (for 1895), 4to., and was published in 1895 (for 1896), each part at 1s. Col. and other illustrations The "English Catalogue" contains no record of any subsequent publication.

Finish to the Adventures of Tom, Jerry, and Logic . . . By Pierce Egan, 1830. Demy 8vo. 36 col. pl and numerous woodcuts by Robert Cruikshank. £19 10s (orig bds, clean copy), £9 (mor ex), £8 8s. (hf. mor)

Another edition, n d (1869), Hotten, with all the col. plates and cuts 15s. (hf. mor, uncut).

Another edition, 1887. Demy 8vo. Reeves and Turner, with all the plates and cuts. £1 10s. (orig. cl.)

See also **Life in London.**

First Ascent of the Kasai, The, being some Records of Service under the Lone Star, by C. S. L. Bateman, 1889. 8vo., with 57 illustrations and 2 maps. 3s. (cl.)

First Lessons in the Art of Wild-fowling, by Abel Chapman, 1896. 8vo. pp. xi. 270. Illustrations by Whymper. 5s. (orig. cl.) Published at 10s. 6d.

Fish and Fishing of the United States, *see* **Frank Forester's Fish and Fishing.**

Fish Hatching, by Francis Trevelyan Buckland, 1863. 8vo. Plates. 9s. (orig. cl.)

Fisherman, The, or the Art of Angling made Easy, *see* **Compleat Fisherman, The.**

Fishing Experiences of Half a Century, with instructions in the use of the Fast Reel, by Major F. Powell, 1895. Post 8vo. Illustrations by the Author. 2s. (orig. cl.) Published at 6s. 6d.

Fishing Miseries, or Six Red Letter Days in the Country, a series of 6 col. plates by Robert Frankland, 1800. Oblong fol. £6 18s. (mor. ex., uncut, fine copy)

Fishing with an Angle, *see* **Here begynneth, &c.**

Five Years of a Hunter's Life in the Far Interior of South Africa, by R. Gordon Cumming. 1st ed. 2 vols. 1850. 8vo. Illustrations. £1 16s. (orig. cl.), £2 7s. (hf. mor., ex.)

Another edition, 1856. 8vo. Issued under the title of "The Lion Hunter of South Africa." This is of no importance, as it is an abridgement. 4s. 6d. (orig. cl.) The same remarks also apply to an issue of (1892), 8vo., Simpkin and Marshall, under the title, "Five Years Hunting Adventures in South Africa."

Floating Flies and how to Dress them, by Frederic M. Halford, 1886. 8vo. pp. 136, with 9 hand col. plates and woodcuts. 10s. (cl.) Published at 15s., or on Large Paper at £1 10s.

Flowers of the Hunt, by G. Finch Mason, 1889. 8vo. pp. viii. 200. Illustrations by the Author. 4s. (orig. cl.)

Fly Fisher's Entomology, The, by Alfred Ronalds. 1st ed., 1836. 8vo. pp. viii. 115, with 19 copper plates.

Second edition, 1839. 8vo. pp. xii. 115, with 20 copper plates. £1 1s. (hf. mor.)

Third edition, 1844. 8vo. pp. x. 115. 20 col. pl. £1 (cloth); 10s. (*ibid.*)

There are later editions of 1849, 1856, 1862 and 1877, all in 8vo., of which the best is that of 1862, which has newly engraved plates.

Fly Fishers' Guide, The, by Geo. C. Bainbridge, *Second edition,* 1828. 8vo. Col. plates of flies. 10s. (orig. cl.)

Third edition, 1834. 8vo. Col. plates. 7s. (orig. cl.)

Fourth edition, 1840. 8vo. Col. plates. 3s. 6d. (orig. cl.)

The First Edition of this well known book appeared in 1816. 8vo., Liverpool. Twelve copies were printed in 4to at £2 2s. with the plates accurately coloured.

Fly Fisher's Text Book, The, by "Theophilus South." 1st ed., 1841. 8vo., with 12 full page plates and cuts in the text after Lee, Cooper, and others. 8s. (cl., uncut). Re-issued in 1845 by Bohn, under the title "The Illustrated Fly-fisher's Text Book," with 23 engravings, front. and pp vi. 231. 8vo. 16s. (orig. cl.) The author was Edward Chitty.

Flyers of the Hunt, by John Mills. 1st ed., 1859. 8vo. 6 plates by Leech, col. by hand. £1 5s. (orig. cl.) Copies with plain plates sell for about 10s. (cl.)

Another edition, 1865. 8vo. £1 4s. (orig. cl.) This is a duplicate of the preceding with a fresh title page.

Foreign Field Sports, Fisheries, Sporting Anecdotes, with the Field Sports of the Native Inhabitants of New South Wales, 1814. 4to. 110 col. pl. from drawings by S. Howitt, Atkinson, and others. £5 10s. (mor. gt.); £1 15s. (mor. ex.)

E

Another edition, 1819. Roy. 4to. Col. plates. £3 10s. (russ.)

Another edition, n. d. 4to. W. Gilling. 50 col. pl. £1 12s. (hf. bd.)

Written by J. H. Clark. Ten of the plates refer to the sports of New South Wales. (A supplement to the main work).

Fores' Sporting Notes and Sketches, Illustrated by Finch Mason and R. M. Alexander. £1 18s. (vols. i. to ix., 1884-92, cf. gt.)

Forest and the Field, by "The Old Shekarry." 1st ed., 1867. 8vo., with 8 illustrations. 6s. (orig. cl.) Published at 21s.

Another edition, 1874. 8vo. 8 illustrations. 2s. (orig. cl.)

Forest Sketches, Deer Stalking and other Sports in the Highlands Fifty Years Ago. 1865. 8vo. Plates. 11s. (orig. cl.) Published at 15s.

Fortnight's Ramble through London, A, or a complete display of all the Cheats and Frauds practised in that Great Metropolis. 1st ed., 1795. Post 8vo. Front and vignette title by Isaac Cruikshank. 7s. (orig. cf.)

Fower Chiefest Offices belongyng to Horsemanshippe, The, That is to say the Office of the Breeder, of the Rider, of the Keeper and of the Ferrer, by Thos. Blundeville, **Black Letter**, numerous engravings, 1565-6. Small 4to. W. Seres. £13 (vellum, some leaves cut). £7 (calf)

Another edition, n. d. (1570?) Willyam Seres. (£12 vellum)

Another edition, 1580. 4to. £1 9s. (cf., fair copy)
Another edition, 1597. 4to. £5 5s. (vellum); £3 (ibid.)
Another edition, 1609. 4to. £1 6s. (cf.)

See **Art of Riding newlie Corrected**.

Fowler in Ireland, The, by Sir Ralph Payne Gallwey, 1882. 8vo. pp. xiii. 503. Illustrations. 12s. (cl.) Published at 21s.

Foxhound, Forest and Prairie, by "Brooksby" (Edward Pennell-Elmhirst), 1892. Roy. 8vo., col. plates and woodcuts by Sturgess and Marshman. 5s. (orig. cl.) Published at 10s. 6d.

Fox-Hunting Atlas of every County in England, by Walker. Col. maps. n.d. 10s (hf. mor.) Another edition appeared in 1892.

Frank Forester's Fish and Fishing of the United States and British Possessions of North America, The, by Henry William Herbert, 1849. 8vo. pp. xvi. 455 Illustrations. 16s. (orig. cl.)

Second edition, 1850. 8vo. New York. Front. pp. 359.

Third edition, 1851. 8vo. New York. Front pp. xviii. 359, with a Supplement.

Another edition, 1859. 8vo. New York. Portraits of Horses on India paper and many woodcuts. 12s (orig cl)

Afterwards reprinted under the title of "Frank Forester's Fish and Fishing . . of North America" (1873). 12mo. New York.

Fur and Feather Series, The, The Grouse, 1894. 8vo. Illustrations. £2 10s. (hf. parchment, as issued, L.P.); 5s. (cl., Small Paper).

The Partridge, 1893. 8vo. £2 10s. (hf. parchment, as issued, L.P.); 5s. (cl., Small Paper)

The Pheasant, 1895. 8vo. £2 10s. (hf parchment, as issued, L.P.), 5s. (cl., Small Paper).

The Salmon, 1898. 8vo. £2 10s. (hf. parchment, as issued, L.P.) 5s. (cl., Small Paper).

The Trout, 1898. 8vo. Prices as before. Large and Small Paper.

The title "Fur and Feather," was subsequently changed to "Fur, Feather and Fin," so as to include books on Angling.

Fysshynge with an Angle, *see* Here begynneth, &c.

Game and Wild Animals of South Africa, *see* **Portraits of the Game, &c.**

Game Birds and Shooting Sketches; illustrating the Habits, Modes of Capture, Stages of Plumage and the hybrids and varieties which occur amongst them, by John Guille Millais. Front. coloured and tinted plates, by Sir J. E. Millais, 1892. Fol. £3 10s. (hf. mor.) Published at £5 5s.

Game Birds and Wild Fowl of Sweden and Norway, by L. Lloyd. 1867. 8vo. Woodcuts 48 chromos and maps (in pocket). £1 5s. (orig. cl.); £2 10s. (*ibid.*)

Game Birds and Wild Fowl, their Friends and their Foes, by A. E. Knox. 1850. 8vo. Plates. 25s (orig. cl.)

Game Fowls, their Origin and History, modes of Feeding, Training and Healing, by J. W. Cooper. 1869. 8vo. Col. plates. 15s (orig. pictorial cl.)

Another edition, quoted as n.d. 8vo., coloured plates. £3 3s (mor. gt.)

Gamekeeper at Home, The, by Richard Jefferies. 1st illustrated edition, 1880. Sq. 8vo. 10s (orig. pictorial cl.) The 1st and 2nd eds. of this work were published in 1878 without illustrations.

Gamekeeper's Directory, The, by "T. B. Johnson," 1820. 8vo. Cuts. 2s (bds.)

Game of Pallone, The, historically considered, by A. L. Fisher, 1865. 8vo. Front. and woodcuts. 5s (cl.) Published at 3s. 6d.

Gamonia; or the Art of Preserving Game, by Lawrence Rawstorne, 1837. 8vo. 15 col. pl. by J. T. Rawlins and others. £5 (mor., ex. g. e.); £3 (mor.)

Genealogy of the English Race Horse, The, by Thomas Hornby Morland, 1810. Front. 14s (hf. cf.); £1 10s. (mor. ex., uncut)

General History of the Lives and Adventures of the most Famous Highwaymen, Murderers, &c., to which is added a genuine account of the Voyages and Plunders of the most Notorious Pyrates, by Charles Johnson, 1734. Folio, the best edition, 26 plates £9 15s. (calf); £15 10s. (russ. gt.) Originally published in 73 weekly numbers, at 2d. each, or 20 monthly parts, at 8d.

Another edition, 1736. Fol. 26 plates £9 15s. (calf)

Another edition Birmingham, 1742. Fol. 26 plates. £5 (cf. ex.)

Another edition, 1814, Edinburgh. 8vo Front. 6s. (hf. cf.)

Another edition. n.d. Hodgson & Co. 8vo. Col. plates. £1 10s. (uncut).

Another edition n.d. Smeeton 8vo Col. plates. £2 5s. (hf. cf.)

General History of the Pyrates, A, with the Adventures of Mary Read and Anne Bonny, by Charles Johnson, 1724 2 vols 8vo Plates £1 5s. (cf.)

Third edition. 1725. 8vo. 14s. (cf.)

Fourth edition. 1726 2 vols 8vo. Plates £1 5s (cf.)

Another edition. 1814 12mo Norwich. Published under the title of "The History of the Pirates." 5s (cf.)

General System of Horsemanship, by the Duke of Newcastle, 1743. 2 vols Folio 63 plates £5 5s. (hf. mor. L.P.); £3 10s. (hf. cf. *ibid.*); £2 10s. (hf. russ., small paper) £1 10s (hf cf *ibid*) The first volume contains 43 plates, the second 20, several of which are coloured The work is a translation of the Duke's "Methode et Invention Nouvelle de dresser les Chevaux," first printed at Antwerp, in 1657. Folio.

Gentleman and Farmer's Guide, for the Increase and Improvement of Cattle, The, by Richard Bradley. 1729. 8vo. Plates. 8s: (cf)

Gentleman Fisher, The, *see* **Whole Art of Fishing, The.**

Gentleman's Academie, The, or the Booke of St. Albans, containing three most exact and excellent Bookes, the first of Hawking, the second of all the Proper termes of Hunting and the last of Armorie, all compiled by Juliana Barnes in the yere 1486 and now reduced into a better method by G. M. (Gervase Markham). 1595. Sm. 4to. Valentine Sims for Humfrey Lowndes. £24 10s. (cf., wanted a blank leaf). Lowndes says that this is printed in Black Letter, but it is not so. The text is Roman throughout. This is a reprint of the Book of St. Albans with re-arrangements and alterations. The treatises of Hunting and Armorie have distinct titles.

Gentleman's Compleat Jockey, with the Perfect Horseman. n.d. 8vo. Engravings. 16s. (cf., cut).

Gentleman's Recreation, The, in two parts, on Horsemanship, Hawking, Hunting, Fowling, Fishing, &c., by Richard Blome. 1st ed. 1686. Folio. About 100 copperplate engravings, coats of arms, &c. £10 5s. (old, cf.), £11 (L. P. mor. gt., Royal folio), £3 5s. (title mounted, fair copy).

Second edition, 1710. Folio, same plates. £5 5s. (good copy, old cf.)

Gentleman's Recreation, The, in four parts, viz. hunting, hawking, fowling, fishing, by Nicholas Cox. 1st. ed. 1674. 8vo. Front. and 4 folding plates. The "Directions for Blowing the Horn" is often missing. £6 (calf, fine and perfect copy).

Second edition, 1677. 8vo. Four folding plates. £1 10s. (old. cf.)

Third edition, 1686. 8vo. Four folding plates. £1 9s. (old. cf.); £2 10s. (ibid.)

Fourth edition, 1697. 8vo. Four folding plates. £1 6s. (old cf.)

Fifth edition, 1706. 8vo. Four folding plates. £1 16s. (mor. ex.)

Sixth edition, 1721. 8vo. Four folding plates. £2 (cf. ex. g. e., fine copy)

Gentleman's Tutor for the Small Sword, The, or the Complete English Fencing Master, by H(enry) B(lackwell). 1730. 4to. Six full page woodcuts of postures. £1 5s. (cf.)

Glaciers of the Alps, The, being a Narrative of Excursions and Ascents, by John Tyndall. 1st ed. 1860. Cr. 8vo. Front and 61 wood engravings. £1 10s. (orig. cl., uncut)

Another edition, with prefatory note by Mrs. Tyndall, 1896. 8vo. pp. xxvi, 445, with 58 engravings. 3s (cl.) Published at 6s. 6d.

Glenmâhra, or the Western Highlands, by Sir Randal Roberts, 1870. Post 8vo. Sporting illustrations by the Author. 2s. 6d (orig. cl.)

Golf, a Royal and Ancient Game, edited with an introduction by Robert Clark, 1875. Sm. 4to. Front and illustrations by Birket Foster, Drummond and others. £3 (orig. cl.) £5 5s (L. P. as issued).

Another edition, 1893. 8vo. pp xxvii, 304

Golf, see **Badminton Library, The.**

Golfing Annual, The. This annual publication was commenced in 1888 under the editorship of C. R. Bauchope. The volume for 1897 forms the tenth of the series and was published at 6s., as also was the volume for 1896. Vols. 1, 2, 3 appeared at 2s. 6d., vols 4, 5 and 6 at 3s. 6d., and vols 7 and 8 at 5s.

Good Grey Mare, The, by George John Whyte Melville, 1870. Oblong 4to. 19 illustrations by G. M. Scarlett. 5s (wrappers)

Gradus ad Cantabrigiam, or Cant Terms peculiar to the University of Cambridge, &c. 1824. 8vo., with 6 col and other plates. 15s. (bds uncut).

Grand Master, The: or the adventures of Qui Hi? in Hindustan. 1st ed., 1816. 8vo. 27 col plates by Rowlandson. £2 (russ.); £1 8s (hf. cf.)

Gretna Green Bolt-a, by Arthur O'Bradley, n.d. (1830). Oblong 4to., Ackermann. Col. front by Henry Alken. £2 5s. (mor. ex., uncut, fine copy)

Greyhound in 1864, The, being a second edition of the art of breeding, rearing and training greyhounds for public running, by "Stonehenge" (John Henry Walsh). 1864. 8vo. Illustrations. 5s. (cl.)

First edition, 1853. 8vo. Illustrations. 12s. (cl.) Published at 21s.

Another edition, 1875. 8vo. Illustrations. 5s. (cl.)

Guide to Norway and Salmon Fisher's Pocket Companion, by J. Jones, edited by Frederic Tolfrey. 1848. 12mo., pp. xxiv. 239, with 8 col. plates of flies. 6s. (cl.) Published at 15s.

Guide to the Cricket Ground, including History of the Game, Definition of Terms, &c., by George H. Selkirk. 1867. Post 8vo., with 9 plates and a scoring sheet. 7s. (cl.).

Gun and Camera in Southern Africa, by H. A. Bryden, 1893. 8vo., pp. xiv. 544. Map and illustrations. 6s. (orig. cl.) Published at 15s.

Gun and its Development, The, with Notes on Shooting, by W. W. Greener. 1st ed., n.d. (1881). 4to., with 342 full page and other engravings of guns in all ages. 4s. (orig. cl.) Published at 10s. 6d. There are many editions of this well-known work; a fourth appeared in 1889, a fifth in 1892, and the sixth and last in 1896.

Gun, Rifle, and Hound in East and West, by "Snaffle," 1894. 8vo. Illustrations. 4s. (cl.) Published at 16s.

Handbook of Angling, A, teaching fly-fishing, &c. with the Natural History of River Fish, by 'Ephemera' (E. Fitzgibbon). 1st ed. 1847. 8vo. Numerous woodcuts. 5s. (orig. cl.)

Second edition, 1848. 8vo. Cuts. 5s. (orig. cl.)
Third edition, 1853. 8vo. Cuts. 5s. (orig. cl.)
Fourth edition, 1865. 8vo. Cuts. 3s. (orig. cl.)

Handbook of Shooting, by "Newtonensis," 1868. 8vo. Illustrations. Published at 6d.

Handbook of Swindling, by "The late Capt. Barabbas Whitefeather" (Douglas Jerrold), 1839. 12mo. With plates by "Phiz." 8s. (orig. pictorial cl.)

Handbook to Boxing; being a Complete Instructor in the Art of Self Defence, and Chronology of the Prize-ring, by Owen Swift. 1848. 8vo. Cuts. 5s. (sewed).

Handley Cross: or Mr. Jorrock's Hunt, by the Author of "Mr Sponge's Sporting Tour" (R. S. Surtees). n.d. (but 1854). Published in 17 parts (March, 1853, to October, 1854), in red wrappers, designed by Leech; afterwards in demy 8vo as above. Contains 17 col. pl. and 84 woodcuts by Leech. £10 10s. (orig. parts); £2 10s. (orig. cl.); £4 15s. (ibid.)

Another edition, n.d. (1888), Bradbury, Agnew & Co. Col. plates by Wildrake and others. 10s. (cl.)

"Handley Cross, or the Spa Hunt," another novel by Surtees, first published in 3 vols. post 8vo., 1843, is not illustrated. £1 10s. (orig. cl.)

Hawbuck Grange; or The Sporting Adventures of Thomas Scott, Esq., by the Author of "Handley Cross; or the Spa Hunt" (R. S. Surtees). 1847. Demy 8vo., with eight full page etchings by "Phiz." £6 (orig. scarlet cloth); £3 10s. (ibid.)

Another edition, n.d. (1884), with coloured reprints of the plates. 10s. (cl.) This series of sketches appeared in *Bell's Life* during the winter season of 1846-7.

Hawking, Hunting, Fowling and Fishing, see **Bokys of Haukyng and Huntyng.** Editions 1586 and 1596.

Helps and Hints to Protect Life and Property, with instructions in Rifle and Pistol Shooting, by Lt. Berenger. 1835. 8vo. Illustrations by G. and R. Cruikshank, Alken and others. 10s. (cl. uncut). Published at 14s.

Here begynneth a Treatyse of Fysshynge with an Angle, by Juliana Barnes, or Berners. Black letter, woodcut on title, repeated on reverse, cuts in text and ornamental initials. London: Wynkyn de Worde. n.d. (1532). Small 4to., the first separate edition. The only copy known sold at the Ashburnham sale for £360. See also " Bokys of Haukyng and Huntyng."

Hibernia Venatica, by Maurice O'Connor Morris, 1878. 8vo. Photographs. 8s. (cl.) Published at 10s. 6d.

A series of letters on Fox Hunting in Ireland, 1876-77, reprinted from *The Field.*

Highland Gathering, A, Sporting Stories, by Edward Lennox Peel, with 31 illustrations by C. & E. Whymper, from original sketches, 1885. Post 8vo. pp xiv. 185. 3s. (cl.) Published at 10s. 6d.

Highland Sport, by Augustus Grimble. 1894. 4to. Ten plates by A. Thorburn. £1 12s. (hf. vel. as issued). Published at 42s.

Highland Sports and Highland Quarters, by Herbert Byng Hall. n.d. (1847). 2 vols. 12mo. Illustrated. 15s (orig. cl.)

Highlands of Central India, The, by Capt. J. Forsyth. 1871. 8vo. Map, col. plates and cuts of sporting trophies. 14s. (orig. cl.) Published at 18s.

Another edition, 1889. 8vo. Illustrations. 6s. (cl.) Published at 12s.

High Life and Towers of Silence, by Elizabeth A. F. Burnaby, 1886. Cr. 8vo., pp. xii. 195. Illustrations. 4s. (orig. cl.)

High Mettled Racer, The, a series of 6 col. engravings after Henry Alken. 1821. Folio. £7. (Good original impressions).

High Mettled Racer, The, to which are added many interesting anecdotes of the Race Horse, by the late Charles Dibdin. 1831. 12mo. Engravings by R. Cruikshank. 5s. (bds.)

Highways and Horses, by Athol Maudsley, 1888. 8vo., pp. xxxii 471. Plates. 6s (orig. cl.)

Hillingdon Hall; or The Cockney Squire, by the author of "Handley Cross" (R. S. Surtees). 1845. 3 vols. Post 8vo. This 1st ed. is not illustrated.

Another edition, 1888. 8vo, with 12 col. plates by Wildrake and others. 7s. 6d (orig. cl.)

Himalayan Journals, or Notes of a Naturalist in Bengal, The Sikkim and Nepaul Himalayas, &c., by Sir Joseph Dalton Hooker. 1st ed., 1854. 8vo. Tinted and coloured plates and engravings on wood. £1 3s (orig. cl., uncut)

Another edition, revised and condensed. 1855. 2 vols. 12mo. Of no importance.

Hints on Horsemanship to a Nephew and Niece; or Common Sense and Common Errors in Common Riding, by George Greenwood. 1839. 8vo. Plates. 2s (cl.)

Another edition, 1861. Sm. 4to. 3s (cl.) Published at 6s.

His Practise, in two Bookes, the first intreating the use of the Rapier and Dagger, the second of Honor and Honorable Quarrels, by Vincentio Saviolo. the two books. 1594-5. Sm. 4to., with woodcuts and ornamental initials. £35 (mor. ex., fine copy); £27 (mor. ex., name cut off title)

Saviolo's "practice" throws much light on the manners of the gallants of Queen Elizabeth's days and elucidates many passages in Shakespeare and Ben Jonson.

Historical Researches on the Wars and Sports of the Mongols and Romans, by John Ranking, 1826. 4to. Map and ten plates. 16s (calf)

A few copies were printed on fine paper, and the value of these is somewhat higher.

History and Art of Horsemanship, The, by Richard Berenger, 1771. Two vols. 4to. Front. and 16 pl. by Baillie. 16s. (cf.) This is a translation of Xenophon's Treatise on Horsemanship, with a dissertation on the ancient chariot, &c., by T. Pownall, added.

History and Delineation of the Horse, The, by John Lawrence, 1809. 4to. 15 plates by J. Scott. 15s. (mor. ex.) £1 1s. (Proof plates, calf). This work was published at £2 2s. or £6 10s. (proofs).

History of Celebrated English and French Thorough-bred Stallions and French Mares, which appeared on the Turf from 1764 to 1887, with preface by the Duke of Beaufort, by "S. F. Touchstone," 1890. Oblong fol. pp. xxv. 165. With 60 col. pl. and 134 hand col. vignettes. 520 copies published. £2 10s. (hf. mor. as issued).

Translated by C. B. Pitman, from "Les Chevaux de Course," Paris, 1889. Oblong fol.

History of Johnny Quæ Genus, the Little Foundling of the late Dr. Syntax: a Poem, by William Combe, 1822. Roy. 8vo. 24 col. pl. (inclusive of front.), by Rowlandson. £3 (orig. boards, broken). £4 (cf. ex., uncut). £2 2s. (cf.)

History of Newmarket and Annals of the Turf, The, by J. P. Hore. 1886. 3 vols. 8vo. Plates. 8s. (orig. cl.)

History of the British Turf, by James Rice, 1879. 2 vols. 8vo. Portraits. 10s. (orig. cl.) Published at 30s.

History of the British Turf, from the earliest period, by James Christie White, 1840. Two vols. 8vo. Portrait to vol. 1 and front. to vol. 2. 16s. (cl.) Published at 28s.

Second edition, 1840. 8vo. H. Bohn. Reduced to 12s.

History of the Lives of the Most Noted Highwaymen, &c. *see* **Compleat History, &c.**

History of the Pirates, *see* **General History, &c.**

History of the Royal Company of Archers, by James Balfour Paul, 1875. 4to. with six col. portraits and six autotype plates. 10s. (cloth)

Hobbinal, Field Sports and The Bowling Green, by William Somerville. 1813. 8vo. pp. 118. Woodcuts. Copies are met with on Large Paper (4to). £1 10s. (L.P., mor. ex., uncut).

This is the title of the above-named Poem, of which there are many prior editions. The first appeared in 1740 under the title "Hobbinal, or the Rural Games," and the sixth in 1773.

Hog Hunting in Lower Bengal, by Percy Carpenter, 1861. Impl fol. Col. plates by the author. £2 5s. (hf mor.)

Hog Hunting in the East and other Sports, by J. T. Newall, 1867. 8vo. Illustrations. 6s. (cl.)

Holiday on the Road, A, by James John Hissey, 1887. 8vo. pp. xviii 408. Illustrated by the Author. 8s. (cl.)

Honor, Military and Civill, contained in four bookes, by Sir William Segar Norroy King-at-Arms. 1602. Small folio, pp. 256, with 8 full length copper-plate portraits. £5. (old cf.)

This work is divided as follows —(1) Justice and Jurisdiction Military (2) Knighthood in general and particular (3) Combats for Life and Triumph. (4) Precedency of Great Estates and Others Some copies were printed on Large Paper.

Hope's New Method of Fencing, *see* **New, Short and Easy Method of Fencing.**

Horse Accomplishments, 12 humorous coloured plates, after Woodward, by Rowlandson, 1799. Oblong fol. Ackermann. £6 6s. (wrappers).

Horse and his Rider, The, by Francis B Head. 1860. 8vo. Plates 3s. (cl.) Published at 5s.

Horse and his Rider, The, by Rollo Springfield, 1847. 12mo. Plates. 3s. (cl.)

Horse and the Hound, The, by "Nimrod" (C. J. Apperley). 1st ed., 1842. Cr. 8vo. with engraved front. by Dobbie. Seven full page col. plates and cuts by Alken. 15s (orig. cl.)

Second edition, 1843. 8vo 8s. (hf. mor.)

Horse in the Stable and the Field, The, by "Stonehenge" (J. H. Walsh). 1861. 8vo. Illustrations. 5s (hf bd.)

There are many editions of this well-known work; a 13th appeared in 1890. 8vo. pp. x. 622, published at 12s. 6d.

Horses and Hounds: a practical Treatise on their Management, by "Scrutator" (K. W. Horlock). 1855. 8vo. 4s. (cl.)

Another edition, 1858. 8vo. Illustrations by Harrison Weir. 6s. (cl.) J. S. Rarey's "Instructions for Taming Horses" (q. v.) was added to this edition of 1858.

Horsemanship, or the Art of Riding and Managing a Horse, by Capt. Mervyn Richardson, 1853. 8vo. Plates by Ansdell. 3s. (hf. cf.) Published at 14s.

Hours of Exercise in the Alps, by John Tyndall. 1st ed., 1871. 8vo. pp. x. 473. Illustrations. £1 10s. (orig. cl.) Published at 12s. 6d.

Second edition, 1871. 8vo. Published at 12s. 6d.

How Pippins enjoyed a day with the ——— Fox Hounds, 1863. Folio. Illustrated title and 12 large coloured lithographic plates by "Phiz." £1 8s. (orig. covers).

How to qualify for a Meltonian, addressed to all would-be Meltonians, a series of six large coloured plates by Henry Alken. 1819. Oblong folio. £11 11s. (Mor. ex., uncut, original wrappers bound in, fine copy).

How to Tie Salmon Flies, a Treatise on the Method of Tying the various kinds of flies, by Capt. Hale. 1892. 8vo. Cuts. 5s. (cl.) Published at 12s. 6d.

Humourist, The, a Collection of Entertaining Tales, Anecdotes, Repartees, &c. 4 vols. 12mo. 1819-20, with 40 col. pl. by G. Cruikshank. £60 (orig. pictorial drab boards); £30 (mor. ex., uncut). The earliest issue of vol. 1 is without "vol. 1" on the title page.

Another edition, 4 vols., 1892. 40 illustrations by Geo. Cruikshank, coloured by hand. £1 15s. (as issued).

Humourist, The, a Companion to the Christmas Fireside, 1831. Cr. 8vo., with 50 illustrations by Thomas Rowlandson. 15s. (orig. green mor.)

Humours of Fleet Street and the Strand; being the Lives and Adventures of the most noted Ladies of Pleasure, &c., by an Old Sportsman. n d. (1749). 8vo. Two parts usually found in one vol. Front. £3 (calf).

Humours of the Hunting Field, by G. Finch Mason n d (1886). Oblong fol. Illustrations. 7s. (bds.)

Hungarian and Highland Broad Sword, 1799. Oblong fol. 24 plates by Rowlandson. Etched under the direction of Henry Angelo & Son. £6 6s (wrappers).
Angelo was fencing master to the Light Horse Volunteers of London and Westminster.

Hunger's Prevention; or, the Whole Art of Fowling by Water and Land, by Gervase Markham, 1655. 12mo. Woodcuts, £6 (orig. sheep, fine copy)
The first edition appeared in 1621. 12mo., pp. 285. Woodcuts

Hunt's Yachting Magazine, Commenced in 1852. Numerous maps, plates, charts, &c. £8 8s. (36 vols. 1852-87. Orig. blue cl.); £2 15s (16 vols 1852 67, hf. cf.)

Hunter's Arcadia, The, by Parker Gillmore, 1886. 8vo., pp. xvi. 300. Full page woodcuts. 4s. (orig. cl.)

Hunt Room Stories and Yachting Yarns, by Augustus Grimble, 1884. 8vo. Plates 3s (cl.)

Hunter's Progress, The, a series of 16 plates illustrating a Hunter's Life n.d. (1850) Oblong 8vo 6s. (orig. cl.)

Hunting, or Six Hours Sport by Three Real Good Ones, six col. plates, by H. Alken, 1823. 4to. £6 6s. (wrappers).

Hunting Bits, a series of 12 large col. plates by "Phiz." Chapman and Hall. n.d. (1865), oblong folio. £2 2s. (orig. bds.)

Hunting Directory, The, containing a compendious view of the ancient and modern system of the chase, &c., by "Thomas B. Johnson." 1826. 8vo. with plates. 14s. (cf.) Published at 9s.

Hunting Field, The, by 'Harry Hieover' (Charles Brindley), 1850. 8vo. Front. 2s (hf. bd.)

Hunting Grounds of the Great West, The. A Description of the Plains, Game and Indians of the Great North American Desert, by Richard Irving Dodge. 1876. 8vo. Port., map and illustrations by Ernest Griset. 10s. (hf. cf.)

This is an English edition of the "Plains of the Great West and their inhabitants," published at New York in 1876.

Hunting Grounds of the Old World, by "The Old Shekarry" (Henry A. Leveson), 1860. 8vo. tinted plates, published in series. 6s (cl., first series relating to India, Circassia and Algeria) Published at 21s.

Another edition, 1867. 8vo. Published at 6s.

Another edition, 1870. 8vo. Published at 5s.

Hunting in Hard Times. n.d. (1889) oblong folio, with letterpress and 20 humorous coloured plates by Georgina Bowers. 3s (original bds.) Published at 12s.

Hunting in the Himalaya, by Robert H. W. Dunlop, 1860. F'cap. 8vo. Map and plates after Wolf. 3s (hf. bd.)

Hunting Reminiscences, by A. E. Pease, 1898. 8vo. Illustrations, including two based upon sketches by Sir Frank Lockwood. Published at 21s. net (hf. bd.)

Hunting Reminiscences: comprising Memoirs of Masters of Hounds, &c., by 'Nimrod' (C. J. Apperley), 1843. Demy 8vo. 32 uncoloured full page plates and maps by Wildrake, Alken, and Henderson. £3 3s. (orig. cl.), £4 5s (*ibid.,* fine copy)

Hunting Sketches, 1859. Oblong folio. Six col. plates, after Alken. £2 10s (orig. hf. binding)

Hunting Songs, Ballads, &c., by Rowland Eyles Egerton Warburton. 1st. ed. 1834. 8vo. Col. port. and plates. £3 10s. (orig. cl., uncut).

Another edition, 1846. 4to. Illustrations. £1 18s. (hf. mor)

Another edition, 1855. Oblong 8vo., with four etchings by "Phiz." £1 2s (orig wrappers).

Another edition, 1859. 8vo An important edition, as it differs considerably from the preceding ones. £1 (cl.)

Another edition. 1877. 2 vols. 8vo. 18s. (hf. bd, uncut). Published at 5s.

See also "Three Hunting Songs."

Hunting Tours, descriptive of various Fashionable Countries and Establishments, &c., by "Cecil" (Cornelius Tongue), 1864. Post 8vo. Col. front. 5s. (cl., uncut).

Hunting Trips of a Ranchman, by Theodore Roosevelt, 1885 4to. New York. pp. xvi. 318. 10s. (orig. cl.)

Another edition, London, 1886. 8vo. pp. xvi 347. 7s. 6d. (cl.) Published at 18s

Illustrated Fly-Fisher's Text Book, The, *see* **Fly Fisher's Text Book.**

Illustrated Handbook of Cricket, by William Lillywhite, 1st. ed 1844 8vo. Portraits. 12s. (orig. cl.)

Another edition, 1888. 8vo. pp. 30. 5s.

Illustrations for Landscape Scenery, 22 coloured plates of hunting, riding, coaching, &c., by Henry Alken, 1821. 4to £3 12s. (hf. rox.)

Illustrations of the Passes of the Alps, by William Brockedon, 1828-9. 2 vols. 8vo. and 4to., with 109 plates by Finden £1 10s. (L P. 4to. proof plates, hf. mor.) Of this work 12 copies were printed in 2 vols. atlas folio, proof plates, at £63. The few sold by auction in recent years have only realised about 35s. each on the average (mor , g.e.)

Brockedon's "Passes of the Alps," as the work is familiarly called, first appeared in 12 parts and was afterwards published in book form as above.

Another edition, n.d. (1877). 2 vols. 4to. 12s. (hf. mor.)

Illustrations to Popular Songs, 1825. Oblong fol. 43 col. plates by H. Alken. £4 4s. (hf. bd.); £5 (hf. mor.); £8 10s. (orig. seven parts, wrappers)

Impartial and Brief Description of the Plaza . . . of Madrid and the Bull-Baiting there, by Jacobus Salgado, 1683. Sm. 4to., folding view. £4 12s. (calf)

Reprinted in the Harleian Miscellany, vol. 7.

Impressions of a series of Animals, Birds, &c., from a Set of Silver Buttons relative to the Sports of the Field, engraved by J. Scott, after drawings by A. Cooper. Edited by T. Gosden, 1821. 8vo. £2 10s (L.P., fine copy in calf, g.e.); £1 10s (calf).

Improved Art of Farriery, The, and a Treatise on Racers, Hunters and Dogs, by James White and W. H. Rosser, 1851. 8vo. Plates. 3s. (cl.)

Improved System of Fencing, wherein the use of the small sword is rendered perfectly plain and familiar, &c., by C. Martelli, 1819. 8vo. Folding plate. 4s. 6d. (cf.)

In and Beyond the Himalayas, a Record of Sport and Travel in the Abode of Snow, by Samuel James Stone, 1896. 8vo. pp. xvi. 330, with 16 plates by Whymper. 6s (orig. cl.) Published at 16s.

Incidents of Foreign Sport and Travel, by Fitzwilliam Thomas Pollok, 1894. 8vo. pp. vi. 427. Illustrations. 4s. (orig. cl.) Published at 16s.

Indispensable Accomplishments, a set of six coloured Hunting Scenes, by R. J. Humphrey, 1811. 4to. £4 4s. (wrappers).

India Sporting Review. Commenced in March, 1845, as a continuation of the "Bengal Monthly Sporting Magazine." Portraits and plates. £10. (16 vols. 8vo., hf. bd.) *See* **Bengal Monthly Sporting Magazine.**

Indian Game, from Quail to Tiger, by William Rice, 1884. 8vo. pp. iv. 221, with 11 tinted Lithographic Plates. 8s. (orig. cl.) Published at 21s.

Indian Spices for English Tables, or a Rare Relish of Fun from the Far East, &c., by George F. Atkinson, 1860. Oblong 4to. 120 humorous sketches. £1 (orig. bds.)

Indian Sports, 1828-9, published in parts, lithographic plates drawn by Sir C. D'Oyly. Folio. £1 8s. (two parts paper covers).

In Haunts of Wild Game, a Hunter-Naturalist's Wanderings from Kahlamba to Libomo, by F. Vaughan Kirby, 1896. 8vo. Illustrations by C. Whymper. Portrait and map. 10s. (cl.) Published at 25s.

Inn-Play, The; or, Cornish Hugg-Wrestler, by Sir Thomas Parkyns. 1st. ed. 1713. 4to. £1 15s. (cf.)

Second edition, 1714. 4to. Woodcuts. £1 12s. (cf. gt.)

Third edition, 1727. 4to. Woodcuts. £1 10s. (cf.); £6 6s. (mor., the author's own copy), £4 (old mor. L.P.)

Another edition, n.d., Bailey. Post 8vo. Two folding plates by R. Cruikshank. 10s. (sewn).

Instruction du Roy en l'Exercise de Monter à Cheval, L', par A. de Pluvinel, Paris, 1625. Folio. Front., 57 folding plates by Crispin de Pass and 4 portraits of Louis XIII, Pluvinel and others. The printed title. is frequently missing. £22 (calf, with title.); £30 (old. cf. gt. The Ashburnham copy).

Another edition, 1627. Folio. £6 (cf.)

Another edition, 1640. Folio. £7 (mor. ex.)

Another edition, 1666. Folio. £2 10s. (cf.)

Instructions for Taming Horses, by John S. Rarey, 1858. 12mo. pp. vi. 233. Illustrations. 4s. (cf.) Several other editions of this work were published under various alterations of title, notably a second of 1858, edited by "Scrutator," 1859. 12mo.; [1874.] 8vo. pp. vi. 236, (Routledge), and 1876. 8vo. *See* **Horses and Hounds.**

Instructions How to Play at Billiards, &c. . . . with the Art and Mysteries of Riding, Racing, Archery, and Cockfighting, 1687. 8vo. Frontispieces £1 18s. (calf, rebacked).

Instructions to Young Sportsmen, in all that relates to Guns and Shooting, by Lt.-Col. P. Hawker, 1st ed., 1814.

Second edition, 1816. 8vo. Plates. £2 2s. (mor. ex., fine copy). £1 5s. (L. P. cf., tinted front.)

Third edition, 1824 8vo. Plates. £2 (bds., uncut); £1 2s. (hf. russ. gt.)

Fourth edition, 1825. 8vo. Plates 18s. (cf., four plates col.)

Fifth edition, 1826. 8vo. Plates. 6s. (cf., plates uncoloured).

Sixth edition, 1830. 8vo. Plates. £1 1s (mor. ex.)

Another edition, 1838. 8vo. Plates. 10s. (orig. cl.)

Another edition, 1844. 8vo. Plates. £1 1s (cf. ex.)

Eleventh edition, 1859. 8vo. Plates. 10s. (hf. bd.)

More often than not some and not all of the plates are hand coloured, the rest being left plain. The value of any given copy depends primarily on the number of *coloured* plates it contains. See also "Diary of Colonel Peter Hawker," *ante.*

Introduction to the Field Sports of France, An, being a Practical View of Hunting, Shooting, &c., by R. O'Connor. 1846. Sm. 8vo. pp. xix. 304 Illustrations of Fish, &c. 5s. (cl.)

Second edition, 1847. 8vo. pp. xxiv. 324. Illustrations. Published under the title of "The Field Sports of France." 3s (cl.)

Introductory Course of Fencing, An, by George Ronald, 1827. 8vo., with five lithographs. 6s (orig cl.)

Another edition, 1846. 8vo. Published at 3s. 6d. *See* **Treatise on the Theory and Practice of the Art of Fencing.**

Irish Melodies, a series of 42 humorous plates illustrative of Moore's "Irish Melodies," by Sir C. E. S n d (1850?) Oblong 4to. £3 3s. (mor. ex., uncut, very fine copy)

Italian Valleys of the Pennine Alps, The, by Samuel Wilham King, 1858. 8vo. Plates. £1 (orig cl.)

Jerks in from Short Leg, by "Quid" (R. A. Fitzgerald), 1866. 4to. Engravings by Du Bellew. 12s. (orig blue cl.)

Johnny Quæ Genus, *see* **History of Johnny Quæ Genus.**

Jolly Angler, The, or Waterside Companion, The, by J. March 1st ed. n d (1833) 8vo. with 80 woodcuts, front, and pp vi , ii , 96. 8s (cf.)

Second edition n d. (1836) 80 woodcuts, front and pp. 106. 8s (cf.)

Third edition, n d. 8vo. 80 woodcuts, front. and pp 106, about the same value.

There are later editions all containing pp. 100, except the fifth (n d), which has 101.

Jorrocks's Jaunts and Jollities . . by R. S. Surtees, 1838. 8vo. Originally published in the *New Sporting Magazine* (July, 1831—Sept 1834), afterwards in volume form, as above. Contains 12 full page plates by "Phiz" £8 8s (orig. cl.)

Another edition, 1839. 8vo. 12 plates as before. £4 5s (cf ex fine copy)

Another edition, 1843. 8vo., with title and 14 plates and Title by H. Alken, all coloured. £8. (orig. cl.)

Another edition, 1869. 8vo., with the col. plates as before. £1 16s. (orig. cl.) This edition contains the extra papers "A Ride to Brighton," "A Week at Cheltenham," and "The Day after the Feast."

Another edition, 1874. 8vo. 16 col. plates by H. Alken. 14s. (cl.)

Journal of the Household Brigade, The, 19 vols. (all published), 1862-80. Ports and plates. £1 4s. (orig. cl.)

Jubilee Book of Cricket, by Prince Ranjitsinhji, 1897. Three issues as follows: 1, *Edition-de-luxe*, on hand-made paper, with 22 photogravures and 85 full page plates, each copy signed. Published at £5 5s. Crown 4to. 2, Fine paper edition, with full page plates on art paper. Published at £1 5s. Roy. 8vo. 3, Popular edition. Published at 6s. Crown 8vo.

Kings of the Turf, by "Thormanby" (Wilmot Dixon), 1897. 8vo., with 32 portraits. 10s. (cl.) Published at 16s.

Kingsclere, by John Porter, edited by Byron Webber, 1896. 8vo., pp. 388. Portraits of the Author and the Duke of Westminster, and 17 plates of race-horses, &c. 5s. (orig. cl.) Published at 18s.

Knapsack, The, with contributions by "Martingale" and others. Parts 1 to 6 (all issued) 1859. Cr. 8vo 5s. (sewn) The illustrations are in gallitype.

Kunopædia, A practical Essay on breaking or training the English Spaniel or Pointer, . . . by William Dobson. 1814. 8vo. Vignette front. 10s. (bds.) Published at 12s.

Land of the Dragon, The, My Boating and Shooting Excursions to the Gorges of the Upper Yangtze, by W. S. Percival, 1889. 8vo. pp. vii. 337. 4s. (orig. cl.) Published at 16s.

Large Game and Natural History of South and South-East Africa, The, by William Henry Drummond. 1875. 8vo. Coloured and other illustrations. 14s. (orig. cl.)

Large Game Shooting in Thibet and the North-West, by Alexander A. A. Kinloch. Series 1 and 2. London 4to. 1869-76 Plates £2 2s (orig cl)

Large Game Shooting in Thibet, the Himalayas and Northern India, by Alexander A. A. Kinloch, 1885 Calcutta. 4to pp vi 237. Illustrated by photogravures. 20s (orig. cl.)

Latham's Faulconry, or the Faulcon's Lure and Cure, by Simon Latham. 1st edition 2 parts. 1615-18. 4to. Each part has a separate title page, pagination and register. £25. (cf., clean copy)

Another edition, 1633. 4to 2 parts. Woodcuts. £6 6s. (vellum).

Another edition, 1653. 4to 2 parts Woodcuts £5. (cf.)

Another edition, 1658. 8vo. 2 parts. Woodcuts. £3 3s. (cf)

Another edition, 1662. 2 parts. Woodcuts. 8vo. £3 (cf.)

Lays of the Deer Forest, by "John Sobieski Stuart" and "Charles Edward Stuart" 1848 2 vols F'cap. 8vo. Fronts. 14s. (orig red cl) Published at 21s. Written by John Hay Allan and Charles Stuart Hay Allan.

Leaves from a Hunting Journal, 1880. Oblong 4to. 20 large plates with lithographed text, by Georgina Bowers. 6s. (hf. leather) Published at 21s

Lecture on the Art of Self Defence, by Pierce Egan (?) Cr. 8vo. Front representing Lord Byron sparring with Jackson, and portraits of prize-fighters. 1845 Cr. 8vo. 10s. (cf.); 17s (cl., uncut)

Le Morvan, its Wild Sports, Vineyards, and Forests . . translated from the French of Henri de Crignelle, by Captain Jesse 1851 Crown 8vo Front 5s. (cloth). Le Morvan is a hunting district in France.

Letters to Young Shooters, by Sir Ralph Payne Gallwey. *1st series,* 1890. 8vo. Published at 7s. 6d. *2nd series,* 1892. 8vo Published at 12s. 6d. *3rd series,* 1896 8vo pp. 660, with 200 illustrations by C. Whymper. Published at 18s £1 10s (the three series, orig. cl.)

Life and Death of a Racehorse, The, exemplified in his various stages of existence till his dissolution, by Thomas Gooch, 1792. Folio 6 aquatinta plates £9 (hf. cf.), £5 (*ibid.*) *See* also **Life of a Racehorse.**

Life in Ireland, *see* **Real Life in Ireland.**

Life in London, or, the Day and Night Scenes of Jerry Hawthorn, Esq . . . by Pierce Egan 1st edition, 1821. Demy 8vo Originally published in parts, afterwards in boards. Three folding sheets of music follow p 118, and there are 36 coloured plates by J. R. and G. Cruikshank. Some copies on Large Paper. £24 (L P , boards); £13 10s. Small Paper, orig bds., fine copy), £6 (mor. ex), £2 16s. (cf); £18 (parts)

Second edition, 1822. Demy 8vo. Plates, &c., as before. £6 10s. (bds., uncut); £3 3s. (mor , uncut)

Another edition, 1823. Demy 8vo Plates, &c., as before. £2 15s (hf russ.); £3 10s (orig bds)

Another edition, 1830. 8vo. Plates, &c., as before. £2 (hf. cf.)

Hotten's Reprint, n d. (1869). Post 8vo, with all the illustrations. 10s (cloth).

A scarce pamphlet entitled "Death of Life in London, or Tom and Jerry's Funeral," by T. Greenwood, is occasionally met with It was published by Lowndes, without date, in wrappers, and contains a coloured folding front, by Geo. Cruikshank £5 5s. (hf. mor. ex., uncut, wrappers bound up).

Lowndes also published several burlesques founded upon "Life in London," all of which are now scarce The most important of these are the following:

(*a*) Tom and Jerry, or Life in London, an entirely new Whimsical, Local, Melo-dramatic, Pantomimical, Equestrian

Drama in Three Acts, entitled Life in London, by Pierce Egan . . . As performed at Davis's Royal Amphitheatre, London 1822. 8vo. One coloured print. Price 1s.

(*b*) Songs, Parodies, Duets, Choruses . . . in an Entirely new Classic Comic Extravaganza Burletta of Fun, Frolic, Fashion and Flash, in three acts, called Tom and Jerry, or Life in London. n. d. (1822). 8vo. One coloured print. Price 1s.

The French version of "Life in London" is entitled "Le Diorama Anglais, ou Promenades Pittoresques à Londres," 1823. 8vo. £1 5s. (calf) ; £1 10s. (hf. mor. t.e g.) This version was published at Paris by Thierry.

Twenty-three extra plates, by Heath (?), are occasionally found with copies of the 1st edition of "Life in London." They are, however, very rare. *See* **Fashion and Folly.**

Life in Paris, comprising the Rambles, Sprees and Amours of Dick Wildfire, &c., by D. Carey. 1st edition, 1822. 8vo. 21 coloured plates and 22 woodcuts by Geo. Cruikshank. Copies on Large Paper are extant. £9 10s. (L. P., mor. ex.); £8 8s. (*ibid*); £14 (bds., *ibid*); £4 10s. (Small Paper, mor.)

Another edition, 1828. 8vo. With the coloured plates, £3 (hf. russ.)

Life of a Fox, by Thomas Smith. 1843. 8vo. Illustrations. £1 5s. (orig. cl., uncut)

Second edition 1852. 8vo. Plates. 5s. (orig. cl.)

Another edition, 1896. 8vo. pp. xiv. 304. Author's illustrations and coloured plates by G. H. Jalland. Vol. 1 of "The Sportsman's Library."

Life of a Foxhound, The, by John Mills. 1st edition, 1848. 8vo. Plates by Leech. £1 10s. (orig. cl.)

Second edition, 1861. 8vo. With 4 coloured illustrations by John Leech. 14s. (orig. cl.)

Life of a Race-horse, The, by John Mills. 1854. 8vo. Front. and vignette. 3s. (wrappers).

Another edition, 1861. Post 8vo. 4 full page plates. 5s. (pictorial cl.)

Another edition, 1868. Post 8vo. Plates by "Phiz." 4s (orig. bds.)

See also **Life and Death of a Racehorse.**

Life of a Soldier, a Narrative and Descriptive Poem, 1823. 4to., with 18 coloured plates, by William Heath. £3 3s. (orig. bds.); £1 1s. (hf. cf.)

Life of a Sportsman, The, by "Nimrod" (C. J. Apperley). 1842. Demy 8vo. With 36 coloured plates by H. Alken. £8 8s. (mor. gt.); £10 10s (orig. cl.); £17 (*ibid.*, very fine copy).

Another edition, 1857. Roy. 8vo. Col. front. and vignette title. by Alken. £1 10s. (orig. cl., uncut).

Life of an Actor, The, By Pierce Egan 1st edition. 1825. Demy 8vo., with 27 col. plates by Theodore Lane (inclusive of Front.), and designs on wood by Thompson. £4 12s. (hf mor.); £3 3s. (*ibid.*); £5 (cf. ex.) Published in pictorial white boards.

Second edition, 1892. 8vo. Pickering. With the col. plates as before. 10s. (orig. red cl.)

Life of John Mytton, *see* **Memoirs of the Life, &c.**

Life of Napoleon, a Hudibrastic Poem, by "Doctor Syntax" (William Combe). 1st ed. 1815. 8vo., with 30 col. aquatint plates (inclusive of title) by Geo. Cruikshank. £5 (cf.)

Another edition, 1817. 8vo. Same plates. £5 (cf.)

Life with the Hamran Arabs, An account of a Sporting Tour of some Officers of the Guards in the Soudan, by A B. R. Myers, 1876. Sm 8vo. Photos of sporting trophies. 3s. (orig. cl.)

Lion Hunter of South Africa, The, *see* **Five Years of a Hunter's Life.**

Lives and Adventures of the Most Famous Highwaymen, &c., *see* **General History, A.**

Lives of the most Remarkable Criminals who have been condemned and executed for murder, &c., from the year 1720 to the present time (1735), collected from Original Papers, 1874. 2 vols. Post 8vo. Front. "Escape of Jack Sheppard." 5s (hf. bd.) Published at 12s. 6d.

The *First edition* of this work was published in 3 vols. 12mo., 1735. 20s. (cf.)

Living made Easy, a series of 12 humorous coloured plates by Robert Seymour, 1830. Oblong fol. McLean £11 15s. (mor. ex., uncut, original wrappers bound in, very fine copy of this rare work).

Living Picture of London, A, shewing the Frauds, Snares, &c., of Rogues, 1828. 8vo. Col. front. 10s. (wrappers).

Log Book of a Fisherman and Zoologist, The, by Francis T. Buckland, 1875. 8vo. Illustrated, 9s. (orig. cl.)

London Angler's Book, or Waltonian Chronicle, The, by John Baddeley, 1834. Post 8vo. Front. 3s. (bds.) Described by Westwood and Satchell in the "Bibliotheca Piscatoria" as "Coarse and Cockney."

London Sharper Detected, The, a complete Exposure of all the Frauds of London, 1802. F'cap. 8vo. Col. folding front. 3s (sewed).

Loose Rein, A, by "Wanderer," n.d. (1886). 8vo. pp. viii. 352, with col. plates by Georgina Bowers. 8s (orig. cl.) Published at 12s. 6d.

Lord Fitzwarine, by "Scrutator" (K. W. Horlock), 1860. 3 vols. Cr. 8vo. Fronts and vignettes. 6s (orig. cl.)

Lyttle Hydrogen, or the Devil on Two Sticks in London, 1819. 8vo. Etchings by C. Williams coloured by hand. £1 1s (cf. gt.)

Maison Rustique, or, the Countrey Farme; also a short collection of the hunting of the Hart, Wilde Bore, Hare, Fox, . . . of Birds and Falconrie, by Charles Stevens and John Liebault, 1606. 4to. Numerous woodcuts. £10 (good copy, old cf.), £4 (hf. mor.)

Another edition, 1616. Folio. Edited by Gervase Markham. Same cuts. £4 (old cf.)

Translated from the French by Richard Swiflet. The first English edition cannot be identified, but it was probably published in 1588. There is also an edition of 1600 in folio.

Malefactors' Register, The, or the Newgate and Tyburn Calendar, n.d. (1778-80). 5 vols. 8vo. Plates by Dodd and others. £1 14s. (cf.); £3 3s. (*ibid.*)

Man of Fashion, The, or Consequences of Gambling, the Memoirs of a Modern Rake, n.d (1805). F'cap 8vo. Folding col. front. 4s. (sewed).

Manual of British Rural Sports, by "Stonehenge" (John Henry Walsh), 1st ed 1856. 8vo. Plates. 4s. 6d. (orig cl.) Published at 10s 6d.

Second edition, 1857. 8vo. Plates. 4s. 6d. (orig. cl.)

Ninth edition, 1871. Post 8vo. Plates. 4s 6d (orig. cl.)

Fifteenth edition, 1881. 8vo. Plates. 4s. 6d. (orig. cl.)

Another edition, 1886. 8vo. Port. of the Author and woodcuts. 6s (orig. cl.) Published at 21s.

Manual of Swimming; including bathing, plunging, diving, floating, &c. By Charles Steedman, 1867. 8vo, with 9 plates. 2s (cl.) Published at London and Melbourne at 5s.

Mars His Field, or The Exercise of Arms, wherein in lively figures is shewn the Right use and perfect manner of Handling the Buckler, Sword and Pike, 1611. 12mo. Sixteen copperplates of positions. No text. A very uncommon work, for which no recent auction price can be given. A copy is in the Bodleian.

Master of the Hounds, The, by "Scrutator" (K. W. Horlock), 1859. 3 vols. Post 8vo. Illustrations by Harrison Weir. 5s (orig. cl.)

Matrimonial Comforts, a series of 6 humorous coloured plates, by Rowlandson, after Woodward, 1st ed 1799. 4to. £4 4s (mor ex, uncut).

Melange of Humour, The, A collection of Comic and Humorous Sketches, 1823. Folio, with 30 col. pl. by H. Alken and others. £9 (hf. cf.)

Memoir of the Rev. John Russell, and his out-of-door Life, 1879. 8vo. Illustrations. 7s. 6d. (orig. cl.) Published at 16s.

A new and cheaper (6s.) edition was published in 1883. Post 8vo.

Memoirs of the Life of the late John Mytton, Esq., of Halston, by "Nimrod" (C. J. Apperley), 1st ed. 1835. 8vo. 12 col. pl. by H. Alken. £10 (orig. cl.)

Second edition, 1837. 8vo. 18 col. pl. (8 new) by H. Alken and Rawlins. £8 (orig. blue cl.); £5 5s. (cf. extra).

Third edition, and the first really complete, as it contains a Memoir of the Author not in the preceding two, 1851. 8vo. £6 (orig. cl.); £4 4s (*ibid.*)

Fourth and fifth editions, 1869. 8vo. Routledge, with the 18 col. pl. £1 (orig. cl.) An edition of 1877. 8vo. Routledge, 18 col. pl. 15s. (orig. cl.) Also an edition of 1892. 8vo. Routledge. 5s. or 6s. (orig. cl.)

Men of the Turf. Anecdotes of their Career and Notes on many famous races, by "Thormanby" (Wilmot Dixon), n. d. (1887). 8vo. Illustrated. Published at 1s.

Methode et Invention Nouvelle de Dresser les Chevaux, La, *see* **General System of Horsemanship.**

Meynellian Science of Fox Hunting upon System, by — Hawkes. 1st edition privately printed, n. d. (1802?). Mr. Meynell died at the beginning of the present century, and this book appears to have been printed shortly after his death.

Another edition, 1848. 8vo. £2 5s (russ. ex.)

Midnight Merriment, a Nocturnal Ramble through St. Giles. n. d. (1803) Hughes. F'cap. 8vo. Front. by G. Cruikshank. 8s. (sewed).

Midnight Scenes and Social Photographs, being Sketches of Life in the Streets, Wynds and Dens of the City, by

"Shadow." 1st edition, Glasgow, 1858. Cr. 8vo. Front. by Geo. Cruikshank. 5s. (cl.)

Second edition, Glasgow. 1858. 8vo. Front. 5s. (cl.)

Midnight Spy, The, or a View of the Transactions of London and Westminster, from the hours of Ten in the Evening till Five in the Morning. 1766. 8vo. Front. £1 5s. (cf.)

Military Adventures of Johnny Newcome, by an Officer, 1815. 8vo. 15 col. plates by Rowlandson. £3 3s. (hf. russ.)

Second edition. 1816. 8vo. Same col. plates. £2 2s. (cf.)

See also "Adventures of Johnny Newcome in the Navy," "My Cousin in the Army."

Miseries of Human Life, *see* **Sixteen Scenes, &c.**

Modern Angler, The, containing the most esteemed Methods of Angling for every species of Pond and River Fish, &c., n. d. (about 1830). 12mo. Derby, T. Richardson. Col. folding front. 4s. (orig. cl.)

The same title was used by Robert Salter (n. d.), Oswestry. 12mo. 2nd edition, 1811. 12mo. Also by James Wallwork, 1847. pp. 108. 8vo. with four plates. Other editions by "Otter" 1864, 12mo., and later. None of these are of much importance.

Modern Art of Fencing, *see* **Art of Fencing.**

Modern Breechloaders, sporting and military, by William Wellington Greener, n.d. (1871). Crown 8vo., with 135 engravings. 2s. 6d. (cl.) Published at 7s. 6d.

Modern English Sports, their Use and Abuse, by Frederick Gale, 1885. 8vo. pp. xx. 201. Plates. 5s. (vellum, uncut).

Modern Falconry, *see* **Treatise of Modern Faulconry.**

Modern Fisher, The, *see* **Driffield Angler, The.**

Modern Horsemanship, a new method of teaching Riding and Training by means of Pictures from the Life, by Edward L. Anderson, 1884. 8vo., with 40 instantaneous photographs shewing various positions. 12s (half leather, as issued). Published at 21s.

Later editions of this work appeared in 1888 (3rd ed.), 1889, and 1895 (5th ed.)

Modern Manhood, or the Art and Practice of English Boxing (by H. Lemoine), 1788. 8vo. Folding front of a Fight. £1 18s (cf. ex.)

Modern Practical Angler, The, a Complete Guide to Fly Fishing, &c., by H. Cholmondeley Pennell, n.d. (1870). 8vo. pp. xvi. 286, with front. and 50 engravings. 2s. 6d (orig. cl.)

Modern Riding Master, The, or a Key to the Knowledge of the Horse and Horsemanship, by Philip Astley, 1775. 8vo. Plates. 12s. (cf.)

Modern Shooter, The, by Capt. R. Lacy, 1842. 8vo. pp 548, with engraved title. by Landells. Front. by T. A. Priors and woodcuts. 5s (orig. cl.) Published at 21s

Moments of Fancy, a series of 13 humorous col. plates by Henry Alken, 1822. Oblong fol. £6 6s. (mor. ex.)

Month in the Forests of France, A, by G. C. G. F. Berkeley, 1857. F'cap. 8vo. Col. front and plate by John Leech. 15s (orig. cl.) Published at 8s. 6d.

Moor and the Loch, The, By John Colquhoun, 1st. ed Edinb. 1840. 8vo. 12 plates. £1 (hf. mor.)

Another edition, 1851. 8vo. Illustrations. £1 (calf ex., fine copy), 4s. (cl.)

Fourth edition, 1878. 2 vols. 8vo. Illustrations. 15s. (orig. cl.)

Fifth edition, 1880. 2 vols. 8vo. Published at 12s. 6d.

Sixth edition, 1884. 2 vols. 8vo. Published at 26s.

Seventh edition, 1888. 8vo. pp. xxiii 496. Published at 21s.

Mountaineering below the Snow-Line, or the Solitary Pedestrian in Snowdonia and elsewhere, by M. Paterson, 1st ed. 1886. 8vo. 4s. (orig. cl.)

Mountaineering in 1861, A Vacation Tour, by John Tyndall, 1862. Cr. 8vo. Front 12s (orig. cl.)

Mountains and Molehills, by Frank Marryat, 1855. 8vo. Illustrations by the Author. 5s. (cl., uncut).

Mr. Barnacles and his Boat, by "A Fly" (Edward Fitzgibbon), author of "Adventures of a Salmon," n.d. Oblong 8vo. Humorous illustrations. 6s. (orig. bds.)

Mr. Crop's Harriers. Illustrations by Georgina Bowers. 20 facsimile water colour sketches and 22 black and white drawings. Oblong. 2s. 6d. (orig. bds., soiled). Published at 10s. 6d.

Mr. Facey Romford's Hounds, by the Author of Handley Cross (R. S. Surtees), 1865. Originally issued in 12 parts, red wrappers designed by Leech, afterwards in demy 8vo., as above. Contains 24 col. pl., the first 14 by Leech and the remainder by "Phiz." £5 (orig. parts); £4 (hf. mor. gt.); £2 12s. (orig. cl.), £1 6s. (hf. cf.)

Mr. Sponge's Sporting Tour, *see* **Sponge's Sporting Tour.**

My Climbs in the Alps and Caucasus, by A. F. Mummery, 1st ed. 1895. Royal 8vo., with 11 full page plates and 21 engravings in the text. 12s. (orig. cl.) Published at 21s.

Second edition, 1895. Roy. 8vo. Illustrations as before. 7s. (cl.) Published at 21s.

My Cousin in the Army; or Johnny Newcome on the Peace Establishment, a Poem, 1822. 8vo. Plates, col. by hand. £2 10s. (mor. ex.) *See* "Military Adventures of Johnny Newcome," "Adventures of Johnny Newcome in the Navy."

My Life and Recollections, by G. C. G. F. Berkeley. Portraits, 1865-66. 8vo. 4 vols. £1 (mor. t e g.)

My Life as an Angler, *see* **Notes and Reminiscences.**

Narrative of an Ascent to the Summit of Mont Blanc on the 8th and 9th August, 1827, by John Auldjo, 1828. 4to. Plates. 10s. (L. P., hf. cf., plates on India paper.)

Second edition, 1830. 8vo. 3s. (cf.)

Narrative of an Ascent to the Summit of Mount Blanc on the 25th July, 1827, by Sir Charles Fellows. 1828. 4to. Coloured plates and engraved title. Privately printed. 12s. (bds.)

Another edition, 1828. 4to. Plates. Of less importance.

National Sports of Great Britain, 1825. 4to., with 50 engravings of Racing, Fishing, Bull-Baiting, &c., by Henry Alken. £5 10s. (orig. cl.)

This is a different work altogether from the one mentioned in the next entry.

National Sports of Great Britain, with descriptions in English and French, 1st edition, 1821. Folio. 50 col. plates by H. Alken. £30 (cf. gt.); £38 (orig. red morocco).

Another edition 1823. Folio. Plates as before. £25 10s. (hf. bd., clean).

Another edition, 1825. Roy. 8vo. Plates as before, but reduced in size. £7 (cloth, clean copy).

Natural History and Sport in Moray, by Charles St. John, 1863. Roy. 8vo. £2 10s. (cl.)

Second edition, 1882. Roy. 8vo. Illustrations. £2 10s. (cl.)

Necessary Qualifications for a Man of Fashion, a series of 12 humorous col. plates by D. T. Egerton. 1823. Oblong folio. £11 (mor. ex., fine tooled copy, uncut); £2 6s. (hf. bd.)

New and Complete Guide to the Art of Riding, A, Teaching the whole System of Horsemanship, by Charles Steward. 1821. 8vo. Plates. 2s. 6d. (orig. bds.)

G

New and Complete Newgate Calendar, by William Jackson. 1800-8. 7 vols. 8vo. Published originally in 112 monthly parts. Plates. £1 6s. (cf.)

Another edition, 1818. 9 vols. 8vo. Plates. £1 16s. (mor.), £1 4s. (cf.); £4 10s. (bds., uncut).

New Complete Sportsman, The, or the Town and Country Gentleman's Recreation, by George Morgan, n.d. (about 1770.) 12mo. pp. iv. 302. Engraved front. 10s. (orig. sheep.)

This is a re-issue, with certain alterations, of Thomas Fairfax's "The Complete Sportsman" (q.v.), first published by J. Cooke, n.d. (but 1760?)

Newgate Calendar, The. 5 vols. 8vo. (1779.) Plates. £3 (hf. cf.); £4 4s. (ibid.)

Another edition, by Knapp and Baldwin. 4 vols. 8vo. 1824-28. Portraits and woodcuts. £2 2s. (hf. cf.)

Another edition, n.d., by Knapp and Baldwin. 5 vols. 8vo. £1 19s. (hf. cf.)

Newgate Calendar Improved, by G. T. Wilkinson. 5 vols. 8vo. n.d. £1 5s. (cl.); £6 6s. (bds., uncut)

New Newgate Calendar, The, being interesting Memoirs of Notorious Characters, comprising Murderers, Ravishers, Pirates, &c., by Knapp and Baldwin. 6 vols. 8vo. n.d. Portraits and plates. £1 10s. (hf. cf.)

New Scrap Book, 1824. Oblong 4to. 20 plates by H. Alken. £1 1s. (cf. ex., good copy). £3 (orig. bds., plates coloured by hand)

New Short and Easy Method of Fencing, A, or the Art of the Broad and Small Sword, by Sir William Hope, 1707. 4to., with large folding sheet containing 16 subjects from copper. £3 15s. (cf.)

Second edition, 1714. 4to. Published under the title of "Hope's New Method of Fencing." £3 3s. (cf.)

The large folding sheet above mentioned is also found in **Vindication of the True Art of Self Defence** (*q.v.*)

New Sketch Book, 1823. Oblong 4to. 40 lithographic plates of sporting and other subjects, by Henry Alken. £3 10s. (orig. pictorial bds.)

New Sporting Magazine. Illustrations. This serial commenced in 1831. £3 10s. (1831-35, 10 vols., hf. cf.); £4 10s (1831-38, 15 vols., hf. cf.)

Newe Booke containing the arte of ryding and breakinge Greate Horses (1565?) Sm. 4to. Black Letter, with 50 woodcuts (at the end) of halters and bits. £3 15s. (cf.); £2 18s (*ibid.*)

Another edition, 1597. 4to. P. Short. Cuts as before. £4 10s. (mor. ex.)

This is a translation by Thomas Blundeville from the Italian of Federico Grisone's "Ordini di Cavalcare," published at Naples in 1550, 4to., and later at Pesaro and Venice.

Newton Dogvane; a story of Country Life, by Francis Francis, 1859. 3 vols. 8vo. Illustrations by John Leech. £1 2s (orig. cl.)

Another edition, 1888. 8vo. Same illustrations. 3s. (cl.) Published at 7s. 6d.

Nimrod's Songs of the Chace: the best Collection of Hunting Songs ever presented to the Lovers of that delightful Sport, 1788. 8vo. Folding front. of a stag hunt. £3 (mor. ex., by Rivière).

Noble Art of Venerie or Hunting, The, translated and collected for the pleasure of all Noblemen and Gentlemen, by George Turberville, **Black Letter**, 1611. 4to. Woodcuts £8 15s (mor.); £2 (mor., title imperfect and several leaves missing); £23 (vellum, fine copy, Ashburnham sale, perfect).

The *First edition* was published in 1576, 4to., and is usually found bound up with the same author's "Booke of Faulconrie" (*q.v.*)

Perfect copies of this scarce work contain two musical leaves of "The Measures of Blowing." These are often wanting.

Noble Science, The, by F. P. Delmé Radcliffe, 1st ed. 1839. 8vo. D. Bogue. Illustrations. £3 10s. (orig. cl., uncut); £2 18s (ibid.) Most copies were issued with cut and gilt edges, and these are of less value. Published at 14s.

Another edition, 1839. 8vo. Bohn, pub. at 10s. 6d.

Fourth edition, 1893. 8vo. Enlarged by W. C. A. Blew. pp. xxviii. 331, with 10 steel-plates col. by hand and 35 wood-cuts in the text. 12s. (orig. cl.)

North Country Flies, *see* **Yorkshire Trout Flies.**

Norway and its Glaciers visited in 1851, by James David Forbes, 1853. Royal 8vo. Ten col. pl., maps and wood-cuts. £1 10s (orig. cl.)

Notes Abroad and Rhapsodies at Home, by "A Veteran Traveller" (William Rae Wilson), 1837. 2 vols. 8vo. Fronts. 2s. 6d. (cl., uncut)

Notes and Reminiscences of My Life as an Angler, by William Henderson, 1st ed., 1876. 8vo. Portrait and 5 illustrations by Clement Burlison. Privately printed. £1 7s. (cl.)

Second edition, published under the title "My Life as an Angler." 1879. 8vo. Portrait and 68 woodcuts by Edmund Evans. 4s. 6d (cl.), 12s. (L. P. Illustrations on India Paper and a "View on the White-adder" added)

Third edition, 1880. 8vo. Published as "My Life as an Angler." Portrait and 12 cuts by Edmund Evans. 3s. (orig. cl.)

Notes and Sketches from the Wild Coasts of Nipon and account of Travel and Sport in China and Japan, by H. C. St. John, 1880. 8vo. Map and 55 engravings. 6s (orig. cl.) Published at 12s.

Notes from a Hunting Box, by Georgina Bowers, 1873. Oblong fol. Illustrations. 6s (orig. pictorial bds.) Published at 15s.

Notes on the Chase of the Wild Red Deer in the Counties of Devon and Somerset, by C. P. Collyns, 1862. 8vo. Tinted lithographic plates and other illustrations. £3 8s. (orig. green cl.)

Notitia Venatica, a Treatise on Fox Hunting, by Robert Thomas Vyner, 1st ed. 1841. 8vo. Illustrations by H. Alken. £3 15s. (orig. cl., fine copy); £2 11s. (*ibid.*)

Another edition, 1847. 8vo.

Another edition, 1892. Roy 8vo., enlarged by W. C. A. Blew. Col. plates by H. Alken and others. 12s. (orig. red cl.)

The *Sixth edition* appeared without date, but 1871. 8vo.

Oakleigh Shooting Code, The, containing two hundred and twenty chapters of information relative to shooting, by Thomas Oakleigh, Esq. (A. K. Killmister) 1836. 12mo. Illustrations, 4s. (cl.) Published at 7s. 6d.

Oberland and its Glaciers Explored, and illustrated, with Ice Axe and Camera, The, by H. B. George, 1866. Impl. 8vo. Map and 28 photographic illustrations. £1 5s. (orig. cl.)

Observations on Fox-Hunting and the Management of Hounds in the Kennel and in the Field, by Colonel John Cook, 1826. 8vo. Plates. £2 5s. (bds. uncut); 18s. (cf.) Published at 31s. 6d.

Observations on Hawking, describing the Mode of Breaking and Managing the several kinds of Hawks used in Falconry, by Sir J. S. Sebright. 1828. 8vo. 14s. (sewed).

Old Bailey Chronicle, The. Edited by J. Mountague. 1st edition, 1783. 4 vols. 8vo., with 40 plates by Valois. 18s. (cf.)

Second edition, 1786. 4 vols. 8vo. Plates as before. 18s. (cf.)

Old Coaching Days, by Stanley Harris, 1882. 8vo. pp. viii. 279. 12 illustrations by J. Sturgess. £1 1s. (cloth); £1 10s. (*ibid.*)

Old Coaching Days in Yorkshire, by Tom Bradley, 1889. 8vo. Illustrations. 9s. (red or green cl.)

Old Coachman's Chatter, An, with some Practical Remarks on Driving, by Edward Corbett, 1890 (1891). 8vo. pp. viii. 304. Col. front. of "The Wonder, a minute to 12," and 7 Lithographs by John Sturgess. 8s. (orig. cl.) Published at 15s.

Old English Squire, The, a Poem in ten Cantos by John Careless, Esq., with upwards of 20 humorous coloured plates in the style of Rowlandson, 1821. Impl. 8vo. £6 (mor. ex., uncut, fine copy).

Old Forest Ranger, The, or Wild Sports of India, by Col. Walter Campbell, 1853. 8vo. Plates. 3s. (orig. cl.)

The First edition was published in 1842. 8vo. It is of little importance.

Old Q, a Memoir of William Douglas, fourth Duke of Queensberry, K.T. by John Robert Robinson, 1895. 8vo. Frontispiece Portrait of the Duke and 5 plates. 3s. (Orig. red. cl.), *see* **Piccadilly Ambulator, The.**

Old Sports and Sportsmen, or, the Willey Country, by John Randall, 1873. Post 8vo. Sketches of Tom Moody and Squire Forester. 3s. (orig. cl.) Published at 7s. 6d.

Another edition, 1875. Post 8vo. 2s. (cl.) Published at 5s.

On a Sunshine Holiday, by "The Amateur Angler." (Edward Marston), 1897. 12mo. Plates on India Paper. 4s. (orig. cl.)

On Plain and Peak: Sporting and other Sketches of Bohemia and the Tyrol, by Randolph Ll. Hodgson, 1898. 8vo. pp. viii. 254. Illustrated. Published at 7s. 6d.

On the Box Seat from London to Land's End, by James John Hissey, 1886. 8vo. pp. xviii. 404, with 16 full page plates by the author. 10s. (orig. cl.)

On the Frontier, Reminiscences of Wild Sports, Personal Adventure and Strange Scenes, by J. S. Campion, 1878. 8vo., with 8 plates. 4s. (orig. cl.)

One Day from the Diary of a Stag, by Mrs. Hanbury, 1st ed. 1847. Oblong 4to. 6 large etchings by E. R. Smyth of the proceedings at a Stag-hunt near Ipswich. 6s. (as issued). Published at 10s.

Second edition, 1847. Oblong 4to. Published at 12s.

Ordini di Cavalcare, *see* **Newe Booke, &c.**

Oracle of Rural Life, The, An Almanac for Sportsmen Farmers, Gardeners, and Country Gentlemen, for the year 1839. 8vo., with 14 illustrations. Continued in 1840, 8vo., 14 plates; then continued as The Sporting Oracle and Almanac of Rural Life for 1841. 8vo. Edited by "Vates," afterwards incorporated in the Sporting Almanac and Oracle of Rural Life for 1842-44. 3 vols. 8vo. Plates. £1 5s. (the 6 vols. calf.)

Oriental Field Sports, by Thomas Williamson, 1807. Oblong folio. 40 col. pl. by S. Howitt and the Author. £5 15s. (hf. cf.); £8 (mor., fine copy); £9 15s. (hf russ.) The best edition, the plates being on a large scale. First published in 20 numbers or parts worth about £20.

Another edition, 1808. 2 vols. Impl. 8vo. 40 col. pl. (reduced). £2 (russ). Large Paper copies were issued in 4to.

Another edition, 1819. Oblong fol. 40 col. pl. £9 (hf. mor.) A reprint of the edition of 1807. This edition is also met with in 2 vols. Roy. 4to., with 40 coloured plates as before, but reduced. £2 (calf)

Oriental Sporting Magazine, The, edited by Raymond. Plates and photos. The 1st volume was published at Calcutta in 1835 and there is a "first" and "new" series. £6 15s. (16 vols. cf.)

Orme's Collection of British Field Sports, by Edward Orme, 1807. Atlas folio, with 20 col. pl. from designs by S. H[owitt]. £50 (russ. gt.); £32 (hf. cf.)

Outline Sketches in the High Alps of Dauphiné, by T. G. Bonney, 1865. 4to. Map and plates. 12s (cl., uncut).

Pallas Armata, or Militarie Instructions for the Learned, &c., by Sir Thomas Kellie, 1627. 4to. Edinburgh. Engraved portrait of Author on title. £2 12s. (cf.)

Reprinted in Richard Bannatyne's "Memorials."

Pallas Armata. Military Essays of the Ancient Grecian, Roman, and Modern Style of War, by Sir James Turner, 1683. 4to. pp. 372. Portrait by R. White. £3 15s (calf)

Pancratia, or a History of Pugilism, 1812. 8vo., with a portrait. £1 (hf. mor.)

Paradoxes of Defence, wherein is proved the true grounds of Fight taken in the short auncient weapons, &c. By George Silver, 1599. Sm. 4to., with arms of the Earl of Essex on reverse of title, woodcut and ornamental initials, £70 (old cf.) An extremely scarce book illustrating some scenes in the Elizabethan dramatists. According to Lowndes the collation is "Sig A, six leaves, A1 probably blank, B to K in fours, E having five leaves, two of which are marked E3." Hazlitt's collation is as follows: "A, 6 leaves, B—K in fours. Dedicated to Robert Earl of Essex, whose arms, gartered, are on the back of the title."

Particulars and Recommendations of the Stadium, or British National Arena for Manly and Defensive Exercises . . . at the Residence of the late Lord Cremorne, on a space of twenty-four acres extending from the King's Road, Chelsea, to the Thames, &c., by Baron De Berenger, 1st ed. 1834. 12mo. Etchings by Geo. Cruikshank. 14s (wrappers), £2 5s. (mor. ex., duplicate set of col. etchings).

Another edition, 1835. 12mo. £2 4s (mor. ex. duplicate set of col. etchings).

Passes of the Alps, *see* **Illustrations of the Passes, &c.**

Peaks and Valleys of the Alps, The, by Elijah Walton, with descriptive text by Thomas George Bonney, 1867. Folio, with 21 col. lithographic plates. £1 16s. (hf. mor., g. e.)

Peaks, Passes and Glaciers, by Members of the Alpine Club first series, 1859. Second series, 2 vols., 1862, together 3 vols., 1859-62. Illustrated. £5 (orig. cl.), £4 4s. (hf. cf., gt.) First series, third edition, 1859. £1 (orig. cl.) First series, 4th ed. and second series, 1st ed., 3 vols. 1859-62. £4 6s. (orig. cl.) First series, 1st ed. £1 5s. (orig. cl.)

Pedestrianism, or an Account of the performances of celebrated Pedestrians . . . with a full Narrative of Captain Barclay's Public and Private Matches, by Walter Thom, Aberdeen, 1813. 8vo. Portrait. £2 (cf. extra, fine copy), 10s. (bds., uncut).

Philosophy in Sport made Science in Earnest, by the aid of popular Toys and Sports [by J. A. Paris] 1st ed. 1827. 3 vols. Post 8vo. Illustrations by George Cruikshank. 12s. (orig. bds.) There are several later editions of this interesting and instructive book, all of them being of little importance from a monetary standpoint.

Piccadilly Ambulator, The, or, Old Q(ueensberry), containing Memoirs of the Private Life of that Ever-Green Votary of Venus, by J. P. Hurstone, 1808. 2 vols. 8vo. Col. front. £1 10s. (2 vols. in 1, hf. mor.) *See* **Old Q.**

Pictorial Gallery of English Race Horses, containing portraits of all the Winning Horses of the Derby, Oaks, and St. Leger Stakes during the last 13 years, by George Tattersall, 1844. 8vo. Bohn. 90 engravings by Alken, Herring and others. £2 10s. (cl.), £7 7s. (mor. ex., fine copy) Published at 21s.

Another edition, "during the last 20 years," 1850. 8vo. Bohn. About the same value.

Picture, A, of the Manners, Customs, Sports and Pastimes of the Inhabitants of England, by Jehoshaphat Aspin, 1825. 8vo. pp. iv 296. Plates. 4s. (bds.)

Pictures of Sporting Life and Character, by Lord William Pitt Lennox, 1860. 2 vols. Cr. 8vo. 5s. (orig. cl.) Though dated 1860 this work was published the previous year.

Pierce Egan's Anecdotes (original and selected) of the Turf, the Chase, the Ring and the Stage, 1827. 8vo., with 13 col. pl. designed and etched by Theodore Lane. £4 10s (cf. ex.); £2 14s (hf. cf.) Originally published in 12 parts, now very seldom met with. £6 10s (11 parts only, with all faults)

Pierce Egan's Book of Sports and Mirror of Life, embracing the Turf, the Chase, the Ring, and the Stage, 1832. 8vo. Originally issued in 25 weekly parts at 3d., woodcut on the first page of each part, afterwards in boards with a pictorial title page. £2 (orig. bds.), 16s (hf. cf.)

Another edition, 1836. 8vo., with the same cuts; of a little less value.

Pioneer Work in the Alps of New Zealand, a record of the first Exploration of the chief Glaciers and Ranges of the Southern Alps, by A. P. Harper. 1896. 8vo. Map and 40 plates. £2 10s (text and plates on Japanese vellum. Only 20 copies printed at £5 5s each)

Pioneers of the Alps, The, a Collection of Sketches of the Lives of those who first conquered the great Peaks, by C. D. Cunningham and Capt. Abney, 1887. 4to. Portraits. 25s (orig. cl.); £3 5s (L. P. as issued)

Piscatorial Reminiscences and Gleanings, by an Old Angler and Bibliopolist (Thomas Boosey), 1835. 12mo. Front. pp. xvi. 255 and 20 unpaged leaves containing a catalogue of books on Angling. 5s (cl.)

Piscatoris Poemata, Vel Panegyricum Carmen in Diem Mangurationis Olivari, &c., London, 1656. Folio. Front of arms, and portraits of Bulstrode Whitelock and Oliver Cromwell, by Faithorne. £3 18s. (mor. ex., title mended).

Piscatory Eclogues, *see* **Angling Sports.**

Plain or Ringlets? By the author of "Handley Cross" (R. S. Surtees), 1860. Originally published in 13 monthly parts, in red wrappers designed by Leech. Afterwards in demy 8vo as above. First title, and 13 plates in colours, 44 woodcuts, all by Leech. £2 18s (orig. cl.); £1 10s (hf. cf.); £2 8s (10 parts only).

Another edition, n.d. (but 1888), Bradbury, Agnew & Co., with Leech's col. plates and cuts, 7s 6d (cloth).

Plaine and Easie Way, A, to remedy a Horse that is foundered in his feete, by Nicholas Malbie, 1583. 4to. Thomas Purfoote. Curious engravings. £14 (mor. ex.)

The first edition of this scarce book was published in 1576. 4to. Four leaves. Sig. A without pagination. There is another edition of 1594. 4to. Same collation.

Plains of the Great West, *see* **Hunting Grounds of the Great West.**

Plaza of Madrid, Bull Baiting there, *see* **Impartial and brief Description.**

Pleasures of Human Life, The (by James Beresford), 1807. 8vo. Engraved title, front, and col. plates by Rowlandson. £1 10s (hf. mor., uncut).

Pocket and the Stud, The, or Practical Hints on the Management of the Stable, by "Harry Hieover" (Charles Bindley), 1st ed. 1848. 8vo. Cuts. 2s (cl.)

Third edition, 1857. 8vo. 2s (cl.)

Polo, by J. M. Brown, 1st ed. 1895. Cr. 8vo. Illustrated by Bradley. 2s (cl.) Published at 5s.

Second edition, 1896. Cr. 8vo. pp. 204. Same illustrations. Published at 5s.

Portraits of Celebrated Race Horses of the Past and Present Centuries (1702-1870), by Thomas Henry Taunton, 1887-88. 4 vols. 8vo. £2 10s. (hf. bd., uncut); £4 4s. (*ibid.*)

Portraits of the Game and Wild Animals of Southern Africa, by Sir W. C. Harris, 1840. Folio. 31 large col. pl. £7 10s. (hf. mor. gt., g. e.); £4 (hf. mor.) Published at £10 10s. or on Large Paper at £21, but reduced by Bohn in 1849 to £6 6s. Originally published in 5 parts. The first edition contains vignettes of heads, horses and skins not reproduced in Bohn's reprint.

Post and Paddock, by "The Druid" (H. H. Dixon), 1862. 3 vols. 8vo. Plates. 5s. (orig. cl.)

Reprinted by Vinton & Co. in "The Druid Sporting Library," 1895.

Practical Angler, The, by "Piscator" (William Hughes), 1842. 8vo., with 6 plates by Beckwith and others. 4s. (orig. cl.) Published at 8s. 6d.

Practical Angler, The, or the Art of Trout Fishing, by W. C. Stewart, 1857. 8vo. Cuts. 4s. (cloth).

Later editions all of the same small value appeared at Edinburgh in 1857, 1857, 1861, 1867, 1874 and 1877, all in 8vo.

Practical Falconry: to which is added, How I became a Falconer, by Gage Earle Freeman, 1869. 8vo. 6s. (cl.)

Practical Fly Fisher, The, more particularly for grayling or umber, by J. Jackson, 1854. 8vo. 10 col. pl. of Flies. 4s. (orig. cl.)

Second edition, 1862. 8vo. Same text with a fresh title-page. 4s. (cl.)

Third edition. 1880. 8vo. 4s. (cl.)

Practical Game Preserving: containing . . directions for rearing . . game and destroying vermin, &c., by William Carnegie, 1884. 8vo. pp. 570. 15s. (cl.) Published at 21s.

Practical Horsemanship, by "Harry Hieover" (C. Brindley), 1850. 8vo. Plates. 2s. (hf. bd.)

Practical Trapping, being papers on traps and trapping for vermin, by William Carnegie, n d (1880) 8vo pp 63 Illustrated, 1s.

Practical Treatise on Farriery, A, by William Griffiths, 1784. 4to Privately printed at Wrexham. Humorous front. by Bunbury. £6 (old cf gt)

Another edition, 1795. 4to Front by Bunbury and portrait 5s (cf.)

Practical Wildfowling: a Book on Wildfowl and Wildfowl Shooting, by Henry Sharp. [1895]. Demy 8vo. Illustrations 8s. (cl.) Published at 12s. 6d.

Prairie and Forest, a description of the game of North America with personal adventures in their pursuit by Parker Gillmore, 1874. 8vo pp x 383 7s. (cl.) Published at 12s.

Another edition 1881 8vo. pp viii 396 3s (cl) Published at 7s 6d

Principles of Modern Riding for Ladies, by John Allen, 1st ed 1825 8vo 23 plates 18s. (hf. mor.)

Another edition, 1835 Roy 8vo 35 plates. 2s 6d. (orig cl.)

Pro Aris et Focis, considerations of the Reasons that exist for Reviving the use of the Long Bow with the Pike, by R. Oswald Mason, 1798 8vo Engraved title, front and folding plates 10s. (calf).

Progress of a Midshipman, The, exemplified in the Career of Master Blockhead, 1st ed. 1820 Oblong folio 8 col. pl by Geo Cruikshank £13 13s. (hf mor. ex)

Another edition, 1821. Oblong folio Same col pl £12 (as issued)

The designs were suggested to Cruikshank by Captain Marryat

Progymnasmata, *see* **Inn Play, The.**

Prosody, *see* **Tour of Dr. Prosody.**

Pugilistica, being one hundred and forty-four years of the history of British Boxing, by H. D. Miles. 3 vols. 8vo. n.d. (1880-81). Portraits. £1 7s. (orig. cl.); £2 10s. (*ibid.*)

Quaint Treatise of "Flees," A, and the Art of Artyfichall Flee Making," by W. H. Aldam, 1876. 4to. 2 chromo-lithographic facsimiles. £2 15s. (cl.)

Qualified Horses and Unqualified Riders, a series of 7 humorous coloured plates and engraved title, by Henry Alken, 1821. Oblong folio. £9 15s. (mor. ex., fine copy).

Queen's Hounds, The, and Stag-Hunting Recollections, by Lord Ribblesdale, with an Introduction on the Hereditary Mastership, by Edward Burrows, 1897. Roy. 8vo. pp. 332. 25 photogravure plates and 37 half-tone plates. 150 copies on Large Paper (4to.) at £2 2s. net. Copies on ordinary paper were published at 25s.

Qui Hi! in Hindustan, *see* **Grand Master.**

Quorn Hunt and its Masters, The, by William C. A. Blew, 1898. Super Royal 8vo. with 12 hand-coloured Illustrations of the Quorn Country, and 12 Head and Tail pieces, all by Henry Alken. Published at 21s. This work is uniform with the same author's editions of Vyner's "Notitia Venatica" and Radcliffe's "Noble Science of Fox Hunting."

Racecourse and Covert Side, by A. E. T. Watson, 1883. 8vo. Illustrations by John Sturgess. 6s. (orig. cl.)

Racehorse in Training, The, with hints on racing and racing reforms, by William Day, 1880. 8vo. pp. x. 323. 5s. (orig. cl.) Published at 16s. Three editions appeared before the close of the year, and a fourth in 1882, all at 16s. In 1885, the fifth edition was published at 9s.

Riding Recollections, by George John Whyte Melville, 1878. 8vo. Illustrations by E Giberne. 8s (cl.)

Race Horses, Pedigree, description, history, translated by "Touchstone" (C B Pitman) from the French, 1890 Oblong folio. 60 col. pl. by Cotlison and others, and vignettes £2 10s (orig cl)

The translation is from ' Les Chevaux de Course," Paris, 1889. Oblong folio. £1 15s (hf mor gt)

Raciana : or Riders' Colours of the Royal, Foreign and Principal Patrons of the British Turf from 1762 to 1883, by J. B Muir, 1890. Roy. 8vo pp. xii 188 Plates and woodcuts. 10s. (white and red boards).

Racing and Chasing : the Road, the River and the Hunt. 50 plates by "Phiz,' n d (1864) Folio. 13s. (orig. illustrated boards)

Racing Life of Lord George Cavendish Bentinck, The, and other Reminiscences, by John Kent, 1892 8vo. pp. xx 482, with 23 full-page portraits and plates 6s (orig cl.) Published at 25s

Rambles and Recollections of a Fly-Fisher, by "Clericus" (W Cartwright), 1st ed 1854 8vo , with 8 full-page plates. 4s (cl gt)

Another edition, 1874. 8vo Same plates 4s (cl. gt)

Ranch Life and the Hunting Trail, containing a complete account of the life and business of an American Ranch, with narratives of shooting expeditions, by Theodore Roosevelt, n d (1888) 8vo pp 186 Illustrated by F Rimington. 6s (orig cl) Published at 21s

Random Shots at all kinds of Game, a series of 12 col pl. by Barrest n.d (1860). Square 8vo 4s (orig pictorial bds)

Real Life in Ireland ; or the Day and Night Scenes of Brian Boru and his elegant friend Sir Shawn O'Dogherty (by

Pierce Egan?) 1st ed. 1821. 8vo. Front. and 18 col. pl. by H. Alken, W. Heath, and others. Some copies on Large Paper. £27 (L. P., very fine unopened copy, pictorial boards); £20 (ibid., good copy), £4 (Sm. Paper, orig. leather).

Another edition, 1822. Demy 8vo., with same col. plates £1 12s. (hf. cf.); £3 10s. (cf. ex.)

Another edition, n.d. 8vo. Evans. Col. pl. 6s. (orig. cl.)

Real Life in London; or, The Rambles and Adventures of Bob Tallyho, Esq. . . . By an Amateur (Pierce Egan?), 1st ed. 2 vols. 1821-2. 8vo. Originally published in 14 parts in pink pictorial wrappers, afterwards in pictorial boards, as above. Some copies on Large Paper. Vol. i. has 19 col. plates (inclusive of front and title). Vol. ii., 13 col. pl. (inclusive of front and title), by Heath, Alken, Rowlandson and others. £15 (parts); £6 6s. (orig. bds.); £8 (L. P., calf); £5 (cf. gt.)

Other editions of 1822-23, 2 vols, demy 8vo., and 1829-30, 2 vols., demy 8vo., with same plates and of about the same value under similar circumstances.

Another edition, n.d., T. Johnson & Co. 2 vols. Demy 8vo. £3 (cf. gt.)

Recollections of a Fox-hunter, by "Scrutator" (K. W. Horlock), 1861. 8vo. Frontispiece. 16s. (orig. cl.); £1 (hf. cf. ex.)

Recollections of Fly-Fishing for Salmon, Trout, and Grayling, by Edward Hamilton, 1884. 8vo. pp. viii. 190. Plates. 12s. (hf. mor.)

Second edition, 1891. Cr. 8vo. Mezzotint by Haden and full page cuts by the author. 4s. (cl.) Published at 6s.

Records of Big Game, by Roland Ward, 1896. 8vo. pp. xvi. 325. Illustrated. 12s. (cl.) Published at 30s. This is the second edition of the same author's "Horn Measurements and Weights of the Great Game of the World." 1892. 8vo. pp. viii. 264. Published at 21s. net.

Records of Old Times, historical, social, political, sporting, and agricultural, by John Kersley Fowler, 1898. 8vo. pp. xix 238. With 9 illustrations. 4s. (cl.) Published at 10s. 6d. A few copies were issued on Large Paper.

Records of Sport in Southern India, by Lt.-Col. Douglas Hamilton, 1892. 4to. pp. xlviii 284. Portrait and illustrations. 14s. (orig. cl.)

Records of Stag Hunting on Exmoor, by John William Fortescue, 1887. 8vo. Folding map and 14 plates by Edgar Giberne, col. by hand. 15s. (orig. cl., uncut); 5s. (orig. cl., plates plain).

Records of the Chase, and Memoirs of Celebrated Sportsmen, by "Cecil" (Cornelius Tongue), 1854. 12mo. Plates. 5s. (cl.)

Another edition, 1877. 8vo. 4s. (cl.)

Another edition, 1880. 8vo. Published at 2s.

Recreations in Shooting, with some account of the Game of the British Islands, by "Craven" (John William Carleton), 1st ed. 1846. 8vo., with 60 illustrations by W. Harvey and A. Cooper. 10s. (orig. cl.) Published at 12s.

Another edition, 1849. 8vo. Bohn's Illustrated Library. 5s. (orig. cl.)

Recreations of a Sportsman, by Lord William Pitt Lennox, 1862. 2 vols. 8vo. Front. 8s. (cl., uncut)

Regular Swiss Round, in three Trips, by H. Jones, 1866. 12mo., with map and 22 wood-engravings by Whymper. 3s. (orig. cl.)

Another edition, 1868. 12mo. 2s. (cl.)

Remarks on Shooting, in verse, by W. Watt, 1839. F'cap. 8vo. Front. 2s. 6d. (cl.)

Remarks on the Condition of Hunters, the Choice of Horses, &c., by C. J. Apperley ("Nimrod"), 1831. Demy 8vo ; mentioned here because though the book contains no illustrations in its normal state, 12 plates by Turner are often found inserted. £1 10s. (orig. cl. with Turner's plates). Later editions are of no consequence.

Reminiscences of a Huntsman, by G. C. G. F. Berkeley, 1854. 8vo. Col. and plain illustrations by Leech. £1 10s. (cf. gt.); £3 (mor. ex., orig. covers preserved); £1 18s. (orig. red cl.)

This work is included (vol. 4) in Maxwell's "The Sportsman's Library," 1896. Published at 15s. Some copies were printed on Large Paper.

Reminiscences of an Old Sportsman, by Col. J. P. Hamilton. 1860. 2 vols. 8vo. 6 full page plates. 6s. (orig. cl.) Published at 18s.

Another edition, 1862. 8vo. Bohn. Published at 7s. 6d.

Reminiscences of the late Thomas Assheton Smith, Esq., by Sir John Eardley Wilmot, 1860. Post 8vo., with 10 portraits and plates by Cooper and others. 8s. (orig. cl.)

Second edition, 1860. Post 8vo. Port. and plates. 8s. (orig. cl.)

Another edition, 1862. 8vo. Revised. 3s. (orig. cl.)

Reminiscences of Frank Gillard. (Huntsman) with the Belvoir Hounds, 1860-96, by Cuthbert Bradley, 1898. Impl. 16mo. pp. 314. Published at 15s.

Reminiscences of the Turf, with Anecdotes and Recollections, &c., 1st ed. 1886. 8vo. pp. xiv. 466. 6s. (cl.) Published at 16s.

Second edition, 1886. 8vo. pp. xiv. 466. Published at 16s.

Third edition, 1891. 8vo. pp. xiv. 345. Portrait. 4s. (cl.) Published at 16s.

Riding Recollections, by George John Whyte-Melville, 1875. 8vo. Illustrations by E. Giberne. 6s. (cl.) Published at 12s. Cheaper editions appeared in 1878 and 1880, at 6s and 2s respectively. Also forms Vol I. of the collective issue of Whyte Melville's works, published 17th October, 1898, under the editorship of Sir Herbert Maxwell, M P. Col. fronts. and other illustrations by Hugh Thomson

Riding Recollections and Turf Stories, by Henry Custance, 1894. 4to. pp xv. 304, with 9 Portraits of Race Horses 6s. (orig cl.)

Rifle and Hound in Ceylon, The, by Sir S. W. Baker, 1st ed. 1854. 8vo. Lithographic plates. 19s. (orig. cl.)

Second edition, 1857. 8vo. Plates. 2s. (orig cl.) Published at 4s. 6d.

Another edition, 1874. 8vo. Plates. 3s. (orig. cl.) Published at 7s 6d.

Rifle Manual, The, and Firing, 1804. Oblong folio. Numerous coloured plates, with descriptive text. £5 (mor. extra, uncut, fine copy).

Rifle and Spear with the Rajpoots: being the Narrative of a Winter's Travel and Sport in Northern India, by Alan Gardner, 1895. Impl. 8vo. pp. xvi 336. Illustrated from photographs and sketches by the author, &c 8s. (orig. cl.) Published at 21s.

Road Scrapings, by Foxe, 1840. Oblong 4to. £1 15s. (hf. mor.)

Road Scrapings, a series of 12 coloured plates by C. C. Henderson, n.d. Oblong folio. £1 5s (hf. bd.)

Road Scrapings; Coaches and Coaching, by Capt. Martin E Haworth, 1882. 8vo pp viii. 202. Illustrations. 5s. (orig cl.)

Rock Climbing in the English Lake District, by Owen Glynne Jones, 1897. 8vo. pp. xxv. 284. Illustrated with 30 full page collotype plates and 9 diagrams of the chief routes. 10s. (orig. cl.) Published at 15s. net.

Rod and the Gun, The, being two Treatises on Angling and Shooting, by James Wilson, 1st ed. 1840. Cr. 8vo. 7 steel plates by Aikman and Miller and about 50 woodcuts 7s. 6d. (orig. cl.)

Second edition, 1841. 8vo. 5s. (orig. cl.)

Third edition, 1844. 8vo. 5s. (orig. cl.)

Originally published in the Encyclopædia Britannica (8th ed.) Revised and enlarged in book form.

Rod Fishing in Clear Water, by Fly, Minnow, and Worm, by Henry Wade, n.d. (1860). 8vo. Col. and other plates of natural and artificial flies. 10s. (orig. cl.)

Rod in India, The, by H. S. Thomas. 1st ed. *Mangalore*, 1873. 8vo. Illustrations of Fish and Tackle. 18s. (orig. cl.)

Second edition, London, 1881. pp. xxvi. 436. 6s. (cl.)

Romford's Hounds, *see* **Mr. Facey Romford's Hounds.**

Rouge et Noir, The Academicians of 1823, or the Greeks of the Palais Royal and St. James, by Charles Persius, 1823. Post 8vo. Col. front. 5s. (orig. bds.)

Rules and Regulations for the Sword Exercise of the Cavalry, published by the War Office, 1796. 8vo., with 29 col. and other folding plates. 12s. (bds., uncut).

An American reprint was prepared by Robert Hewes of Boston and published there in 1798. A second edition appeared in 1802. These American editions are much scarcer than the English issue above-named.

Run with the —— Stag Hounds, A, 1863. Folio. 12 chromolithographic plates by "Phiz." £2 10s. (as issued).

Rural Chivalry, a series of six plates of Fighting Cocks, engraved by J. Fahey from drawings by Weigall. 4to. Ackermann. £2 10s. (wrapper).

Rural Life of England, The, by William Howitt, 1st ed. 2 vols. 1838. 8vo. Published at 24s.

Another edition, 1844. 8vo. 9s. (cl.) Published at 21s.

Another edition, 1862. 8vo. Cuts by Bewick and Williams. 5s. (cl.) Published at 12s. 6d.

Rural Sports, by W. B. Daniel, with a supplement, 1st ed. 3 vols. 8vo. 1801-2-13. Plates by J. Scott and others. £2 15s. (russia); £1 16s. (bds.) Also met with on Large Paper (4to.) Value about the same.

Another edition, with supplement, 1812-13. 4 vols. 8vo. Plates by J. Scott and others. £2 10s. (russ.) Published at £7 7s.

Another edition, 1805-13. 4 vols. 4to., including supplement. Revised and enlarged, with additional plates and proofs, sometimes met with coloured. £1 12s. (calf.)

The edition of 1805 was much enlarged, and contains additional plates. The supplement, which is dated 1813, is found in 8vo., 4to., and imperial 4to.; as also is the edition of 1812, 3 vols., to which it was first appended. As will be seen above, this supplement is often added to earlier editions by way of ensuring completeness. Every copy of Daniel's "Rural Sports" is valued with reference to its "make up," which varies very much.

Rural Sports, by "Stonehenge," *see* **Manual of British Rural Sports.**

Saddle and Sirloin, by "The Druid" (H. H. Dixon). 8vo. Plates. 5s. (orig. cl.)

Another edition, revised and re-edited (1880), 8vo., belonging to "The Druid" Sporting Series.

Sailing Tours, the yachtman's guide to the cruising waters of the English and adjacent coasts, by Frank Cowper. Vol. I., the coasts of Essex and Suffolk, containing descriptions of every creek from the Thames to Aldborough, with charts and illustrations. Pub. 5s. Vol. II., the coast from the Nore to the Scilly Isles, with 25 charts. Pub. 7s. 6d. Vol. III., the coast of Brittany ; descriptions of every creek, harbour, and roadstead from L'Aberviach to St. Nazaire, and an account of the Loire, with 12 charts, printed in colours. Pub. 7s 6d. Vol IV., the west coast, from Land's End to Mull of Galloway, including the east coast of Ireland, with 30 charts, printed in colours. Pub. 10s. 6d. Vol. V., the coasts of Scotland and the N E. of England down to Aldborough, with 40 charts. Pub. 10s. 6d. All these books are at present in print

Salmon Casts and Stray Shots, being fly-leaves from the note-book of John Colquhoun, 1858. 8vo. pp. x. 205. 7s. (orig. cl.)

A *Second Edition* appeared the same year at 5s.

Salmon-Fishing in Canada. By a Resident. Edited by Col. Sir J. E Alexander, 1860. Post 8vo Front., map and humorous cuts. 5s. (orig. cl.)

Salmonia, or Days of Fly Fishing, by Sir Humphrey Davy, 1st ed. 1828 12mo Illustrated. 5s. (bds.)

Second edition, 1829 8vo., with six plates and woodcuts. £1 (mor. ex)

Third edition, 1832. 12mo., with six plates 4s. (cf.)

Fourth edition, 1851 12mo Woodcuts 4s. (cf.)

The first two editions were issued without any author's name. In the fourth a number of woodcuts take the place of the engraved plates, which had by that time become much worn.

Saviolo's Practise of Duelling, *see* His Practise.

Scandinavian Adventures during a residence of upwards of 20 years, by L. Lloyd, 1854. 2 vols. 8vo. Map, 12 tinted plates and 102 woodcuts. £1 5s. (original figured cl.)

Scenes and Recollections of Fly Fishing in Northumberland, Cumberland and Westmoreland, by "Stephen Oliver" (W. A. Chatto), 1834. 8vo Woodcuts. 4s. (orig. cl.)

Scenes and Sports in Foreign Lands, by Edward H. D. E. Napier, 1840. 2 vols. 12mo. Plates. 10s (cl.) Published at 21s.

Scenes from the Snow Fields, being illustrations of the Upper Ice-World of Mont Blanc, 1859. Folio. With 19 col. pl. by E. T. Coleman, from sketches made on the spot. £2 10s (orig. cl.) Published at £3 3s.

Scenes on the Road, a series of 18 coloured plates by C. Newhouse, n.d. Oblong folio. £1 18s (hf. bd.)

School of Fencing, The, with a general explanation of the principal attitudes and positions, by Henry Angelo. Text in English and French. 1765. Roy. oblong folio. 47 plates. £2 16s (hf. cf.)

Another edition, 1787. Oblong 4to. pp. viii 150. 47 plates. £1 2s (bds.); £1 18s (*ibid*, very clean copy).

This work was first published, *Londres*, under the title of " L'Ecole des Armes," 1763. Oblong folio. 47 plates. £2 10s. (uncut).

School of Recreation, The, or the Gentlemen's Tutor to those ingenious Exercises of Hunting, Racing, &c., by R. H. 1719. 12mo. Front. in 6 compartments. £1 (cf. ex.)

First edition, 1684. 12mo. Front. £1 12s (calf).

Another edition, 1696. 12mo. Front. £1 18s (cf. ex.)

Another edition, 1701. 12mo. Front. £1 16s (old cf.)

Another edition, 1732. 12mo. Front. £2 (orig. sheep)

Schoole of the Noble and Worthy Science of Defence, The, by Joseph Swetnam. 1617. Small 4to., 7 woodcuts. £22 (cf.)

This scarce treatise is very similar to the work written by Vincentio Saviolo under the title " His Practise " (q. v.) It contains 115 leaves, the last of which is occupied by the monogram of Nicholas Okes, the printer.

Schools and Masters of Fence, from the Middle Ages to the 18th Century, by Egerton Castle. 1st ed. 1884. 4to., pp. lii. 254, with 141 woodcuts in the text. Front. and 6 carbon plates. 15s. (orig. cl.) Published at 31s. 6d.

Another edition, 1892. 8vo., pp. lxxviii. 355. Revised. 3s. 6d. (cl.) Published at 7s. 6d.

Schreiner's Sporting Manual, a Complete Treatise on Fishing, Fowling, and Hunting, as applicable to this Country, by William H. Schreiner. Philadelphia, 1841. 12mo. pp. 147. Front. and illustrations. 5s. (cl.)

Science of Gunnery, The, as applied to Military and Sporting Arms of England, &c. by W. Greener. 1846. 8vo. Engraved title and illustrations. 7s. (orig. cl.)

A prior edition of somewhat less value was published in 1841. 8vo.

Scientific Angler, The, a general and instructive work on Scientific Angling, by David Foster. n.d. (1882) 8vo. Port. coloured and other plates. 3s. (orig. cl.) Published at 6s.

Another edition, 1886. 8vo. 4s. (orig. cl.) Published at 7s. 6d. An edition also appeared in September, 1898.

Scientific Swimming, being a series of instructions by which Swimming may be readily attained, by John Frost. 1816. 8vo., with 12 plates. 6s. (calf). Published at 8s.

Another edition. 1818. 8vo. *New York.*

Most of the plates in this work are reproduced in 'British Manly Exercises,' by Donald Walker. 1834, 12mo., 1837, 12mo., 1847, 18mo (the eighth ed., edited by "Craven.") These and other editions of the same book are of small importance.

Scots Fencing Master, The, or Compleat Small Swordman, in which is fully described the whole guards, etc., by W(illiam) H(ope), Gent. 1687. 8vo., with 12 illustrations in the text. £6 18s (old cf.)

Second edition, 1692. 8vo., published under the title of "The Compleat Fencing Master." *See* **Compleat Fencing Master, The.**

Scott and Sebright, by "The Druid" (H. H. Dixon), 1862. 8vo. Plates. 8s (orig. cl.)

Another edition. Revised and re-edited (1880). 8vo, pp. xi. 418, belonging to "The Druid Sporting Series."

Scourge, The, or Monthly Expositor of Imposture and Folly, 1811-16. 12 vols., 8vo. Col. caricatures by G. Cruikshank and others. £11. (11 vols. only, hf. cf.)

This Periodical commenced in January, 1811, and was carried on until the end of 1816. Complete sets of volumes are very rarely met with.

Scrambles amongst the Alps in 1860-69, by Edward Whymper. 1st ed. 1871. 8vo, map and illustrations. £1 10s (orig. cl.)

Fourth edition, 1893. 8vo. £1 9s (orig. cl.), £2 (edition de luxe, hf. mor.)

Scraps from the Sketch Book of Henry Alken, 1821. Oblong folio. 42 plates of sporting subjects. £5 10s (cf. ex., plates coloured, fine copy); £1 5s (orig. bds. broken, plates plain). *See also* **New Scrap Book.**

Sea Fishing as a Sport, by J. H. Lambton Young. 1st ed. 1865. F'cap. 8vo. Plates. 2s. 6d. (cl.)

Second edition. 1872. 8vo, pp. xvi. 220, with coloured plates and woodcuts. 2s. 6d. (cl.) Published at 5s.

Secrets of Angling, The, teaching the choicest Tooles, Baits and Seasons for the taking of any Fish, in Pond or River, by I. D. (John Dennys), 1613. 8vo, woodcut on title. £25 (cf. ex.)

Second edition. n.d. (1620?) 8vo. Only one copy known.

Third edition, 1630. 8vo. Only one copy known.

Fourth edition, 1652. 18mo. Front. £15 (mor. ex.)

Another edition. 1811. 8vo. 100 copies printed. £3 10s. (bds.)

This work was reprinted in Edward Arber's "An English Garner," 1877.

Select Trials at the Sessions House in the Old Bailey, for Murder, Robberies, etc., from 1720 to 1764. Two Series, in 8 vols. 8vo. 1742-64, with fronts. to the first four vols £5 5s. (cf. ex. by Bedford, fine copy)

Self Defence, or the Art of Boxing, by Edward Donnelly; edited by J. M. Waite (1879) 8vo. Illustrations. Published at 2s. 6d. and 1s.

Seventeen Trips through Somaliland: A Record of Exploration and Big Game Shooting, 1885 to 1893 . . . by Capt. H. G. C. Swayne 1895. 8vo. pp. xx. 386. Illustrations and maps. 6s. (orig. cl.)

Severale wayes of Hunting, Hawking, and Fishing, according to the English manner . . . by Francis Barlow, 1671. Oblong 4to. Engraved title and 12 etchings by Hollar, under each of which is a four-line verse. A copy of this very scarce book realised £7 10s. at the sale of the library of the late Edward Snow, held at Sotheby's on November 30, 1898.

There is a set of 12 prints of Hunting, Hawking, and Fishing, which is usually catalogued under the name of Francis Barlow. These are sometimes extracted from the above-named work, and at others reprinted from retouched plates.

Seymour's Sketches, illustrated in prose and verse, by Alfred Crowquill, 1841. 2 vols. 8vo. 8s. (hf. cf.)
Includes numerous sporting subjects.

Seymour's Sketches. *See* **Sketches by Seymour.**

Shooter's Guide, The, by "B. Thomas" (Thomas B. Johnson). 1st ed. 1809. 12mo. Illustrated. 5s. (orig. bds.)

The second, third and fourth editions, the last being considerably enlargèd and improved, appeared respectively in 1810, 1811 and 1814. The sixth edition appeared in 1820. All these are unimportant.

Shooting, a series of 8 representations and engraved title by Robert Frankland, 1813. Oblong folio. £7 7s. (mor. ex., uncut, fine copy)

Shooting, or One Day's Sport of Three Real Good Ones, however ignorant of Sporting Rules, 1823. Oblong fol. 6 large col. plates by Henry Alken. £5 10s. (mor. ex., good set).

Shooting and Fishing Trips in England, France, Alsace, &c., by "Wildfowler," "Snapshot," and others, 1876-7. 4 vols. 8vo., plates. 20s. (orig. cl.)

Consists of papers contributed to *Bell's Life in London*, and other journals. The above-mentioned work is in two series, the second comprising Shooting, Yachting, and Sea Fishing Trips.

Shooting and Salmon Fishing, by Augustus Grimble, 1892. Large Paper in 4to., pp. xi. 259, with 18 full page illustrations by Thorburn and others. £2 5s. (hf. vellum); 8s (Small Paper in 8vo., orig. cl.) The Small Paper copies were published at 16s.

Shooting Directory, The, by Richard Badham Thornhill, 1804. 4to., col. port. and plates. £2 2s. (hf. cf.)

Shooting in the Himalayas, a Journal of Sporting Adventures and Travel in Chinese Tartary, &c., by Frederick Markham, 1854. 8vo. Tinted plates. £1 10s. (orig. cl.)

Shooting in Thibet. *See* **Large Game Shooting, &c.**

Short Introduction for to learne to Swimme, A, gathered out of Master Digbie's Booke of the Art of Swimming . . . by Christopher Middleton, 1595. Sm. 4to., with 40 woodcuts after those in Everard Digby's "De Arte Natandi" (q.v.) A copy of this scarce book is in the Bodleian.

Short Sketches of the Wild Sports in the Highlands, by Charles William George St. John, 1878. 8vo. Woodcuts. 15s. (cl.)

Short Stalks, or Hunting Camps, North, South, East, and West, by Edward North Buxton, 1892. Roy. 8vo. pp. xii. 405, with 67 illustrations by Whymper, Wolf, and others. 10s. (buckram, as issued). Published at 21s.

Second edition. 1893. 8vo. pp. xiii. 405. 8s. (cl.) Published at 21s.

A Second Series, comprising Trips in Somaliland, Sinai, the Eastern Desert of Egypt, &c., 1898. Impl. 16mo. (9¼ in. by 6½ in.), pp. 238. Numerous illustrations and maps. Published at 21s.

Short Treatise of Hunting, A, compyled for the delight of Noblemen and Gentlemen, by Sir Thomas Cockaine, 1591. Sm. 4to. Woodcuts. £15 10s. (calf, one leaf missing.) Printed in Black Letter.

Shot-Gun and Sporting-Rifle, The, and the Dogs, Ponies, Ferrets . . . used with them in the various kinds of Shooting and Trapping, by "Stonehenge" (John Henry Walsh), 1859. 8vo. Illustrations. 5s. (cl.) Published at 10s. 6d.

Another edition, 1862. 8vo. Illustrations. 2s. 6d. (cl.)

Show Folks, The, by Pierce Egan, 1831. 12mo., with 9 woodcuts, by Theodore Lane. 5s. (wrappers, as issued).

Silk and Scarlet, by "The Druid" (H. H. Dixon), 1859. 8vo. Eight portraits of Hunters, Jockeys, &c. 5s. (orig. red cl.)

Another edition, Revised and re-edited (1880). 8vo. Belonging to "The Druid Sporting Series."

Sixteen Scenes taken from the Miseries of Human Life, by "One of the Wretched," 1807. Oblong 4to., with vignette, title, and 16 coloured plates by J. A. Atkinson. £3 10s. (mor. ex., uncut, fine copy).

Sketch Book, The, by Henry Alken, a series of 42 plates by Henry Alken, 1821. 4to. £1 10s. (cf.)

Another edition, 1826. 4to. £3 5s. (hf. bd., plates coloured).

Sketches, the Stable, the Road, the Park, the Field A series of 6 coloured plates, by Henry Alken, 1854. Folio. £1 15s. (cf. ex., orig. wrappers bound up).

Sketches, by Seymour. Five parts, containing 180 etchings of sporting subjects, and five title pages, printed on papers of different tints, n d (1835-36), G. S. Tregear £5 (mor. ex.); £6 10s. (ibid.)

Another issue, n d 4to Published by Fry, with 2 engraved titles. and 24 etchings, by R. Seymour. £1 5s. (orig. bds.)

A reprint was published by Hatten, n d , oblong 4to. It contains the 180 humorous designs. "Seymour's Sketches, illustrated by prose and verse by A. Crowquill," appeared in 2 vols., 8vo., 1841. Neither of these works is of much value.

Sketches in the Hunting Field, by Alfred E. T. Watson, 1880 8vo., pp x. 256 19 illustrations by Sturgess. 6s. (orig. cl.)

Sketches of Field Sports, as followed by the Natives of India, with observations on the Animals; a Description of the Art of Catching Serpents, with remarks on Hydrophobia and Rabid Animals, &c., by Daniel Johnson, 1822. 8vo. Front. 7s. (bds.) Published at 10s 6d

Sketches on the Road, 1835. Oblong 4to. Sporting plates by Newhouse, engraved by Reeve, col. by hand. £1 15s. (orig cl)

Sketching Rambles, or Nature in the Alps and Appennines, by Agnes and Maria E Catlow, 1861. 2 vols. 8vo., with 20 tinted plates. 5s. (orig, cl.)

Slang, a Dictionary of the Turf, the Ring, the Chase, the Pit, &c., by "John Bee" (J Badcock), 1823. 12mo. Folding col. front £2 (bds. uncut).

Smoking Hunt, The. Hand-coloured plates, by C. L. Smith, 1826. Oblong folio. £2 (cloth).

Snob à L'Exposition, by "Crafty," 1867. Small oblong fol. 40 humorous plates of racing, hawking, &c. 16s. (orig. pictorial boards).

Snob à Paris, by "Crafty," 1867. Small oblong fol. 40 caricatures of racing, chasing, shooting, &c. 16s. (orig. pictorial bds.)

Snobson's Seasons, being Annals of Cockney Sports, n.d. 8vo., with 92 col. plates. 18s. (cl. as issued)

Solitary Rambles and Adventures of a Hunter in the Prairies, by John Palliser, 1853. Post 8vo. Plates. 5s. (calf).

Some Account of English Deer Parks, by Evelyn Philip Shirley, 1867. 4to. Illustrations. £2 10s. (orig. cl.); £3 15s. (*ibid.*)

Songs of the Chace. *See* **Nimrod's Songs of the Chace.**

Songs of the Chace, &c., 1811. 8vo. Front. and engraved title by J. Scott. 18s. (calf). £1 1s (mor. g e.)

Songs of the Edinburgh Angling Club. Probably printed 1858. Vignettes by members of the club. £2 18s. (hf. mor. gt.)

Another edition, enlarged, 1879. 8vo. Vignettes. £1 8s. (orig. cl., uncut).

Songs, Parodies, Duets, Choruses, &c., in an entirely new . . . Burletta of Fun, Frolic, Fashion, and Flash, n.d. 8vo. One coloured plate. Published by John Lowndes at 1s. *See* **Life in London.**

Specimens of Riding near London, Drawn from Life, by H. Alken, 1823. Fol. 18 col. plates. £9 9s (mor. ex., fine copy); £10 10s. (orig. hf. binding); £7 15s. (original 3 parts, with wrappers)

Sponge's Sporting Tour, by the author of "Handley Cross" (R. S. Surtees), 1853. Originally published in 13 monthly parts, red wrappers designed by Leech; afterwards in demy

8vo. as above. Contains 13 col. plates and numerous woodcuts all by Leech. £2 15s. (orig. cl.); £2 10s. (ibid.); £3 10s. (ibid.); £8 8s. (orig. parts).

Another edition, 1860. 8vo. £1 6s. (orig. cl.), £1 10s. (ibid.)

Another edition, n.d., 1888. Col. plates by Wildrake and others. 10s. (cl. as issued).

Sport, Fox Hunting, Salmon Fishing, Covert Shooting, &c., by William Bromley Davenport. 1st ed. 1885. 8vo. plates by H. H. Crealock. 15s. (hf. mor. gt.), £2 15s. (L. P., illustrations on India paper, 250 copies printed).

Another edition, 1888. Post 8vo. Illustrations. 2s. (cl.) Published at 6s.

Sport and Photography in the Rocky Mountains, by Andrew Williamson, 1880. Folio. pp. vi. 55 Photographs. £1 3s. (cl.) Published at 42s.

Sport and War, or Recollections of Fighting and Hunting in South Africa, by General John Jarvis Bisset, 1875. 8vo. 5s. (cl.) Published at 14s.

Sportfolio: Portraits and Biographies of Heroes and Heroines of Sport and Pastime, 1896. Folio; pp. 144; 144 portraits. 3s. (cl.) Published at 6s.

Sport in Moray, *see* **Natural History and Sport in Moray.**

Sport in Norway, and where to find it, by M. R. Barnard, 1864. F'cap 8vo. Illustrations. 4s. (orig. cl.)

Sport in the Alps in the past and present . . with . . . some sporting reminiscences, &c., by W. A. Baillie Grohman, 1896. 8vo., pp. xv. 356. Illustrations. 7s. (cloth). Published at 21s.

Sport in the Highlands and Lowlands of Scotland with Rod and Gun, by Thomas Speedy, 1884. 8vo., pp. xviii. 412. More than 60 illustrations by Crealock. 5s. (orig. cl.) Published at 15s.

Second edition, 1886. 8vo., pp. xx 444. Illustrations. 5s. (orig. cl.) Published at 15s.

Sport, Travel, and Adventure in Newfoundland and the West Indies, by Capt. W. R. Kennedy, 1885. 8vo., pp. x 399. Illustrations by the author. 8s. (orig. cl.)

Sport with Gun and Rod in American Woods and Waters, by A. M. Mayer, 1884. 2 vols. 8vo. Illustrations. £1 8s. (hf. rox. t.e.g.) A few copies were published on Large Paper at £4 4s., with Japan proofs and other illustrations. £2 8s. (hf. rox.)

Sporting, edited by "Nimrod" (C. J. Apperley), 1838. Impl. 4to. 38 steel plates and woodcuts, after Gainsborough, Landseer, and others; text by Tom Hood and others. £1 10s. (orig. cl.)

Sporting Adventures in the Far West, by John Mortimer Murphy, 1879. 8vo. 5s (orig. cl.) Published at 18s.

Sporting Adventures in the New World, or Days and Nights of Moose Hunting, by Lt. Campbell Hardy, R.A., 1855. 2 vols. 12mo. Fronts. 12s. (orig. cl.)

Sporting Adventures of Mr. Popple, The, by G. H. Jalland, 1898. Oblong 4to., with 10 coloured plates and other illustrations. Published at 6s.

Sporting Almanac, *see* **Oracle of Rural Life.**

Sporting Alphabet, The, a series of 26 humorous engravings and a titlepage, by William Heath, n.d. (1840) 8vo. £1 14s. (hf. cf.)

Sporting Anecdotes, original and select, including characteristic sketches of eminent persons who have appeared on the turf, &c., by an Amateur Sportsman. 1st ed. 1804. 8vo., with 16 illustrations, by Bewick. £1 (cf.), £2 10s. (cf. ex., fine copy)

Another edition, n.d. (1807). 12mo. 8s. (cf.)

Sporting Anecdotes, original and selected, including numerous characteristic portraits of persons in every walk of life, by Pierce Egan. Best ed. 1825. 8vo Plates and woodcuts by R Cruikshank and others, and 2 col. plates by J R. Cruikshank £3 12s. (pictorial bds. uncut); £3 (cf. ex , g.e.)

New York edition. 2 vols., 1823 8vo. Woodcut frontispiece £2 (cf. ex , uncut).

The First English edition appeared in f'cap 8vo., 1820, with front. by J. R. Cruikshank, and 8 plates of hunting, fishing, &c. £1 10s. (orig. bds.)

Sporting Annual, *see* **Finch Mason's Sporting Annual.**

Sporting Architecture, by George Tattersall (1841). 4to., with 43 full page and other illustrations by Vyner and others. 10s. (orig. cl.)

Sporting Days in Southern India, by Lt.-Col. A. J. O. Pollock, 1894 8vo. pp xx 252 Illustrations. 7s. (orig. cl) Published at 16s.

Sporting Dictionary, The, and Rural Repository of General Information upon every Subject, &c., by William Taplin. 1803. 2 vols. 8vo. Plates. 8s (cf.)

Sporting Discoveries: or, Miseries of Shooting, being Hints to Young Sportsmen, a series of 7 coloured plates by "Ben Tally Ho." S. and J Fuller, 1816. Oblong 4to £4 4s. (orig. wrappers.)

Sporting Facts and Sporting Fancies, by "Harry Hieover" (Charles Brindley), 1853. 8vo 13s. (hf. mor.)

Sporting Fish of Great Britain, with notes on Ichthyology, by H. Cholmondeley Pennell 1886. 8vo., pp. 185, with 16 lithographs of fish in gold, silver, and colours, £2 (Large Paper, hf bd.) Published at 15s , or on Large Paper at 30s.

Sporting in Algeria, by Edward Vernon Harcourt, 1860. (1859?). F'cap. 8vo. Map and col. front. 2s. (cl.)

I

Sporting Incidents in the Life of Another Tom Smith, Master of Fox-hounds, by Tom Smith, 1867. Cr 8vo front. and illustrations on tinted paper. £2 4s (cl. uncut)

Sporting Magazine, The, or Monthly Calendar of the Turf, the Chace, &c. Illustrations. This serial commenced in 1792. £250 (1792 to 1870. 156 vols. 8vo. 2 vols. missing, and 7 in half cf.; all the rest in green cf. gt uniform) £190 (1828-70. 84 vols. in the orig. parts, nearly all clean and fresh). £17 10s (1792-1803. 22 vols orig hf. cf.) *See* **New Sporting Magazine.**

Sporting Mirror, The, edited by Diomed, 1881 6. Complete in 10 vols. 8vo. Portraits. £1 12s. (10 vols. hf. cf.)

Sporting Notions, n d Oblong 4to 20 col plates by Henry Alken. £5 10s. (wrappers.)

Sporting Oracle, The, and Almanac of Rural Life, for 1841, edited by "Vates." 12 whole page sporting plates, by R. B. Davis. 6s. (paper covers.)

This periodical was afterwards incorporated in "The Sporting Almanack," which was then produced as "The Sporting Almanack and Oracle of Rural Life." 1842-44. 8vo. *See* **Oracle of Rural Life.**

Sporting Recollections, by G. Finch Mason, 1885. 8vo, pp. xv. 200, with 102 illustrations. 4s. (orig. cl.)

Sporting Reminiscences of Hampshire, 1745 to 1862, by Æsop, 1864. 8vo 4s (cl.) Published at 6s 6d

Sporting Repository, The: Horse Racing, Hunting, Coursing, Shooting, Pugilism, &c., 1822 8vo McLean. 19 col plates, by Henry Alken. £17 (mor. ex, uncut, fine copy.)

Sporting Review, The, a monthly Chronicle of the Turf, the Chase, &c., edited by "Craven." Illustrations by H. Alken and others. This serial commenced in 1839. £3 (1839-44; 12 vols, hf. cf.)

Sporting Rifle, The, and its Projectiles, by James Forsyth, 1863. Post 8vo. 3 plates. 2s. (cl.) Published at 7s. 6d.

Second edition, rewritten and enlarged, 1867. 8vo. Illustrations. 2s. (cl.) Published at 7s. 6d.

Sporting Satirist, The, a series of 12 col. plates, by Henry Alken, 1839. 4to. £2 5s. (cf. ex.)

Sporting Scenes and Country Characters, by "Martingale" (— White), 1840. 8vo. Illustrations by Alken, Landseer, and others. 16s. (cl., uncut), £1 5s. (cf. ex.)

Sporting Scenes among the Kaffirs of South Africa, by Alfred Wilks Drayson, 1858. 8vo. Col. plates by Harrison Weir. 5s. (cl. uncut).

Sporting Scrap Book, The, a series of 50 col. plates designed and engraved by Henry Alken. McLean, n.d. (about 1824). Oblong 4to. £4 15s. (hf. mor.), £9 *(ibid.)*

Sporting Sketch Book, The, by J. W. Carleton, 1842. 8vo. 11 engravings. £1 8s. (cf. ex. uncut, original covers bound up, fine copy).

Sporting Sketches, 1826. 4to., with 17 plates, four etchings on each, by H. Alken. £4 10s. (cf.)

Sporting Sketches, by G. Finch Mason, n.d. (1879). Oblong folio. 7s. (bds.)

Fourth edition. n.d. (1882). Oblong fol., pp. 22. 3s. (bds.)

Sporting Sketches at Home and Abroad, by "The Old Bushman," n.d. Cr. 8vo. Coloured illustrations by Georgina Bowers. 5s. (cl.)

Sporting Sketches with Pen and Pencil, by Francis Francis and Alfred W. Cooper, 1878. 4to., with 36 engravings. £1 10s. (cl.) Published at 21s.

Sporting Songster, The, *see* **Fairbairn's Sporting Songster.**

Sporting Tour through various parts of France, in the year 1802, by Col. Thomas Thornton, 1806. 2 vols. 4to. Portrait of the author and 49 plates by Merigot and Scott, and tail pieces by Scott and Bewick. £2 5s. (hf. cf.)

Sporting Tour through the Northern Parts of England, and parts of the Highlands of Scotland, by Col. Thomas Thornton, 1804. 4to. 16 plates after Garrard. £1 10s. (bds. uncut).

Another edition, 1806. 2 vols. 4to. Portrait of the author in colours, plates. £7 (L.P. old russ. ex.), £1 15s. (cf. gt., Small Paper).

Reprinted in "The Sportsman's Library" (q.v.) with coloured plates by G. E. Lodge. Portraits and selections from the original illustrations, pp. xviii. 332.

Sporting World, The, by "Harry Hieover" (Charles Brindley), 1858. F'cap 8vo. Front. 2s. (cl.)

Sports and Adventures in the Highlands, see **Wanderings in the Highlands.**

Sports and Anecdotes of Bygone Days, in England, Scotland, Ireland, &c., by C. T. S. Birch Reynardson, 1887. 8vo. 6 col. pl. 6s. (orig. cl.)

Sports and Pastimes, a series of 10 large coloured plates, by John Leech, 1865. Atlas folio. £7 7s. (in cover), £9 (*ibid.*)

Sports and Pastimes of Merry England, by Thomas Miller, n.d. (1859). Crown 8vo. 21 illustrations by Harrison Weir and others. 3s. 6d. (orig. cl.) Published at the same amount.

Sports and Pastimes of the People of England, by Joseph Strutt. 1st ed., 1801. 4to., col. plates. £2 8s. (L.P. hf. russ.), £3 10s. (*ibid.* bds.)

Second edition, 1810. 4to. 40 col. plates. £1 15s. (hf. mor.); £2 10s. (russ.)

Another edition, 1830. 8vo. 140 plates. £1 3s. (L.P., cl. uncut). 15s. (orig. 10 monthly parts).

Another edition, 1833. 8vo., with 140 engravings. 3s. (cl.); 7s. (L.P., cl.)

Another edition, 1838. 8vo., with 140 engravings. 3s. (cl.)

Another edition, 1841. 8vo.

Another edition, 1845. 8vo., with 140 engravings. £1 5s (L.P., plates coloured); 7s. (L.P., plates plain).

Another edition, 1876. 40 copperplates and 140 woodcuts. £1 12s. (L.P., hf. mor.)

Sportsman, The. This periodical commenced in 1834, a "New Series" being published in 1836, and a "Second Series" in 1839. From and inclusive of the year 1845, the volumes are precisely the same as "The New Sporting Magazine," a new title page, &c., being added to meet the exigencies of the case. *See* **New Sporting Magazine.**

Sportsman and Naturalist in Canada, The, by William Ross King, 1866. 8vo. 6 col. plates and woodcuts. £1 10s. (cl.)

Sportsman and Naturalist's Tour in Sutherlandshire, A, *see* **Tour in Sutherlandshire.**

Sportsman in Canada, The, by Frederic Tolfrey, 1845. 2 vols. F'cap. 8vo. 6s. (orig. cl.) Published at 21s.

Sportsman in France, The, by Frederic Tolfrey, 1841. 2 vols. F'cap 8vo. 12 plates by R. J. Hamerton. 6s. (orig. cl.) Published at 21s.

Sportsman in Ireland, The, with his Summer tour through the Highlands of Scotland, by a Cosmopolite, 1840. 2 vols 8vo. Illustrations. 2s. 6d. (cl.)

Probably written by R. Allan. Reprinted in the "Sportsman's Library." (q.v.)

Sportsman's Annual, The. 1st series (Dogs), 1836. Folio. Plates by Sir E. Landseer, Cooper, and Hancock. 18s (hf. mor., proof plates).

No second series appears to have been published.

Sportsman's Cabinet, The, or a Correct Delineation of the various dogs used in the Sports of the Field, 1803-4. 2 vols. 4to. Large Paper. 25 plates by Scott, and numerous woodcuts by Bewick. £1 10s. (hf. cf.); £2 10s. (cf. gt.); £4 10s. (uncut).

Sportsman's Cabinet, The, and Town and Country Magazine, edited and conducted by T. B. Johnson, Nov., 1832, to Oct., 1833. 2 vols. 8vo. Plates borrowed from "The Sportsman's Cyclopædia" (q.v.). 10s. (cl.)

Sportsman's Cyclopædia, The: being a complete elucidation of the science and practice of the field, the turf, and the rod, by "Thomas B. Johnson." 1831. 8vo. Illustrations. 16s. (cl.)

Second edition, 1848. 8vo. Bohn. Illustrations. 5s. (cl.)

Sportsman's Dictionary, The, or the Country Gentleman's Companion in all Rural Recreations, 1735. 2 vols. 4to. 25 plates. £1 5s. (calf).

Another edition, 1744. 4to. Plates. 10s. (calf).

Sportsman's Dictionary, The, or the Gentleman's Companion, for town and country. 1st ed., 1778. 4to. with 17 plates. 10s. (cf.)

Second edition, 1782. 4to. 17 plates as before. 10s. (cf.)

Other editions, of 1785, 4to., 1786, 4to., Dublin, 1792. 4to., 1800. 4to., and lastly, 1807. Folio. Improved and enlarged by H. T. Pye. All of about the same value.

Sportsman's Directory, The, or Park and Gamekeeper's Companion, The, by John Mayer. 1st ed., 1815, 12mo. Cuts. 5s. (bds.)

Second edition, revised and enlarged, 1817. 8vo. Cuts. 5s. (bds.)

Third edition, 1819. 12mo. Cuts. 5s. (bds.)

Other editions, of 1823, 12mo.; 1828, 12mo., 1845, 12mo., 1860, 12mo., all of small value.

Sportsman's Friend in a Frost, The, by "Harry Hieover" (Charles Brindley), 1857. 8vo. Front. 5s. (cl.) Published at 12s., but reduced to 5s. in 1861.

Sportsman's Handbook, The, to practical collecting. Preserving . . . of trophies and specimens. To which is added a synoptical guide to the hunting grounds of the world, by Rowland Ward. 1st ed. 1880. 8vo. pp. viii. 103. Illustrated. 3s. 6d. (cl.) Published at the same amount.

Second edition, 1882. 8vo. pp. x. 119, with additional Illustrations. Published at 3s. 6d.

Several other editions of this well-known book have appeared, notably a fourth in 1888, a sixth in 1891, and a seventh in 1894, all at 3s. 6d.

Sportsman's Library, The, by John Mills, 1845. 8vo. Portraits and tinted plates. 10s. (cl. uncut).

Sportsman's Library, The: a re-issue of Rare, Valuable and Entertaining old Books on Sport, edited by Sir Herbert Eustace Maxwell, Bart., and published at 15s. each (vellum, gilt tops) or on Large Paper at £2 2s., 200 copies of each issued. These volumes contain all the plates found in the original editions, supplemented by engravings after Millais, Whymper, and other modern artists. The following volumes have already appeared (November, 1898):—

Life of a Fox, The, by Thomas Smith, 1896. 14 plates, 6 by Jalland (coloured) which have not previously appeared.

Sporting Tour through the Northern Parts of England and Part of the Highlands of Scotland, by Colonel T. Thornton.

Sportsman in Ireland, The, by Cosmopolite.

Chase, the Turf, and the Road, The, 1898. Illustrated by Alken. Portrait by Maclise, and other portraits.

Reminiscences of a Huntsman, by G. C. G. F. Berkeley, 1897. Coloured and other plates.

Art of Deer Stalking, by William Scrope, 1897. Illustrations.

Days and Nights of Salmon Fishing, by William Scrope, 1898.

Sportsman's Magazine, The, or Chronicle of Games and Pastimes, 1823-4. 3 vols. 12mo. Plates and portraits. 12s. (calf).

Sportsman's Pocket Companion, The, being a Striking Likeness or Portraiture of the Most Eminent Race Horses and Stallions, n.d. (1760). 8vo. 40 plates by James and Henry Roberts. £4 10s. (hf. mor.)

Sportsman's Repository, The, by John Scott, 1820. 4to. 40 plates after Marshall, Stubbs, and others. Front and vignettes by Bewick. £1 8s. (hf. russ.), £1 10s. (orig. bds.)

Another edition, 1845. 4to. Plates. £1 5s. (cf., sound copy)

Sportsman's Vocal Cabinet, The, by Charles Armiger, 1830. Post 8vo. Front. 5s. (bds. uncut).

Sportsman's Year Book, The, edited by C. S. Colman and A. H. Windsor. Vol. 1 appeared on December 15, 1898.

Spring Tide, or the Angler and his Friends, by John Yonge Akermann, 1850. 12mo. Portrait and woodcuts. 2s. (cl.)

Second edition, 1852. 12mo. Portrait and woodcuts. 2s. (cl.)

Stable Practice, or Hints on Training for the Turf, the Chase, and the Road, by "Cecil" (Cornelius Tongue), 1852. Post 8vo. 4s. (orig. hf. binding).

Stable Talk and Table Talk, or Spectacles for Young Sportsmen, by "Harry Hieover" (Charles Brindley), 1845-6. 2 vols. 8vo. 8s. (cl. uncut)

Stadium, The, *see* **Particulars and Recommendations of the Stadium.**

Stag Hunting on Exmoor, *see* **Records of Stag Hunting, &c.**

Stage Coach, The, or the Road of Life, by John Mills, 1843. 3 vols. 8vo. 9 plates by "Standfast." £1 15s. (cl. uncut).

State Lottery, The: a Dream, by Samuel Roberts, 1817. 8vo. Folding col. front. £1 5s. (bds. uncut).

Steeple Chase, The: A series of 6 oblong folio coloured plates, by Henry Alken. £4 10s. (fair)

St. James's, a Satirical Poem, 1827. Post 8vo. £1 5s. (cf.) Published by Colburn at 6s.
This Poem has reference to Crockford's Gaming Rooms, then situate in St. James's Street, W.

Story of Mont Blanc, The, by Albert Smith. 1st ed., 1853. Post 8vo. Published at 10s. 6d. Col. front. and numerous cuts in the text. 10s. (orig. orange cl.)
Second edition, 1854. 8vo. Enlarged, plates. 5s. (cl.)

Stranger's Safeguard, The, against Cheats, Swindlers, and Pickpockets, 1819. 12mo. Front. 5s. (hf. cf.)

Stray Notes on Fishing and Natural History, by Cornwall Simeon, 1860. 8vo. Front and woodcuts. 3s. (cl.)
Second edition, 1863. 8vo. Front and woodcuts. 3s. (cl.)

Stray Sport, by J. Moray Brown, 1893. 2 vols. Post 8vo. 50 illustrations. 6s. (orig. cl.) Published at 21s.

Stud Farm, The, or Hints on Breeding for the Turf, the Chase, and the Road . . by "Cecil" (Cornelius Tongue), 1873. F'cap 8vo. Front. 3s. (cl.)

Stud, for Practical Purposes and Practical Men, The, by "Harry Hieover" (Charles Bindley), 1849. 12mo. Plates. 2s. (cl.)
Another edition, 1858. F'cap 8vo. 2s. (cl.)

Such Things Are: a series of 26 coloured plates by Henry Heath, Heidman, and others, 1835. 4to. £7 (mor. ex., uncut, fine copy)

Summer Months among the Alps, with the Ascent of Monte Rosa, by T. W. Hinchliff, 1857. Cr. 8vo. 4 col. plates and maps. 15s. (orig. cl.)

Sword Exercise of Cavalry, The, 1796. 8vo. 26 folding plates. 3s. (bds., uncut).

A book entitled "Sword Exercise for Cavalry," with 6 engravings, London, 1799, 8vo., is mentioned by Mr. Egerton Castle in his "Schools and Masters of Fence."

Symptoms of being Amused: a series of 42 coloured plates by Henry Alken, 1822. Oblong folio. £6 10s. (orig. half binding with label on side), £5 (ibid.) First published in 7 parts.

Syntax, *see* **Tour of Dr. Syntax; Tour of Dr. Syntax through London; Syntax (Dr.) in Paris.**

Syntax (Dr.) in Paris: a Tour in Search of the Grotesque, 1820. 8vo. 18 coloured plates in the style of Rowlandson. £2 (hf. russ.), £5 5s. (bds., uncut)

System of Equestrian Education, A Exhibiting the Beauties and Defects of the Horse, by Philip Astley, 1801. 8vo. Portrait and plates. 2s. (bds.)

A fifth edition appeared the same year, and an eighth at Dublin in 1802.

Takings: or the Life of a Collegian, 1821. 8vo. 26 plates by R. Dagley. 4s. (boards), £1 5s. (plates coloured; russ.)

Tales and Traits of Sporting Life, by Henry Corbet, 1864. Post 8vo. Col. front. and vignette of "Ascot Heath, 1838," on title. 2s. 6d. (bds., uncut).

Tales of Humour, Gallantry and Romance, Selected and Translated from the Italian. 1st ed., 1824, 8vo., with 16 etchings by George Cruikshank. £1 10s. (hf. mor.)

Another edition, 1827. 8vo. Etchings as before. £1 (cf. ex., with the cancelled plate of the Dead Rider)

Tauromachia: or the Bull Fights of Spain, by Luke Price. 1852. Imp. folio. 26 chromo-lithographic plates mounted on cardboard, with text. £4 4s. (in a portfolio), £2 (hf. mor.)

Terrific Register, The: or Record of Crimes, Judgments, Providences, and Calamities, 1825. 2 vols. 8vo. Engravings. £1 5s. (hf. mor.)

Theory and Practice of Fencing, *see* **Army and Navy Gentleman's Companion.**

Thirteen Years among the Wild Beasts of India, by George P. Sanderson, 1878. 8vo. Plates. £1 (hf. mor.); published at 15s.

Second edition, 1879. 4to. Col. front., map and plates. 10s. (cl.); published at 15s.

Sixth edition, 1896. 4to. Illustrated. 6s. (cl.), published at 15s.

Thoughts on Hunting, in a series of Familiar Letters to a Familiar Friend, by Peter Beckford. 1st ed., 1781. Small 4to. Front by Bartolozzi (Diana preparing for the chase), and plans of Kennels. Sarum. £1 5s. (cf. gt.)

Second edition, 1782. 4to. Front. 13s. (hf. cf.)

Third edition, 1796. 8vo. 20 plates (1st illustrated ed.) £2 5s. (hf. cf. ex.)

Fourth edition, 1802. 4to. pp. 360. Front by Bartolozzi. £1 1s. (hf. russ.)

Another edition, 1810. 8vo., with 11 plates by Scott, and woodcut by Bewick on title. £1 5s. (bds., uncut), £1 16s. (L.P., bds., uncut), £4 (L.P., mor. ex.)

Another edition (1820). 8vo. Front and numerous vignette cuts by Bewick. £3 (mor. ex., g. e., fine copy), £1 1s. (russ. gt.)

Another edition, 1840. 12mo., with a chapter on Coursing.

Another edition, 1879. 8vo. 5s. (orig. cl.), published at 14s.

Another edition, 1881. 8vo. pp. xi. 269. Illustrated. 5s. (orig. cl.), published at 14s.

Three Bookes of Colloquies concerning the Arte of Shooting in Great and Small Peeces of Artillerie, by Cyprian Lucar, 1588. Small folio. Folding and other woodcuts. £3 (hf. cf.)

This work is a translation from the Italian of Nicolo Tartaglia.

Three Great Runs, the Waterloo, the Greatwood, and the Harlequin Run, 1889. 4to. Photographs. £2 (orig. cl.)

Three Hunting Songs, by Rowland Eyles Egerton Warburton, 1855. Oblong 8vo. 4 plates by "Phiz." £1 10s. (orig. wrapper). Only 250 copies printed. *See* also "**Hunting Songs, Ballads,**" &c.

Through a Field Glass, by George F. Underhill and H. S. Sweetland, 1896. 8vo. Illustrations by L. Thackeray. 1s. 6d. (pictorial boards). Published at 3s. 6d.

Tiger Shooting in India, by William Rice, 1857. Roy. 8vo., with 12 lithographic plates from sketches by the author. £2 15s. (orig. red cl.)

Tit Bits of the Turf, by Finch Mason, n.d. Oblong folio, with 16 tinted plates. £1 1s. (bds., as issued).

To all Sportsmen. . . . Above thirty years practice in Horses and Dogs; . . . The Rat-Catching Secret; On Fowling Pieces, &c., by Colonel George Hanger, 1814. 8vo., with folding frontispiece after Reinagle. 10s. (bds.)

Another edition, n.d. (1816) 8vo. Folding front. 10s. (bds.)

Tom and Jerry, *see* **Life in London.**

Tom and Jerry: or Life in London; the songs, parodies, &c., in the Burletta, founded on Pierce Egan's work, 1821. 8vo. Col. front. of Mr. Wilkinson as Bob Logic, by George Cruikshank. £1 (wrappers).

Tom and Jerry: or Life in London; an entirely new Whimsical, Local, Melodramatic . . . Drama . . . as performed at Davis's Royal Amphitheatre, London, 1822. 8vo. One coloured plate. Published by John Lowndes at 1s. £1 (wrappers). *See* **Life in London.**

Tom and Jerry: or Life in London, with a copious Vocabulary of Flash and Cant. Dublin, 1822. Post 8vo. Col. front. 12s. (sewn).

Tom and Jerry, Songs, Duets, &c., in the Burletta, produced at the Adelphi Theatre, 1821. 1st ed. 1821. 8vo. Col. front. of Mr. Wrench as Corinthian Tom, by J. R. Cruikshank. £1 5s. (sewed)

Another edition, n.d (1822) Lowndes Col front. £1 5s (sewed) *See* **Life in London.**

Tommiebeg Shootings, The: or a Moor in Scotland, by Thomas Jeans, 1860 8vo Illustrated by P. Skelton 6s. (orig. cl.)

Tom Moody's Tales, edited by Mark Lemon, 1864 (1863). 8vo., with 13 plates by H. K. Browne. 18s. (cl.)

Tom Raw, the Griffin, a Burlesque Poem [by Sir Charles D'Oyley], 1828. Roy 8vo. 25 humorous col. plates by Rowlandson. £4 (bds. uncut); £2 14s. (hf. russ., uncut).

Touch at the Fine Arts, A: a series of 12 humorous coloured plates, with descriptions, by Henry Alken, 1824 Impl. 8vo. McLean. £8 (mor ex., uncut, fine copy); £3 3s. (orig. bds.)

Tour in a Phæton Through the Eastern Counties, A, by James John Hissey, 1889. 8vo. pp. xiv. 403. Map and 16 illustrations by the author. 12s (orig. cl.)

Tour in Sutherlandshire, A, by Charles William George St. John, 1849. 2 vols. 12mo. 10 full-page illustrations. £1 8s. (orig. cl., uncut).

Second edition, with an appendix on the Fauna of Sutherland, by J. A Harvie-Brown, 1884. 2 vols. 8vo 12s. (cl.) Published at 21s

Another edition, 1891. 8vo. pp. 320. Published at 4s. 6d. under the title of "A Sportsman and Naturalist's Tour in Sutherlandshire." 2s (cl)

Tour of Dr. Prosody in Search of the Antique and Picturesque, 1821. 8vo. 20 col plates by W. Reed. £1 10s. (hf. mor.); £3 (cf. ex.); £4 (orig. bds.)

Tour of Dr. Syntax in Search of the Picturesque: a Poem, by William Combe. 1st ed. 1812. 8vo. First appeared in the *Poetical Magazine* (May, 1809, to April, 1811), afterwards in volume form, as above, at 21s. 31 col. plates (inclusive of front. and engraved title) by Rowlandson.

Many later editions, notably a 4th and 5th in 1813, a 6th in 1815, and a 9th in 1819, all with the same col. plates. "Crowquill's Edition" appeared in 1838.

Second Tour of Dr. Syntax in Search of Consolation: a Poem, by William Combe. 1st ed. 1820. 8vo. First appeared in the *Poetical Magazine*, afterwards in volume form, as above. 25 col. plates by Rowlandson. There are several later editions with the same coloured plates.

Third Tour of Dr. Syntax in Search of a Wife: a Poem, by William Combe. 1st ed. 1820. 8vo. First appeared in the *Poetical Magazine*, afterwards in volume form as above. 25 col. plates by Rowlandson. There are several later editions of this tour, all having the same coloured plates.

The *Miniature edition* of the three Tours was published by Ackermann in three small volumes in 1823-28, at 21s., with Rowlandson's plates, coloured but reduced in size.

Nattali and Bond's reprint. 3 vols. 8vo., n.d. (1855). Green cloth; with all the col. plates.

Hotten's Reprint. 8vo., n.d., with 80 col. plates. Green cloth.

Prices of single volumes and of two or more volumes vary greatly according to date, binding, and quality. The following are recent auction values:—

Tour in Search of the Picturesque. 1st ed. 1812. £1 6s. (calf); £1 (half calf); £1 9s. (boards, uncut); £4 12s. (mor. ex.); £4 4s. (cf. gt.); £2 (boards, uncut).

First Tour, 1813; Second and Third Tours, together 3 vols. the last two 1st editions, £4 18s. (calf); £4 4s. (*ibid.*)

Nattali and Bond's Reprint. 3 vols., n.d. £2 16s. (calf gilt); £1 14s. (cloth).

The Three Tours. First, 9th ed. 1819 ; second, 2nd ed. 1820 ; third, 1st ed. 1821. £6 (orig. bds., backs broken).

Second Tour in Search of Consolation. 2nd ed. 1820. £1 1s. (calf; binding broken).

The Three Tours ; Ackermann's "Miniature Edition." 3 vols. 16mo. 1823-28. £1 12s. (orig. boards, uncut); £2 (ibid.)

First and Second Tours. First Tour, 3rd ed. 1813; Second Tour, 2nd ed. 1820. £2 8s (hf. mor. and hf. cf.)

The Three Tours. First, 6th ed. 1815 ; Second and Third, 1st eds. 1820-21 ; together 3 vols. £6 10s. (cf. extra, by Tout).

Third Tour; in Search of a Wife. 1st ed. 1820. £5 10s. (orig. boards, fine copy).

Tour of Dr. Syntax through London, 1820. 8vo. Coloured vignette title ("Dr. Syntax and his Spouse"), and 19 plates, by Williams. £2 (hf. russ.) Originally issued in 8 parts. Very scarce in this form. £14 (orig. parts in wrappers) ; £5 10s. (orig. bds., fine copy).

Tour of Mont Blanc and of Mont Rosa, The, by James David Forbes, 1855. 8vo., with two maps and several woodcuts. 3s. (orig. cl.)

Tournament, The : or Days of Chivalry; a Poem, 1823. Roy. 8vo., with 24 col. plates. 16s (cf.); £1 15s. (mor. ex., uncut). Published at 15s.

Toxophilus, the Schole of Schootinge, conteyned in two Bookes, by Roger Ascham. 1st ed. 1545. 4to. Front. of Royal arms. £1 17s (5 leaves inlaid and some stained, Ashburnham copy); £18 10s (old cf., ibid.), £12 15s (russ. gt., ibid.); £30 10s (orig. cf., presentation copy, ibid.)

Another edition, 1571. 4to. Black Letter ; woodcut on title. £2 15s. (old cf., title stained).

Another edition, 1589. 4to. £3 10s. (old mor., gt.); £5 (ibid.)

Another edition, 1788. 12mo A nearly verbatim reprint of the edition of 1545. 16s. (cf., sound copy).

Another edition, 1866. 12mo. 3s. (cl.)

The chief title "Toxophilus" is the same in all these editions, but the second title often varies from that given above.

Training in Theory and Practice, by Archibald Maclaren, 1866. 8vo. Illustrated. 3s (cl.)

Second edition, revised and enlarged, 1874. 8vo 4s. (cl.)

Traité de Fauconnerie, par Schlegel and Wulverhorst, 1845-53. Atlas folio. Front. and 16 col. plates. £8 8s. (hf. mor.)

Trapper's Guide, The: a Manual of Instructions for Capturing Fur-Bearing Animals, &c., by S. Newhouse. 1st ed. 1865. 8vo. Illustrations. 13s. (orig. cl.)

Second edition, 1867. 8vo 5s. (cl.)

An American book, written by a practical trapper and inventor of the "Newhouse Trap," a description of which is given in the work.

Travel and Adventure in South East Africa, being a narrative of eleven years spent on the Zambesi and its tributaries, with an account of the colonization of Mashunaland . . . by F. Courteney Selous, 1893. 8vo pp. xviii. 503. Map and 58 engravings of scenery, hunting subjects, &c. 20s. (cf. ex., good copy); 8s. (cloth). Published at 25s. net.

Travel and Adventure in the Congo Free State and its Big Game Shooting, by Bula N'Zau, 1894. 8vo. Illustrations 5s (cl.) Published at 14s

Travels amongst the Great Andes of the Equator, by Edward Whymper, 1892. Roy. 8vo. Maps and illustrations 10s (orig. cl.) Published at 21s.

There is a Supplementary Appendix to this work, with contributions by H. W. Bates and others, 1892. 8vo pp. xxii. 147. Illustrated. 7s. 6d. (cl.) Published at 15s

A *Second edition* of the work appeared in 1892 at 21s.

Travels in the Air: being a History of Balloon Ascents, by James G. Glaisher, Flammarion, and others, 1871. Roy. 8vo. 118 engravings, some coloured. 10s. 6d. (orig. cl.) Published at £1 5s.

A new and revised edition. The first was published in 1871 (1870). 8vo.

Travels through the Alps of Savoy and other parts of the Pennine Chain, by James David Forbes. 1st ed. 1843. Impl. 8vo. Maps and illustrations. £1 (orig. cl.), £1 10s. (*ibid.*)

Another edition, 1845. 8vo. Maps and illustrations. £1 10s. (orig. cl.)

Travels through the Rhetian Alps in the year 1786, by Albanis Beaumont, 1792. Folio, with 2 large plates in aquatint. 15s. (cf.) Published at £3 3s.

Tread Mill, The, or Tom and Jerry at Buxton: a Serio-comic Burletta. 1st ed., n.d. (ca. 1820). Col. front by R. Cruikshank. £2 10s. (pictorial wrappers)

Treatise of Modern Faulconry, A, to which is prefixed an Introduction shewing the Practice, &c., by James Campbell, 1773. 8vo. Front. 5s. (ct.), 14s. (bds.)

Treatise on English Shooting, *see* **Art of English Shooting.**

Treatise on Equitation, or the Art of Horsemanship, by J. G. Peters, 1835. 8vo. 27 full page plates. 5s. (bds. uncut)

Treatise on Falconry, *see* **Treatise upon Falconry.**

Treatise on Fencing, A, by Captain Miller, 1738. Folio. Consists of 15 plates engraved by Scotin, and one column of text. 14s. (hf. cf.), £1 12s. (mor. g. e.)

Treatise on Fly and Fly Hooks, by Jackson, 1885. Impl. 8vo., with 10 coloured plates, only 120 copies printed. £2 (hf. mor.)

Treatise on Greyhounds, with Observations on the Treatment and Disorders of them, by a Sportsman, 1819. 12mo. Front. 4s. (cf.)

Treatise on Modern Education, *see* **Compendious Treatise, &c.**

Treatise on Skaiting, A, founded on Certain Principles deduced from many years' experience, by Capt. Jones, 1797. 8vo. Copper plates. 10s. (cf., sound copy).

Treatise on the Art of Dancing, A, by Giovanni Andrea Gallini, 1762. 2 vols. 8vo. Plates. 19s. (calf).

Treatise on the Art of Riding, by H. G. English, 1890. Cr. 8vo. Portrait and illustrations. 4s. (orig. cl.) Published at 10s. 6d., and afterwards reduced to 5s.

Treatise on the Care, Treatment, and Training of the English Racehorse, by Richard Darvill, 1828. 8vo. Plates. £1 17s. (orig. bds.)

A second volume appeared in 1834, but the third, which it announced, never appeared. A second edition appeared in 2 vols., 8vo, 1840, 8s. (hf. bd.), and a third in 1846, 8vo, 8s. (hf. bd.)

Treatise on the New Broad Sword Exercise, with 14 divisions of movements as performed at Newmarket, 1798. F'cap. 8vo., with 5 plates. 5s. (cf.)

Treatise on the Proper Condition for all Horses, by "Harry Hieover" (Charles Brindley), 1852. 12mo. Illustrations. 2s. (cl.)
Fourth edition, 1861. F'cap. 8vo. 2s. (cl.)

Treatise on the Science of Defence, A, for the Sword, Bayonet, and Pike, by Anthony Gordon, 1805. 4to., with 18 numbered plates and one without number. £1 14s. (mor. ex.)

Treatise on the Theory and Practice of the Art of Fencing, A, by George Roland, 1823. 8vo., with 12 lithographic plates. 14s. (calf).

Second edition, 1824. 8vo. *See* **Introductory Course of Fencing.**

Treatise on the Utility and Advantages of Fencing . . . to which is added a dissertation on the use of the Broad Sword, by Mr. Angelo. 1817. Oblong folio. 47 plates by Gwyn and Ryland, and 6 etchings by Rowlandson. Mezzotint portrait of the Chevalier St. George, by William Ward, after Brown. £5 (cf.); £4 8s. (wrappers).

The author was the son of the well-known Henry Angelo. The plates are the same as those in "The School of Fencing" (q.v.) with the portrait and Rowlandson's etchings added.

Treatise upon Falconry, A, by J. C. Belamy, 1841. 8vo. Front. 10s. (orig. cl.)

Trials for Adultery; or the History of Divorces, being Select Trials at Doctors Commons, 1781, &c. 7 vols. 8vo. Plates. £15 (hf. cf.), £3 (cf., no plates).

Copies of this book are frequently found to have been denuded of all or some of the plates.

Trip to Town, A; a series of 12 oblong folio coloured plates, with descriptive verse above each, by Rowlandson, 1822. Roy. folio. £17 (mor. ex., fine copy, uncut).

Triviata: or Cross-road Chronicles of Passages in Irish Hunting History, during the Season of 1875-6, by Maurice O'Connor Morris, 1877. 8vo. Illustrations. 5s. (orig. cl.)

Troller's Guide, The: a new and Complete Practical Treatise on the Art of Trolling or Fishing for Pike, by T. F. Salter. 1st ed. 1820. 8vo. Illustrations. 5s. (bds. uncut).

Second edition, 1830. 12mo. with 28 cuts. 2s. (bds.)

Third edition, 1841. 8vo., with 28 cuts. 12mo. Revised by the author. 5s. (cl.)

Trout and Salmon Fishing in Wales, by George Agar Hansard, 1834. 8vo. pp. xix. 223. Vignette on title. 6s. (cl.)

Trout Flies of Devon and Cornwall, and when and how to use them, by G. W. Soltau, 1847. 8vo. 2 tinted plates of flies. 4s. (orig. cl.)

Second edition, 1856. 8vo. Same plates. 4s. (cl.)

True Art of Angling, The : or the Best and Speediest way of Taking all Sorts of Fresh-Water Fish, &c., by S. (J.) *Gent,* 1696. 24mo. Published at 6d. Front. and woodcuts. pp. vi. 160. Scarce. £2 15s. (without covers).

Second edition, 1697. 24mo.

Third edition, 1704. 24mo. Issued under the title of "The Compleat Fisher, or the True Art of Angling."

Fourth edition, 1716. 24mo. Issued as "The Compleat Fisher."

Fifth edition, 1725. 24mo. A reprint of the last.

All the above editions were published at 6d., and copies of the earlier ones are now very scarce. Several later editions appeared, e.g., n.d. Price 9d., n.d.; price 6d. 1740 and 1770; the last in 12mo. Some of these were published under the title of "The Complete Fisher."

True Arte of Defence, The, plainlie teaching . . . . the manner and forme how a man may safelie handle all sorts of weapons as well offensive as defensive. With a treatise of Disceit or Falsinge, by Giacomo di Grassi; Englished by J. G., gentleman, 1594. 4to. Cuts. Extremely rare. There is a perfect copy in the Bodleian.

True Enjoyment of Angling, The, by H. Phillips, 1843. 8vo., with portrait, songs and music. 8s. (cl. uncut). 100 copies of this book were printed on Large Paper (roy. 8vo.), with over 60 engravings, some of which are occasionally found coloured by hand. £11 11s (mor. ex., very fine copy, 20 of the plates coloured, L.P.)

True Treatise on the Art of Fly-Fishing, Trolling &c., by William Shipley, edited by Ephemera (E. Fitzgibbon), 1838. 12mo. pp. xii. 264. The Large Paper copies, of which a few were printed, have the cuts on India Paper. £1 (L.P., calf gilt).

Turf, the Chase, the Ring and the Stage, The, *see* **Pierce Egan's Anecdotes.**

Tutor's Assistant, The: a series of 6 humorous coloured plates, by Henry Alken, 1823. Oblong folio. £5 15s. (mor. ex., tooled to a pattern, very fine copy)

Tutor's Assistant, The: Involuntary Thoughts and New Symptoms; 26 lithographic plates by Henry Alken, 1824. Folio. £1 10s. (pictorial covers)

Tweed and Don: or Recollections and Reflections of an Angler, by James Locke, 1860. Cr 8vo. Front. 4s. (cl.)

Twelve Months, The: or a Pleasant and Profitable Discourse of Every Action Proper to each Particular Month . . As also of Hunting, Hawking, Fishing, &c., by Matthew Stevenson, 1661. Small 4to., with 12 copperplate engravings of the months. £25 (hf. mor.)

Twelve Packs of Hounds: being a Collection of Sketches of some of the Hounds and their Masters, by John Charlton, 1891. Oblong folio. Full page col. plates and sketches in sepia. 12s. (white cloth as issued). Published at £3 3s.

Tyburn Chronicle, The: or Villany Displayed in all its Branches; Lives, Tryals and Adventures of Notorious Malefactors. 4 vols., n.d. 8vo. J. Cooke. Plates. £2 10s. (hf. cf.)

Types of the Turf, Anecdotes and Incidents, &c., by "Rapier" (Alfred E. T. Watson). 1883. 8vo. Portraits. 3s. (orig. cl.)

Reprinted, with alterations and additions, from *The Illustrated Sporting and Dramatic News*.

Tyrol and the Tyrolese: the People and the Land in their Social, Sporting and Mountaineering Aspects, by W. A. Baillie Grohman, 1876. 8vo. Illustrations. 5s. (orig. cl.) Published at 14s.

Second edition, 1877. 8vo. 3s. (cl.) Published at 6s.

Unpleasant Discoveries: or Miseries of Driving, being Hints to Young and Inexperienced Drivers, a series of 7 coloured plates, by "Ben Tally Ho," S. and J. Fuller, 1817. Oblong 4to. £4 4s. (orig. wrappers).

Untrodden Peaks and Unfrequented Valleys, by Amelia Blandford Edwards, 1873. 4to. Maps, plates, and cuts. £1 3s. (orig. cl.)

Upland Game Birds and Water Fowl of the United States, by A. Pope, 1878. Oblong folio. New York. Published in 10 parts with 20 coloured plates. £2 (parts, in a portfolio).

Vagabondiana: or Anecdotes of Mendicant Wanderers Through the Streets of London, with portraits of the most remarkable, by J. T. Smith, 1817. 4to. 7s. 6d. (bds.)

Valentine Verses, 1827. 8vo. Sporting plates. 7s. (orig. bds.)

Venationes Ferarum, Avium, Piscium, pugnæ bestiariorum, per Johannes Stradanus, editæ a Gallæo, n.d. (*Antv* 1580). Oblong folio. Engraved title and 104 plates by Galle and Collaert. £2 5s. (some plates mounted, vellum)

The plates are sometimes found coloured by hand, and when this is the case the value of the book is considerably augmented. The full number is as above mentioned, but some are generally missing.

Venationis, Piscationis et Aucupii Typi, by Hans Bol. (1582?) Small oblong 4to. 46 narrow oblong engravings, by Philipp Galle. £22 (mor. ex.)

The number of plates varies in different copies. The above, as will be observed, had 46, but the full complement consists of 48, including the frontispiece.

Views in the Tyrol, being a series of 46 plates of Tyrol, Auer, Mayenburg, &c., after drawings by Allom, with letterpress descriptions by a companion of Hofer, n.d. 8vo. Tilt. 8s. (cl., plates on India paper). Published at 21s.

Vignettes: Alpine and Eastern, by T. G. Bonney, 1872. 4to. Vol. I., Alpine. Vol. II., Eastern. Each with chromo illustrations in imitation of the original drawings. £1 18s. (2 vols., cloth extra). Published at £2 2s. per vol.

Vincentio Saviolo, His Practice, *see* **His Practice.**

Vindication of the True Art of Self Defence, with a proposal, &c., by Sir William Hope, 1724. 8vo., with folding sheet containing 16 engraved figures. £1 13s (old cf.)

Second edition, 1729. 8vo. Folding sheet as before. 10s. (hf. cf.)

The same engraved sheet is found in **New, Short and Easy Method of Fencing** (q v.)

Voyage in the Sunbeam, A: Our Home on the Ocean for Eleven Months, by Annie Brassey. 1st ed. 1878. 8vo. 118 illustrations, chiefly after drawings by A. G. Bingham. 10s. Published at 21s.

Second edition, 1878. 8vo. Published at 21s.

Fourth edition, 1878. 8vo. Published at 1s.

Cheaper editions were subsequently published in 1880, and the text has been revised for the use of schools.

Voyage of the Nyanza, being the Record of a Three Years' Cruise in a Schooner Yacht in the Atlantic and Pacific, by James Cumming Dewar, 1892. 8vo. pp xviii 466, with two photogravures and numerous full page and smaller engravings. 7s (orig cl.) Published at 21s.

Vue du Simplon. 40 full page col. plates of Alpine Scenes, n d (published 1835). Oblong 4to. 3s. (as issued).

Wanderings among the High Alps, by Alfred Wills. 1st ed. 1856. 12mo. 3 tinted plates. £1 5s. (orig. cl.)

Second edition, 1868. F'cap. 8vo. Enlarged. 5s (cl.)

Wanderings in Patagonia, or Life Among the Ostrich-Hunters, by Julius Beerbohm, 1879. 8vo. Map and woodcuts. 5s. (hf. cf.)

Wanderings in the Highlands and Islands: . . . being a Sequel to "Wild Sports of the West," by William Hamilton Maxwell. 1st ed. 1844. 2 vols. 8vo. Portrait of the author. 18s. (orig. cl.)

Another edition, 1852. 2 vols. 8vo. 18s. (orig cl.) Published under the title, "Sports and Adventures in the Highlands and Islands of Scotland."

Wanderings of a Pilgrim in the Shadow of Mont Blanc and the Jungfrau Alps, by George B. Cheever, n.d. (circa 1847). 8vo., with 3 plates. 2s. 6d. (cl.)

Wars of Wellington, The: a Narrative Poem in 15 cantos, by "Dr. Syntax," with "six engravings" (coloured), 1821. 4to. Sometimes met with having 25 additional col. plates by W. Heath. £5 (hf. mor. extra, with the 25 plates), £2 8s. (orig. hf. mor., g.e., 6 col. pl., fine copy).

Warwickshire Hunt, The, from 1795-1836, describing many of the most splendid runs, etc., by "Venator" (John Cooper), 1837. 8vo. Front. and vignettes. £4 10s. (hf. mor., uncut).

Way to Get Wealth, A, containing sixe Principall Vocations or Callings ... by G(ervase) M(arkham), 1st collected issue (according to Hazlitt), 1625. 4to. Woodcuts.

Sixth edition, 1638. Sm. 4to. Cuts. £2 2s. (cf. gt.)

Seventh edition, 1648. Sm. 4to. Cuts. £2 5s. (old cf.), £1 5s. (cf. gt.)

Eighth edition, 1653. Sm. 4to. Cuts.

Ninth edition, 1657. Sm. 4to. Cuts.

Tenth edition, 1660. Sm. 4to. Cuts. £1 17s. (old cf.), £2 16s. (orig. cf., fine copy).

The second book (there are six, the last by Master W. L.) treats of Hawking, Angling, and Cock Fighting. The compilation consists of a re-issue of Markham's "Farewell to Husbandry," 1625; "Cheap and Good Husbandry," 1623; "Country Contentments," 1623, and Lawson's "New Orchard and Garden," 1623, each with the several title-page, pagination, and register. There are a number of other editions than those mentioned, notably a 15th published in 1695.

Where There's a Will There's a Way: an Ascent of Mont Blanc without Guides, by Charles Hunt and E. S. Kennedy, 1856. Post 8vo. Map and plate. 16s. (orig. cl.) Published at 5s. 6d.

Whole Art of Fishing, The, to which is added the Laws of Angling. E. Curll, 1714. 12mo. Front. of an angling scene. 7s 6d (cf.)

Second edition, 1727. 8vo. Published under the title of "The Gentleman Fisher." No frontispiece. 2s. (cf.)

Wilderness Hunter, The: An Account of the Big Game of the United States, by Theodore Roosevelt, 1893. 8vo. Coloured and plain plates. 10s (orig. cl.); £1 4s (L.P., 4to., orig. cl.)

Wild Beasts of India, The, see **Thirteen Years Among the Wild Beasts, &c.**

Wild Fowler, The, a Treatise on Ancient and Modern Wild Fowling, historical and practical, by Henry Coleman Folkard. 1st ed. 1859. 8vo. £1 5s (orig. cl.) Published at 21s.

Third edition, 1875. Plates. 13s. (orig. cl.) Published at 15s.

Fourth edition, 1897. 8vo. pp. xviii 386. Published at 12s. 6d.

Wild Fowler, The: a treatise on Ancient and Modern Wild Fowling, by Henry Coleman Folkard, 1859. 8vo. Plates. £1 5s (green cloth).

Second edition, 1864. 8vo. Plates. 16s (orig. cl.)

Third edition, 1875. 8vo. Plates. 13s (orig. cl.)

Wild Men and Wild Beasts: Scenes in Camp and Jungle, by Lt.-Col. Gordon Cumming, 1871. Sq. 8vo. Illustrations by Col. Baigrie and others. 12s. (orig. cl.) Published at 21s.

A later edition appeared in 1872 in 8vo. at 18s. and 4to at 24s.

Wild Sports in Europe, Asia, and Africa, by Edward H. D. E. Napier, 1844. 2 vols. 8vo. Plates. 10s (cl.) Published at 21s.

Wild Sports in Ireland, being Picturesque and Entertaining Descriptions of several Visits paid to Ireland, by "John Bickerdyke" (Charles Henry Cook) 1897. 8vo. pp. xii 227. Illustrations from photographs by the author. 4s. (orig. cl.) Published at 6s.

Wild Sports in the Far West, by Friedrich Gerstaecker, 1854. Post 8vo. Tinted plates by Harrison Weir. 3s. (cl.)

Second edition, 1856. 12mo.

Translated from the German "Streif und Jagdzuge durch die Vereinigten Staaten Nordamerikas," published at Dresden in 1844.

Wild Sports in the Highlands, *see* **Short Sketches of the Wild Sports, &c.**

Wild Sports of India, The, with Remarks on the Breeding and Rearing of Horses, by Henry Shakespear. 1st ed. 1860. F'cap 8vo. Not illustrated. 4s. (cl.)

Second edition, 1862. F'cap 8vo. Much enlarged, with a portrait. 6s. (cl.)

Wild Sports of Southern Africa, being the Narrative of a Hunting Expedition, . . . by Sir W. C. Harris, 1839. 12mo. 3s. (cl.) Published at 10s. 6d.

Third edition, 1841, with coloured plates. 15s. (orig. cl.) Published at 42s. Reduced by Bohn in 1849 to 21s.

Wild Sports of the West, with Legendary Tales and Local Sketches, by William Hamilton Maxwell. 1st ed. 1832. 2 vols. 8vo. Plates. £1 8s. (hf. cf.); £2 5s. (orig. cl.)

Other editions appeared in 1838 and 1842, both in 8vo.

The sequel to this work is "Wanderings in the Highlands and Islands." (q. v.)

With Axe and Rope in the New Zealand Alps, by George Edward Mannering, 1891. 8vo. pp. viii 139. Illustrations. 5s. (orig. cl.) Published at 12s. 6d.

Wolf Hunting in Lower Brittany, by Henry Hope Crealock, 1875. 8vo., with tinted illustrations by the author. 10s. (orig. cl.)

Wrinkles: or Hints to Sportsmen and Travellers upon Dress, Equipment, Armament and Camp Life, by H. A. L. "The old Shekarry," 1867. Post 8vo. Illustrations. 2s. (orig. cl.) Published at 6s.

Yacht Designing: a Treatise on the Practical Application of the Scientific Principles, upon which is Based the Art of Designing Yachts, by Dixon Kemp, 1876. Folio. Illustrations. £1 5s. (cl.) Published at *The Field* office.

Year of Sport and Natural History, A, by Oswald John F. Crawfurd, 1895. 4to. pp. x. 331. Illustrations by Stanley Berkeley and others. 10s (orig. cl.) Published at 21s.

Yoicks, by C. H. Ross, n.d. (1870). 8vo. Col. and other illustrations by "Phiz" and others. 3s. 6d. (wrappers).

Yorkshire Hunt, The, by W. Cowper, 1830. 12mo., with 6 cuts, by M. V. Sears. 5s. (original wrappers).

Yorkshire Trout Flies, ... comprising Plates ... , with particulars of the Dressing and Season of each Fly, &c., by Thomas Evan Pritt, 1885. 8vo. pp. 63. Coloured plates. 8s. (as issued).

Second edition, 1886. 8vo. pp. 63. Plates. Published under the title of "North Country Flies." Coloured plates. 8s. (as issued). Published at 10s. 6d.

Young Angler's Pocket Companion, The, by Ralph Cole, 1795. 12mo. R. Bassam. Front. and 2 plates. 7s. (bds.)

Another edition was published the same year by W. Lane. 7s. (bds.)

Another edition, 1813. 12mo. Front. and 2 plates. 7s. (bds.)

Another edition n.d. (1816), W. Mason. Front. Abridged. 2s. (bds.)

Young Sportman's (*sic*) **Instructor in Angling, Fowling, Hawking, &c., The,** by G(ervase) M(arkham). n.d. Sold at the Gold Ring in Little Britain. Price 6d. n.d. Frontispiece. £6 (mor. gt.)

This little pamphlet, which measures some 2½in. by 2in., is extremely scarce. The Huth Catalogue, Vol. III. p. 908, states that the one in that library formerly belonging to Mr. Heber and Mr. Corser, is the only copy known. Other editions appeared in 1652, also n.d. S. Ganudge, bookseller in Worcester, and 1820, T. Gosden, 32mo.

Young Sportsman's Miscellany in Hunting, Shooting, Racing, &c., 1826. 12mo. Front. and 22 woodcuts. 5s. (cf.)

Contains a reprint of Thomas Barker's "Art of Angling" (q.v.)

ADDITIONS AND CORRECTIONS

Accomplish'd Lady's Delight, The, in Preserving, Physick, Beautifying, Cookery, Gardening, and Angling, 1st ed. 1675. 12mo. £6 10s (old cf., sound copy).

Second edition 1677. 12mo. Portrait, engraved front. and cuts. £3 10s. (fine copy).

Third edition, 1683. 12mo. Portrait, front. and cuts. £3 18s. (orig. cf.)

Tenth edition, 1719. 12mo. Portrait, front. and cuts. £2 (mor. ex.)

Adventures of a Salmon in the River Dee . . . with Notes for the Fly Fisher in North Wales (by W. Ayrton), n.d. (1853). 12mo. Plates. 6s. (hf. mor.)

Almanac of Twelve Sports, The, by W. Nicholson. 4to. Published December, 1897 (for 1898). The popular edition, 5s. The library edition, lithographed in colours on Dutch Hand-made Paper, mounted on brown paper, and bound in cloth, gilt edges. 12s. 6d. net. Also a few sets, printed from the original wood blocks hand-coloured, and signed by the artist. In vellum. Portfolio. £21 net. See *ante* p. 3.

The Almanac for 1899, with the Rhymes by Rudyard Kipling, was published in December, 1898, at 2s. 6d. This is a re-issue with a new calendar for 1899.

Alps, The, by F. Umlauft, translated by Louisa Brough, 1888. Roy. 8vo. pp. xii. 523. Illustrations. 5s. (orig. cl.). Published at 25s.

Angler's Complete Guide to the Rivers and Lakes of England, The, by Robert Blakey, see *ante* p. 6. A new edition of this book has just been published (November, 1898). The text is preserved in its entirety, but there are copious Notes at the end of each chapter, and a Biographical Introduction by "Red Spinner" (William Senior). Illustrations by Avery Lewis. Published at 3s. 6d. under the title ' Angling, or How to Angle and Where to Go."

Angler's Hand-Book, The, 1st ed. 1838. 24mo. Two coloured plates of Flies. £1 16s. (mor. ex. by Zaehnsdorf)

Second edition, 1838. 24mo. Two col. plates. 12s. (cf. gt.)

Third edition, 1840. 24mo. Two col. plates. 14s. (mor. ex. by Zaehnsdorf).

Another edition, 1846. 24mo. Two col. plates. 6s. (hf. mor.)

Angler's Library, The: a series of books on Angling, edited by Sir Herbert Maxwell, Bart. Published in crown 8vo. at 5s. and 7s. 6d., or on Large Paper (130 copies only), at 21s. All are illustrated. The following have already appeared:—

Vol. I. Coarse Fish, by C. H. Wheeley. pp. viii. 268. 5s.

Vol. II. Sea Fish, by F. G. Aflalo. pp. xii. 256. 5s.

Vol. III. Pike and Perch, by Alfred Jardine. pp. xii. 204. 5s.

Vol. IV. Salmon and Sea Trout, by Sir Herbert Maxwell. 7s. 6d. 130 numbered copies on Large Paper at 21s.

Angler's Museum, The, or the Whole Art of Float and Fly Fishing by Thomas Shirley, 1st ed. n.d. (1784). 12mo. Printed for John Fielding. Portrait. 5s. (cf.)

Second edition n.d. (1784.) 12mo. Portrait. 2s. (sewn).

Third edition, n.d. 12mo. Portrait. 2s. (sewn).

The portrait is that of John Kirby, the keeper of Newgate Prison, and a celebrated Fisherman in his day.

Angling, being the first part of a series of familiar letters on sporting, by Robert Lascelles, 1st ed., n.d. (1815). 8vo pp. 123. The complete work is in three parts and deals with the subjects of Angling, Shooting, and Coursing, 1819. 8vo., with 3 engraved plates. £2 2s. (hf. mor.)

Badminton Magazine of Sports and Pastimes, The, edited by A. E. T. Watson. No. 1 of this Periodical appeared in August, 1895, and No. 41, in December, 1898. Each number is fully illustrated and published at 1s. In November, 1898, a series of six half-yearly volumes (August, 1895, to July, 1898), in half morocco, g.t., realised £1 15s.

Book of the Sword, The, by Capt. R. F. Burton, 1884. 8vo. pp. xxxix. 299. Illustrations. 20s. (orig. cl.)

Booke of Fishing with Hooke and Line, A, and of all other instruments thereunto belonging. Another of sundrie Engines and Trappes to take Polcats, Buzards, Rattes, Mice by L(eonard) M(ascall), 1st ed. 1590. 4to. Woodcuts, including a folding one. £12 10s. (hf. calf, several leaves stained and others wormed), £6 15s. (cf. ex., folding plate in facsimile and head lines cut into).

Another edition, 1596. 4to.

Another edition, 1600. 4to.

Another edition, 1606. 4to.

The edition of 1590 was reprinted in 1884 under the editorship of Mr. T. Satchell. 4s. (hf. bd., uncut).

British Deer and their Horns, by John Guille Millais, 1897. Impl. 4to. This book has materially increased in value since it was catalogued on p. 22 (*ante*). The edition was limited to 100 copies, and the booksellers are now (Dec., 1898), asking as much as £7 7s. for a good and clean one.

British Sportsman, The, by Samuel Howitt. *See ante* p. 23. There is a prior edition of 1800, oblong 4to., with 72 plates. £1 5s. (hf. bd.), £2 (bds.)

British Sportsman, The, by S. Scott, 1806. Oblong 8vo., with 72 plates. 9s. (hf. bd.)

Chase, The, by William Somerville. The 1st ed., 1735, 4to., described on p. 24 (*ante*), as not illustrated, has a frontispiece by Gravelot.

Chronicles of Blackheath Golfers, by W. E. Hughes, 1897. 8vo. pp. xxii. 245. Illustrations and portraits. 7s (orig. cl.) Published at 21s.

Compleat Husbandman and Gentleman's Recreation, The with Directions in Angling, Fowling, Hawking, &c., by Gervase Markham. 1707. 12mo. Front. and woodcuts. £2 2s. (russ. gt.)

This book is in two parts the second of which has a separate title page, "The Husbandman's Jewel."

Compleat Troller, The, or the Art of Trolling by Robert Nobbes, 1st ed. 1682. 8vo. £2 4s. (mor. ex.)

Facsimile Reprint, n. d. (1790) 6s (cf. gt.)

Other editions were published as follows, n. d. 8vo. Norwich, J. Payne; n. d., 8vo., London, 1805. 12mo., London, and 1814, 12mo., London.

Compleatest Angling-Booke that ever was writ, being done out of ye Hebrew . . . by a person of Honour (Joseph Crawhall) The first edition was published at Newcastle in 1859. 4to., with etchings and woodcuts, illustrations of fish, &c. £4 18s (hf. mor.) *See ante* p. 31.

Deer of all Lands, The, a history of the family Cervidæ living and extinct, by Richard Lydekker, 1898. 4to. pp. xx. 329. Only 500 copies printed. 24 hand-coloured plates. £5 (orig. cl.)

Defensive Exercises, comprising Wrestling as in Cumberland, Westmoreland, &c., Boxing, Fencing and Broadsword, &c., by Dr. Walker, 1st ed. 1840. 8vo., with 100 illustrations. 6s (orig. cl.) Published at 8s. A new and cheaper (4s.) edition was issued by Bohn in 1842.

Discourse of Fish and Fishponds, A [by Roger North] *See ante* p. 38. There is an edition, n. d. (1730), 4to. with 18 large coloured specimens by E. Alben. 18s. (nearly uncut).

Encyclopædia of Sport, The. *See ante* p. 41. This work was completed in October, 1898. 20 parts at 2s. each. Vol. 2 runs from Lion to Zebra. The bound volumes were published at 25s. each, but on January 1st, 1899, the price of the parts was raised to 2s. 6d. each, and of each volume, in buckram, to 30s., or in half morocco, to £2 2s. The engravings of the drawings by Archibald Thorburn, J. G. Millais and other artists have also been published in sets apart from the work as follows :—156 signed artists' proofs (16in. by 9½in.), India Paper, at £2 2s. per plate; plates on plate paper (same measurements), at 10s. 6d. each. The 40 photogravure plates, reduced to the same size as in the Encyclopædia, 15s. net, in a portfolio.

English Masters of Defence, The, or the Gentleman's A-la-Mode accomplishment. Containing the true art of single-rapier . . . broadsword, and quarter-staff . . . also the . . . rules of wrestling, &c., by Zachary Wylde, 1711. 8vo. No copy of this scarce book appears to have been sold by auction in this country during the last 12 years.

Englishman's Mentor, The : Picture of the Palais Royal, describing its spectacles, gaming-rooms, gamesters, sharpers, epicures, courtesans, filles, &c., and other remarkable objects in that high change of the Fashionable dissipation and vice of Paris. With characteristic sketches and anecdotes of its Frequenters and Inhabitants, W. Hone, 1819. 12mo., with coloured folding frontispiece of the Palais Royal and some of its frequenters, by George Cruikshank, extra illustrated by the insertion of 5 coloured etchings by the same Artist who illustrated Carey's Life in Paris. £3 3s. (half vellum, uncut, top edges gilt).

Fisherman's Magazine and Review, The, edited by H. Cholmondeley-Pennell. Vol. I., 1864; Vol. II., 1865. 8vo. Coloured and other illustrations. 10s. (orig. cl.)

Greyhound, The : its History, Points, Breeding, Rearing, Training, and Running, by Hugh Dalziel, 1886. Demy 8vo. Coloured front. 2s. 6d. (cl. gt.)

Guide to the Perfect Knowledge of Horses, wherein everything necessary for the Choice, Management, and Preservation of that Noble and Useful Animal are clearly laid down . . . by Gaspar de Saunier, 1769. 8vo. Copperplates. 8s (calf).

Hollybush Hall, or Open House in an Open Country. a series of 29 large plates, containing nearly 50 col. engravings with descriptions, by Georgina Bowers, n.d (1870) Oblong 4to. 6s (pictorial cl., g.e.)

How to Chuse, Ride, Traine and Diet, both Hunting Horses and Running Horses. Also a discourse of horsemanship . . . together with a newe addition for the cure of horses diseases of what kind or nature soever, by Gervase Markham 1st ed. 1593. 4to. Woodcuts Only one copy known (Huth Library).

Second edition, 1596. 4to. A copy, said to be the only one known, was recently on sale by Messrs Robson and Co., 23, Coventry Street, Piccadilly, W., at £35 (mor. ex. by Rivière, fine copy).

Other editions, of 1599 and 1606, both in 4to. These are the only editions represented in the British Museum Library.

Hunt Cup, A, or Loyalty before all, by Wat Bradwood, 1873. Post 8vo. Illustrations. 2s. 6d. (cl. extra)

Hunter's Wanderings in Africa, A, being a Narrative of Nine Years' Sport amongst the Game of the Far Interior of South Africa . . . by Frederick Courteney Selous, 1881. 8vo. pp. xvii. 455. Illustrated with map and 19 full page plates by Whymper, Smit, and Miss Selous. 7s (cloth). Published at 21s.

Second edition, 1890. 8vo. pp. xvii. 455. 13s. (cf. ex. fine copy). Published at 18s.

Hunting Trips in the Caucasus, by Anatol Demidov, Prince de San Donato, 1898. 8vo. pp. xvi. 319, with 96 illustrations and a map. 8s. (orig. cl.)

Incompleat Angler, The, after Master Izaac Walton, edited by F. C. Burnand and illustrated by Harry Furniss. 1st ed 1887. 8vo. 5s. (wrapper). The only edition of any material value.

Indian Alps and How we Crossed Them, The, being a Narrative of Two Years' Residence in the Eastern Himalaya, and Two Months' Tour into the Interior, by a Lady Pioneer, 1875. Impl. 8vo. Front. in colours, and illustrations in the text 10s. (orig. cl.) Published at £2 2s.

Isaac Walton, a Drama in Four Parts—Moonlight, Sunrise, Noon, Sunset—by Charles Dance. 12mo., n.d Front. by Pierce Egan, the Younger. 3s (orig. covers).

Italian Alps, The: Sketches in the Mountains of Ticino, Lombardy, the Trentino and Venetia, by Douglas W. Freshfield, 1875. Post 8vo. 9s. (orig. cl.) Published at 15s

Kings of the Hunting Field: Memoirs and Anecdotes of Distinguished Masters of Hounds and other Celebrities of the Chase, with histories of famous packs, and hunting traditions of great Houses, by "Thormanby" (Wilmot Dixon), 1898. Demy 8vo., with 32 portraits. Published at 16s.

Life and Extraordinary Adventures of Samuel D. Hayward, denominated the Modern Macheath, with an address to the rising generation, by Pierce Egan, 1822. 12mo pp. viii. 208. Col. portrait by J. R. Cruikshank. 16s. (bds.)

Life of a Nobleman, published in three parts, containing text and 9 col. plates, n.d. 4to £3 (orig. pictorial wrappers, title missing)

Life of Izaac Walton, The, including notices of his contemporaries, by Thomas Zouch 1st ed., York, 1790. 4to.

Second edition, 1823. 8vo. 20 plates. 25 Large Paper copies in 4to. India Proof plates £3 (hf. rox., L.P.); £2 (Small Paper, uncut).

Another edition, 1826. 8vo. Portrait and plates. £2 5s. (mor. ex, fine copy); £1 (hf. russ).

Another edition, 1830. 4to. Portrait. Privately printed without author's name.

The illustrations to the editions of 1823 and 1826 are mostly borrowed from Hawkins's edition of "The Compleat Angler," 1822. 8vo.

List of Natural Flies, A, that are taken by Trout, Grayling, and Smelt, in the Streams of Ripon (by M. Theakston), 1853. 8vo. Plates of flies. 8s. (hf. cf. gt.)

The "addenda" which is sometimes found in serted in copies of the work is very rare. It was missing from the above copy.

Lover's Panorama, The, or Cupid's Vagaries on St. Valentine's Day, n.d., Hodgson and Co. Sm. 8vo., with 2 col. etchings by George Cruikshank and 10 by R. Cruikshank. £2 5s. (wrappers).

Maxims and Hints for an Angler, and Miseries of Fishing . . . [by Richard Penn], 1833. 12mo. pp. iv. 59, with 12 drawings on stone by R. Seymour. £1 5s (mor. ex., g.e.); 10s (calf).

Second edition, 1839. 12mo. pp. iv. 79. Frontispiece. 10s (cl.)

Another edition, 1855. 8vo. Woodcuts. 4s. (orig. cl.) Published under the title "Maxims and Hints on Angling."

Modern Angler, The, containing instructions in the art of Fly-Fishing, Spinning, and Bottom Fishing . . . with an account of the best places for angling, including the Thames, &c., by "Otter" (H. J. Alfred), 1864. 12mo. 5s. (orig. cl.) *See ante* p. 78. Many other editions, notably those of 1859, 1860, 1876, and 1878, all in 12mo.

Last edition, 1898. 8vo. 2s (orig. cl.)

Modern Angler, The: comprising Angling in all its Branches; being the result of more than thirty years' practice and strict observation . . . by James Wallwork, 1847. 8vo. pp. 108, with 4 illustrations. 5s (cl.) *See ante* p. 78.

Mont Blanc, The Annals of, a Monograph . . . by C. E. Mathews, 1893. 8vo. pp. 392. Published at 21s. net. The Geology of the Mountain is by T. G. Bonney.

Month in the Midlands, A: a series of 24 col. prints by Georgina Bowers, n.d. (1869). Oblong 4to. 6s. (pictorial cl., g.e.)

New Method and Extraordinary Invention to Dress Horses, and work them according to Nature, as also to perfect Nature by the Subtility of the Art, which was never found out but by the Noble William Cavendish, Duke of Newcastle, &c., 1740. 8vo. *Dublin.* 6s. (cf.) *See* also **General System of Horsemanship,** *ante* p. 53.

Notes on Game and Game Shooting, by John Jackson Manley (1880). 8vo. pp. viii. 389. Illustrations. 4s. (cl. gt.) Published at 7s. 6d.

Old Flies in New Dresses: How to Dress Dry Flies with the Wings in the Natural Position and some Wet Flies, by Charles Edward Walker, 1898. Demy 8vo. Illustrations. Published at 7s. 6d. net.

Parfait Mareschal, Le, or Compleat Farrier, to know the Shapes and Goodness, as well as Faults and Imperfections of Horses . . . together with a Treatise how to raise and bring up a True and Beautiful Race of Horses, &c., by Sir William Hope, 1696. Folio. Plates. 16s. (old cf.) *See ante* p. 31, **Compleat Horseman, The,** by Jacques de Solleysell.

Perfect Horseman, The, or the Experienced Secrets of Mr. Markham's Fifty Years' Practice, shewing how a Man may come to be a General Horseman by the knowledge of these seven offices. viz.:—The Breeder, Feeder, Ambler, Rider, Keeper, Buyer, Farrier, 1680. 12mo. Engraved front., having portrait of Gervase Markham. 15s. (old cf.)

Piscatorie Eclogs and other Poetical Miscellanies, by F. P. (Phineas Fletcher). 1st ed., Cambridge, 1633. 4to. Two plates in the style of William Marshall. £3 12s. (mor. sound copy). One or other of the plates is nearly always missing. Copies containing them both are rarely met with.

Another edition, 1771. 8vo. 16s. (cf.)

The above-mentioned edition of 1633 is really a portion of the same author's "Purple Island," with a separate title and distinct pagination. *See* also **Angling Sports,** by Moses Browne, *ante* p. 8.

Practical Boat Sailing for Amateurs, containing particulars of the most Suitable Sailing Boats and Yachts for Amateurs and Instructions for their proper Handling, &c., by G. Christopher Davies. 1st ed. 1880. 8vo. Illustrated. 3s. (orig. cl.)

Second edition, 1886. 8vo., with several new plans of yachts. Published at 5s.

Practical Hints on Shooting, by "20-Bore." *Lond.*, 1887. 8vo. pp. xiv. 472. Illustrations. 4s. (orig. cl.) Published at 12s.

Rambler's Magazine, The, or Fashionable Emporium of Polite Literature, the Fine Arts, Politics . . . Gallantry, and all the gay variety of Supreme Bon Ton. 5 vols. 8vo. 1822-25. With portraits of Lord Byron, Napoleon, &c., and plates. Published in parts. Complete sets are very seldom met with. Messrs. Robson and Co., 23, Coventry Street, Piccadilly, W., price the 5 vols., bound in 3, at £21 (calf ex., t.e g., by Rivière). Another publication, bearing an almost similar title, is, however, scarcer still. This is "The Rambler's Magazine, or Annals of Gallantry, Glee, Pleasure and Bon Ton." 9 vols. 8vo. 1783-90. Plates. £20 (hf. cf., auction). £24 (*ibid.*)

Reminiscences of the Course, the Camp, the Chase, by Col. R. F. Meysey Thompson, 1898. Cr. 8vo. Published at 10s. 6d.

Sea Fishing for Amateurs; Practical Instructions to Visitors at Sea Side Places for Catching Sea Fish . . . by Frank Hudson, 1888. 8vo. Illustrations. Published at 1s. in paper covers.

Sea Fishing on the English Coast: The Art of Making and Using Sea Tackle . . . by F. G. Aflalo, 1891. 8vo. pp. viii. 190. Illustrations. 2s. (cl. gt.)

Turf, The: a Treatise on Racing and Steeplechasing, by "Rapier" (A. E. T. Watson), 1898. Demy 8vo. Illustrated. Published at 6s.

Welsh Mountaineering, a Compleat and Handy Guide to all the best Roads and Bye Paths, &c., by A. W. Perry, 1896. Cr. 8vo. pp. 172, with maps. 2s. (cl. gt.) Published at 2s. 6d.

Whippet and Race Dog, The : How to Breed, Rear, Train, Race, and Exhibit the Whippet . . . by Freeman Lloyd. 1894. Post 8vo. 2s. (orig. cl.) Published at 3s. 6d.

APPENDIX
OF
SPORTING PRINTS.

APPENDIX

OF

PRINTS RELATING TO VARIOUS SPORTS.

BALLOONING.

BOXING.

BULL & BADGER BAITING, DOG FIGHTING, RATTING.

COACHING, DRIVING, RIDING.

COCK FIGHTING.

COURSING.

FISHING.

HUNTING.

PORTRAITS OF SPORTING CELEBRITIES.

PORTRAITS OF RACE HORSES.

RACING.

SHOOTING (INCLUDING SPORTING DOGS).

VARIOUS.

APPENDIX

OF

SPORTING PRINTS.

NOTE.—The quoted values represent average auction prices realised for prints of the quality described during the year 1898. Prices vary, of course, with quality, some impressions being often better than others, although all may be from the same plate. For this reason great judgment has to be exercised in all questions relating to the value of prints, especially those *printed* in colours. It must be remembered that Sporting Prints, if of good quality, are, on the whole, increasing in value. In the following list, prints which are not stated to be coloured must be regarded as uncoloured. Prints published in a series, under distinctive and well-known titles, in wrappers or other coverings, are classed as "Books," and will be found in the front part of the work. It is advisable to consult the Index in every case. (*See* Introduction).

BALLOONING.

"**The Aerial Ship**," advertised to start from "the Dockyard of the Æronautical Society, in Victoria Road, opposite Kensington Gardens." Good. 8s.

"**All on Fire: or the Doctors disappointed**," the attempted ascent from the garden of Lord Foley's house, September 29, 1784 (the site now occupied by the Langham Hotel, &c.); and a satirical print relating to the balloon catching fire on the above occasion, in the manner of Paul Sandby. Both scarce. 19s.

The "**Ariel**" **Flying Ship**: an aquatint, published by Ackermann, and "**The Aerostat**" Flying Machine, a lithograph, published by the same, both coloured. Good. £1 5s.

APPENDIX OF SPORTING PRINTS.

Ascent of Messrs. Charles and Robert from the Gardens of the Tuilleries, December 1, 1783, three engravings, by French artists. Vue d'Optique, or a Treat for the Curious, a humorous print relating to the same, together 4 plates. Good impressions. £1 5s.

The Triumph of Messrs. Charles and Robert, by Alessandri, coloured; Expérience faite à Versailles par M Montgolfier, after D Lorimier, by N. de Launay. The pair. Fair. 3s.

Mr. Blanchard and Dr. Jefferies Crossing the Channel from Dover to Calais in a balloon, January 7, 1785, an etching in the manner of Rowlandson, proof before letters; and another of the same, an aquatint. Both scarce. £1 2s.

J. P. Blanchard's Ascent from the Grounds of Chelsea Military Academy, October 16, 1784; Admission Ticket to the Grounds on the above occasion, signed by Blanchard, rare, and a Satirical Print in the manner of Paul Sandby Good. £1 12s.

Portrait of J. P. Blanchard, the Æronaut, by J Newton, after R. Livesay, and His Ascent from Lille, August 26, 1785, after L Watteau, inscription cut Both good £1 5s.

Blanchard's Ascent from Lille, the same as above, proof before the dedication; and the same, engraver's unfinished proof. Fair. 7s 6d

Coxwell's Mammoth Balloon Ascent, 1862, coloured lithograph Good 3s. 6d

Mr. Garnerin's Ascent from St George's Parade, North Audley Street, and Descent in a Parachute, September 21, 1802. Portrait of N. Charles, the French æronaut, together 3 plates. Fair. £1.

Lunardi's Ascent, by Jukes, after Brewer, 1781. Perilous Situation of Major Murray, a mezzotint, two prints. Both good. £1 10s.

Lunardi's Ascent from the Artillery Ground, an aquatint, by F. Jukes, after J. J. Brewer, proof before letters. Very good. Rare. £2 4s.

Mr. Lunardi's Balloon, as exhibited in the Pantheon in 1784, after F. G. Byron, by V. Green, in colours. Good. £1 2s.

Vincent Lunardi with his dog and his cat; Lunardi's Ascent from the Artillery Ground, September 15, 1784; and Handbill advertising the exhibition of his balloon "at the Lyceum, near Exeter Change." Good. £1 4s.

The Enterprising Lunardi's Grand Air Balloon, which took its flight from the Artillery Ground, September 15, 1784, first state; the same, in the second state. £1.

An Exact Representation of Mr. Lunardi's New Balloon, as it ascended with himself, 13 May, 1785; a mezzotint published by Carington Bowles; and two Caricatures relating to Ballooning, coloured. Good. £3 16s.

Montgolfier in the Clouds: a Satirical Print; View of the Town of Rodez, with Montgolfier's Balloon. August, 1784, engraved by Blanchon, two prints. Good. 16s.

Representation of the Air Balloon of Mr. Montgolfier in the Field of Mars, near Paris, August 27, 1783; Montgolfier's Experiments at Versailles, September 19, 1783. Both good. £1 6s.

The Three favourite Aerial Travellers, after Rigaud, by Bartolozzi. Good. In black. £1 10s.

BOXING.

The Champion Triumphant, in colours; The Bruiser Bruised, and Sparring, by Cruikshank. Fair. 13s.

Crib Uncorking Black Strap, a Boxing subject, 15in. by 12in., published 1811, Tegg. Fair. 3s. 6d.

The Fight between J. Broughton and G. Stevenson in 1742, by John Young, after Mortimer, a very rare print, proof. £52. Again, lettered impression. Good. £6.

APPENDIX OF SPORTING PRINTS 157

The Fight between Humphreys and Daniel Mendoza, by Joseph Grozer, after S Einsle, full margins Good £4. Another impression Good £2 15s Again, later impression, coloured. £1 18s. Again, proof, with etched letters, plain £2 2s

The Fight between Humphreys and Daniel Mendoza, three engravings, published by Fores, one with letterpress description under. Good. £1 14s. This celebrated fight took place at Odiham on January 9, 1788.

The Fights between Humphreys and Mendoza, Mendoza and Ward. Fair 13s.

The Fight between Broome and Hannan, after Heath. In colours, with key Fair 14s. Again, in colours. Good £2 5s

The Fight between Crib and Molineux, after Rowlandson; Fight between Benjamin Brian and Thomas Johnson, both coloured Fair £1 12s

The Fight between Pearce and Gully, by Woolnoth and Lopez. Good. £3.

The Fight between Sayers and Heenan, 1860, after Machrell, etching. Good. 10s.
Ditto, after Walton, coloured, framed, with key. Good £4 15s.
Ditto, by Jem Ward, coloured, framed. Fair. £1 1s.

The Fights between Mendoza and Ward; between Randal and Martin; and between Dutch Sam and Medley, three prints. All fairly good impressions £2

The Fight between Spring and Langan, by Clements and Pitman, in colours. Good. £3 5s.

The Fight between Ward and Cannon, with descriptive letterpress. Fair. 10s.

The Fives Court, after Collins; The Bruiser Bruised, in colours. The latter good £2 5s.

Going to the Fight; the Return. Two long strips about 4ft. long by 2in. wide. Coloured. Each in a black and gilt frame. Very rare. £36 15s.

The Interior of the Fives Court, with Randall and Turner sparring, after Blake, by C. Turner, first state, in colours. Very fine. £14.

Ditto, later state, in colours. £5 5s.

Ditto, in colours, with key inlaid in the mount. £6 6s. The same, uncoloured. Good. £2 2s.

A Milling Match, after Rowlandson, in colours. The Triumph. Fair. 9s.

Scenes on the Road to a Fight, by Henry Alken, a pair. Fair uncoloured impressions. 9s.

BULL AND BADGER BAITING, DOG FIGHTING, RATTING.

Badger-Baiting: a Match at the Badger, &c., after H. Alken; a Dog Fight, by J. Scott, old coloured impressions. Fair. £1 16s.

A Bull Baited by Dogs, by Johann Jacobé, after Rembrandt. Good. 15s.

Bull-Baiting, two plates, after H. Alken; Bear-baiting by the same, old coloured impressions. Good. £3 4s.

Bull-Baiting, Badger-Baiting, Bear Baiting, Cock-Fighting, &c.: a series of 7 oblong 4to. coloured plates, after H. Alken, published 1823-24, good impressions, sewed. £8 15s.

The Bull Ring, a series of 33 plates, representing Scenes in the Bull Ring, by Francisco Goya. Fair. £1 10s.

The Westminster Pit: a Dog Fight, printed in colours. Fair. £2.

Billy, the Rat-killing Dog, killing 100 rats in five and a half minutes, coloured. Fair. £1 10s.

COACHING, DRIVING, RIDING.

An Airing in Hyde Park, showing the "Ring" in the Park, 1793, by T. Gaugain, after E. Dayes. Proof before letters. Very fine and rare. £44

The Birmingham Mail Fast in the Snow, 1836, The Guard goes on to London with the Letter Bags, by J. Pollard, in colours. Fine. £3 10s.

The Blenheim Coach leaving the Star Hotel, Oxford, in colours. Good. £2 2s.

The Brighton Age Coach, 1852, original impression in colours. Good. £1 10s.

The Cambridge "Telegraph" starting from Fetter Lane, by Charles Hunt, after Pollard, in colours. Good. £2 2s.

The Louth Mail Snowed Up, 1836; the Letter Bags sent on in a Post Chaise and Four, by J. Pollard, in colours. Good. £1 14s.

Chaise Horses, Coach Horses, both by John Young, after Garrard. Good. £4 10s.

The Chaise Match, after Seymour. Good. £1 1s.

Changing Horses at Clermont, by C. G. Lewis, in colours. Good. £2 2s.

Coach Horses, a mezzotint, by John Young, after Garrard. Fair. 9s.

Coaches in Snowstorms: a series of six plates, by Havell, after Henry Alken. 21s. (fair coloured impressions).

Coaching, two coloured prints, "One Mile from Gretna," and "A False Alarm on the Road to Gretna," by R. G. Reeves, after Newhouse. About 14in. by 12in. Good. £1 10s.

Coaching, a set of 4 coloured prints (22½in. by 15in.), by J. Pollard, representing Mail Coach in a Flood; Mail Coach in a Drift of Snow; Mail Coach in a Snow Storm; and Mail Coach in a Thunderstorm, 1825-27. Fair. 20s.

Coaching Incidents, three coloured plates, after Cooper Henderson, very rare. £15 10s. (fine impressions).

Coaching Scenes, a pair by John Harris, after Harrison, in colours. Good. £2 10s. Again, fair, in colours. 16s.

Driving and other Caricatures: a series of six coloured plates, by William Heath, 1829. Fair. 14s.

The Duke of Beaufort's Coach, after Shayer; and The Resolute Team, after C. Henderson, in colours. Good. £7 10s.

The Edinburgh Express; the Reading "Telegraph," in colours. Very fine £10.

Equestrian Sketches, six coloured plates, by H. Alken, published in 1821. Good. £2 15s.

"A Favourite Turn-Out," a scene at Hyde Park Corner. Coloured lithograph. Good. 16s.

A Fine Young English Gentleman, after Alken; and A Stanhope Phaeton. Both fair. £1 8s.

Four-in-Hand; Royal Mail Coach; and A Stage Coach, after Pollard, in colours. Fine impressions. £15.

Four-in-Hand, after Pollard, by Gleadah; Mail behind Time, after ditto, in colours. Fine. £14.

The Four-in-Hand Club, after J. Pollard, by J. Harris; and East India House, in colours. Fine impressions. £9.

The Four-in-Hand Club in Hyde Park, 1838, by J. Harris, after J. Pollard, coloured impression. Very fine. £18.

The Four-in-Hand Club in Hyde Park, 1838, by Charles Hunt, after Pollard, in colours. Good. £5 10s.

General Post Office, north-east view, after Pollard, by Ryall, in colours. Very fine. £26 5s.

General Post Office, The New Building, after Pollard, in colours. Very fine. £28.

General Post Office, with Mails Departing, by Reeves, after Pollard, in colours. Fine. £11 11s.

Highgate Tunnel; View on the Highgate Road, both after Pollard, by Charles Hunt, in colours. Good. £7 7s

Hyde Park Corner, after Pollard, by Rosenberg, in colours. Very fine. £22.

Inn Yard at Calais, The, by C. G. Lewis, after Byron, in colours. Good. £2 2s.

Lioness Attacking the Exeter Coach, after Pollard, in colours. Fine. £7 10s.

The Liverpool "Umpire"; The Manchester Day Coach, in colours. Both fair. £2 2s.

The London and Birmingham Tally-ho; the Red Rover, both in colours. Fine. £11 6s.

London Fire Engines, after Pollard, by Reeve, in colours. Very fine. £13 13s.

Mail Changing Horses; Mails preparing to Start, both after Pollard, in colours. Very fine. £30.

Mail Coach by Moonlight, in colours. Fair. £1 1s.

Mail Coach in a Storm, after Newton, by Alken, in colours. £3 5s.

Mail Coach in a Storm of Snow, published August 5, 1826, by Thomas Reeve, after Pollard, in colours. Good. £3 3s.

Mail Coach in a Flood; In a Drift of Snow; and In a Thunderstorm, after Pollard, in colours. Good £6 16s. 6d

Mail Coach behind Time, after Walter, and Stage Coach, after Jones, in colours. Both good. £7 5s.

Mails arriving at Temple Bar; Mails Starting from the Post Office, both in colours. Fine. £10 10s.

Manchester and London Coach; Stage Coach in a Fog, in colours. Good. £4.

M

Manchester Day Coach; The New London Royal Mail; and The Blenheim, in colours. Fair £3 10s.

The Modern Phaeton; and A Coach and Six, after Rowlandson, in colours. Fair. £1 10s.

The New London Royal Mail, by Charles Hunt, after Pollard. Fair. 5s. The same, in colours. Fine. £2 15s.

North Country Mails; West Country Mails, after Pollard, by Sutherland and Rosenberg, both in colours. Very fine £23.

On the Highgate Road, "The Woodman," by J. Pollard. Good 12s. Again, in colours. Fine. £2 12s. "The Woodman" is the name of the tavern, still standing, on the Great North Road between Highgate and Finchley. It was here that Fowler and Milsom called just prior to the Muswell Hill murder, for which they were convicted and hanged in 1896.

Postboys Watering their Horses; Approach to Christmas; and A Four-in-Hand, after Pollard, in colours. Fine £10 15s.

The Reading Coaches; Paris and Dover Coach; and The "Eagle," in colours. Very fine. £33 12s.

Relay in the Snow; Mail Coach Delayed; and Mail Coach in a Storm, after Pollard. Fair. £1 1s.

Regent Circus; The Angel Inn, both by Reeve, after Pollard, in colours. Fine. £16.

Riding and Driving in Hyde Park, with portraits of Lord Petersham and others, coloured lithograph. Good. £1 4s.

The Roadsters; and The Birthday Team, by C. Hunt, in colours. Good. £3.

The Royal Glasgow and London Mail Coach, after J. F. Herring, original impression in colours. Good. £1 10s.

Royal Mail Coach, by and after Pollard, in colours. Very fine. £14 14s.

Scenes during the Snowstorm, 1836, after Pollard A set of four, in colours. Fine. £12.

Scenes on the Road to Epsom, after Pollard, by J. Harris. A set of four, in colours. Fair. £2 8s. £16 (very fine)

Stage; and Mail, after M. E., by C. Hunt, in colours. Good. £8.

The Stage Coach, by Himely, after Jones, in colours. Fair. 15s.

Stage Coach; and Mail Coach, after Pollard, in colours. Good. £5.

Stage Coach; and Mail Coach, by M. Dubourg, in colours. Good. £3.

Stage Coach Arriving; Changing Horses, and Setting Off, after Pollard, by Havell, a set of three, in colours. Very fine. £26 5s.

Stage Coach, with News of Peace and News of Reform, after Pollard, by Havell, a pair, in colours. Very fine. £17.

Stage Coach Travelling; and Opposition Coaches at Speed, after Pollard, in colours. Fine. £12 12s.

The Taglioni, after G. Henderson; The Original Bath Mail Coach. Both good. £5 10s.

Two of His Majesty's State Horses; the Earl of Chesterfield's State Carriage, both by William Ward, after Chalon. Good. £7.

Under Weigh without a Pilot; and No Time for Refreshment, after Newhouse, in colours. Good. £9.

The Windsor Coach; The Southampton Coach; and the "Age" (Brighton), in colours. Very fine. £21.

COCK FIGHTING.

A Game Cock, coloured; Cock Fighting; and Articles for a Cock Match. Good. £2.

Game Cocks: A Black-breasted Dark Red, and a Streaky-breasted Red Dunn, proofs, a pair. Good. £8 8s.
The same, printed in colours. Good. £3 3s.

Cock-Fighting. The set of 6 plates, drawn and engraved by N. Fielding, fine old coloured impressions. Scarce. £6 5s.

Cock-Fighting. The set of 4 plates, by Sutherland, after H. Alken, fine old coloured impressions. Scarce. £3 14s.

Cock-Fighting. Two plates by J. Clark, after H. Alken; and another, after S. Alken, old coloured impressions. £4 6s.

Cock-Fighting, after Welch, a pair, in colours. Very fine. £16 10s.

Cock-Fighting, by C. R. Stock, a series of 4 small (6in. by 5in.) coloured plates, entitled, Set-to, Fight, Throat, Death. Good. 12s.

Cock-Fighting, by Thomas Reeve, after Alken: a series of four small plates, in colours. Good. £1 1s.

Cock in Feather, The; The Streaky Breasted Red Dunn, both by Charles Turner, in colours. £5 15s. (good).

Colonel Mordaunt's Cock Match, with key, by Richard Earlom, after Zoffany. £3 5s. (open letter proof, fine); £6 (engraver's proof, full margin).

Rural Chivalry: a series of 5 col. plates of Fighting Cocks, by J. Fahey, after Weigall, published by Ackermann, 1839. Oblong folio. £2 10s. (in wrappers as issued). The subjects comprise: "Stand at Ease," "Make Ready," "Present," "Fire," "Victory."

The Trimmed Cock; and The Cock in Feather, after B. Marshall, by C. Turner, a pair. Very fine. £13 2s. 6d.

The same subjects, printed in colours, before the alteration in the title. Fine. £4 10s.

The same, printed in colours, with titles "Peace and War." Good. £3 15s.

COURSING.

Coursing; Shooting, a pair, by Robert Pollard, proofs before letters, plain. Good. £2 2s.

Coursing. Five various engravings, after H. Alken and S. Alken, all coloured, five plates. Fair. £2 4s.

Coursing at Hatfield, after Robert Pollard, in colours. Good. £1 10s.

Coursing Scenes, a set of four coloured plates, by Reeve, after Wolstenholme. Fine. Full margins. £11 11s.

Coursing Scenes, a set of four plates by Sutherland, after Wolstenholme, in colours. Good. £2 5s. *Again*, very fine, £10 10s.

Finding; and Coursing, after R. Jones, by C. Turner, a pair. Very fine. £13 13s.

Return from a Course on Lambourn Downs, by Thomas Major, after Seymour. Good. 14s.

FISHING.

The Angler's Repast; a Party Angling, both by George Keating, after Morland, in colours. Very fine. £23 2s.

Children Fishing; Children Gathering Blackberries, by George Dawe, after Morland, both in colours. Very fine. £31 10s.

Mr. Briggs and his Doings, a series of 12 coloured plates by John Leech, n.d. (but 1848), published by Bradbury and Evans. £2 10s. (early issue, in wrappers).

The Fisherman, by Nicolaas Van Haeften. Good lettered impression. 7s. 6d.

Fishermen and the Monstrous Fish, by Adamo Ghisi, after Giulio Romano. Good. 18s. Again, very fine, £1 16s.

Illustrations to Walton's Angler, a series of plates by J. Mitan, 1822. 4to. £1 (bound in book form, half morocco).

A Lady Fishing, by E. Dumée, after Cruikshank, printed in colours. Good. £4 4s.

Pike Fishing; and Fishing in a Punt, after H. Alken, a pair; and two others after S. Alken, all old coloured impressions. Four plates. £4 4s.

HUNTING:

At Fault, by John Harris, after Pollard, in colours. Good. £1 12s. Again, very fine. £5.

Badger Catching, Otter Hunting, Hawking, &c, after H. Alken and S. Alken, old coloured impressions. Six plates. £3 5s.

Beagles, Fox-Hounds, Harriers, and Stag-Hounds, after D. Wolstenholme, by Reeve, a set of four aquatints, in colours. Good. £5 15s. 6d.

The Bear Hunt, coloured mezzotint by William Ward, after Morland. Fair. £2 10s.

A Boar Hunt, by François Joullain, after Desportes. Fair. 4s. Again, good, 10s. 6d.

A Boar Hunt, by Pieter Soutman, dated 1642. Good. 10s.

Breaking Cover; The Death of the Fox, both by James Scott, after Reinagle, lettered impressions. Good. £5

Breaking Cover, by James Scott, after Reinagle. A good proof. £3 10s.

Breaking Cover; The Death, both by James Scott, after S. Gilpin. Good. £3 3s.

Breaking Cover; and The Death, after H. Alken, by T. Sutherland, a pair, in colours. Good. £4 4s.

Breaking Cover; Morning, or a Few of the Right Sort, and The Refreshment, after Alken, all three in colours. Fair. £3 10s.

Breaking Cover; Full Cry, A Check; and The Death, a set of four, in colours. Indifferent. £1 12s.

Breaking Cover; and The Death, after Pollard, by Havell, proofs, in colours. £5 10s.

The Chase of the Roebuck, by H Alken, after Hodges, a rare print. Fair. £1 2s.

The Chase; and Death of The Roebuck, after Alken and Reeve, a pair, in colours. Indifferent. 10s.

The Chase, after Davis; and The Death, after Alken, by T. Sutherland, in colours. Good. £7 10s.

A Check; and Crowding at a Gap, both after Alken, in colours. Good. £4

The Cover Hack, by C. G. Lewis, after Sir E Landseer. Presentation proof. £10 10s.

Drawing a Cover; Gone Away; The Leap, &c., after H Alken. Set of five, in colours. Fine. £24 3s

The Drive of Deer, by T. Landseer, A.R A , proof before letters; "There's Life in the Old Dog Yet," by H T. Ryall, artist's proof; the pair, £7 7s.

An Easter Hunt, after Pollard, by Dubourg; and Easter Monday, both in colours. Good. £8 18s. 6d

A Fox Chase, after Wolstenholme, by R. Reeve, set of four, in colours. Good. £3 12s. 6d.

The Fox Chase; The Stag at Bay, both by R. Pollard, after W. Ellis, old coloured impressions. Good. £6 10s.

The Fox Chase, a series of four coloured plates, by Charles Hunt, after J. F. Turner, published by Ackermann in 1835. Good. £5 10s.

Fox Hunters, after Alken, by Reeve, a set of four, in colours. Good. £9.

Fox Hunters Meeting; Breaking Cover; Fox Chase; The Death, a set of four coloured plates, by C. Hunt, after Pollard. Good. £12 10s.

Fox Hunting, a series of four rare plates, by E. Bell, after Morland, in colours. Very fine. £45 Again, good, £28.

Fox Hunting, the set of four plates in colours, after Herring, in oak and gilt frames. Fine. £14.

Fox Hunting, a series of eight plates, from drawings by W. P. Hodges, by H. Alken, coloured by Rosenberg. £13 (orig. wrappers, proofs, three plates missing).

Fox Hunting. Various incidents after H. and S. Alken, all old coloured impressions, seven plates. Good. £4 12s.

Fox Hunting, a set of four coloured prints, after H. Alken. Good. £8. Again, better impressions, £12.

Fox Hunting, a series of four plates by John Havell, after Pollard, open letter proofs, in colours. £25.

Fox Hunting, after D. Wolstenholme, by Reeve, the pair, in colours. Good. £6.

Fox Hunting, after Rowlandson, a set of four, aquatints. Very fine. £18.

Full Cry; and Going Home by Moonlight, after Pollard, by Havell, in colours. Fair. 18s.

Full Cry; and The Death, after Pollard and Gill, a pair. in colours. Proofs. £3 10s.

A Gentleman, with two hunters and groom, in a landscape. Very fine. £11.

George III. returning from Hunting; a Royal Hunt in Windsor Park, both by L. F. Dubourg, after Pollard, jun., in colours. £4 15s. (tolerably good); 15s. (inferior); £14 (very fine).

Going Down; Coming Up; A Hunter, and The Death, after Alken, in colours. Fair. £1 10s.

Going Out; Entering Cover; In Full Cry, and The Fox Run Down, a series of four plates, engraved in the chalk manner, by J. Wright, old coloured impressions. Good. £4 4s.

Going Out in the Morning; The Death, both by Walker, after Seymour. Good. £2 15s.

Going to Cover; Going to the Moors, a pair, after S. Alken, in colours. Fair. 14s.

Going to Cover; Full Cry, and The Death, after Alken, by C. Bentley, in colours. Fair. £1 12s.

Going to Cover; The Leap, Full Cry, The Death, the set of four coloured plates by C. Bentley, after H. Alken. Good. £5 12s. Again, better impressions, £9 9s.

Going to Cover; Full Cry; The Leap, The Death, a series of four coloured prints, by Thomas Reeve, after Henry Alken, 1828. Folio (fair impressions) £4 3s.; £10 10s. (good).

Going to Cover; Breaking Cover, Full Cry; Freeing the Fox, a set of four coloured plates, by Thomas Sutherland, after Henry Alken. Good. £7. Again, £9 9s.

Going to Cover; The Chace, at Fault; and The Death, a set of four plates, by T. Burford, after J. Seymour, in colours. Good. £10 10s.

Hare-Hunting. Finding; and Ware Turnips! after Hodges, by Reeve, a pair, in colours. Good. £3 10s.

Hold Hard; Going at a Stone Wall, both in colours, by J. Clark. Good. £3 15s.

Horse and Hounds in a Stable, by Thomas Burford. Good. 10s.

The Hunted Stag, by Thomas Landseer, after Sir Edwin Landseer, proof, signed by the painter. £12 12s.

The Hunters' Annual, a set of seven lithographs, after Davis. Good. £4 10s.

Two Hunters, after Stubbs, by C. T. Stubbs; and An Arabian, after the same, fair impressions. £1 1s.

Hunters at Grass, after B. Marshall, by W. Ward, proof. Fine. £9 19s. 6d.

Hunters at Grass, by Thomas Landseer, after Sir Edwin Landseer, £35 (artist's proof), signed by Sir E. Landseer).

Hunting and Shooting, a series of 8 coloured lithographs, by P. Reinagle—5 relating to Hunting and Shooting subjects, n.d. (1830). Atlas folio. £1 5s. (wrappers).

Hunting Accidents, a set of four, in colours. Fair. £2 2s.

Hunting Accomplishments, a series of 6 plates, by John Harris, after Henry Alken, published by Fores, and sometimes called "Fores' Hunting Accomplishments." £2 (in colours, fair).

Hunting in Cover; the Chase; and the Death, after Davis, by Sutherland, a set of three, in colours. Good. £12 10s.

Hunting Notions, a set of six subjects, by Henry Alken, printed in colours. Good. £5 10s. A reprint of this series was subsequently published at 3s. 6d. The value is trifling.

Hunting Scenes. Fourteen subjects on six plates, in colours, on vellum. Fine. £10.

A Hunting Scene, after Sartorius, by Pollard; and Death of the Fox, both in colours. Fair. £2.

Hunting Scenes, a series of four plates, in colours, after Henry Alken. Inferior. £1 6s.

Hunting Scenes, a series of four coloured plates, by Thomas Reeve, after Wolstenholme. Fine. £9 9s.

Hunting Subjects, after Loraine Smith, a set of six, in colours. Very fine. £21.

Hunting Subjects, after Alken, by Thomas Sutherland, a set of four, in colours. Good. £8 8s

Hunting Subjects, a series of 4 plates, after Wolstenholme, by Thomas Sutherland, in colours. Good. £5 10s.

Hunting Subjects, after H. Alken, by J. Gleadah, a set of four. In colours. Very fine. £15 15s.

Hunting Subjects, a series of 12 coloured plates, by "Phiz," published by Ackermann, n.d. (1860) £4 10s

Hunting Subjects, Sett of Prints of Hunting, Hawking, and Fishing, by Francis Barlow. 11 plates to the set. Good. £1 15s. *See* **Severale Wayes of Hunting, &c.,** *ante* p 106.

Hunting Subjects, a set of eight plates, by G. L. Jukes, after C. Lorraine Smith, in colours. Good. £10 10s.

Huntsman Taking Hounds to a Cover, by C. G. Lewis, after Rosa Bonheur, artist's proof. £1 10s.

The Huntsman Rising, and The Gamester Going to Bed, two coloured plates, by Rowlandson, 1807. 20s (original impressions)

In Full Cry, by Samuel Howitt, in colours. Good. £1 12s

The Leicestershire Hunt, a set of four coloured plates: "A Struggle for the Start," "The First Ten Minutes," "Symptoms of a Skurry in a Pewy Country," and "The Death," folio. £2 10s (fan set)

Leicestershire, a set of four hunting subjects, after J. Dean Paul in colours. Good. £10 10s. Again, very fine £26 5s.

The Leap, The Death, after Alken, by Bentley, in colours. Good. £4.

The Life and Death of Tom Moody, a series of four plates, by Charles Hunt, after Pollard, in colours. Good. £3 18s. Again, fair, £1 6s

The Lion Hunt, by Scheltius à Bolswert, after Rubens. £1 8s (fine impression)

A Litter of Foxes, after G. Lorraine Smith, by J. Grozer. Good. £1.

The Lucky Sportsman, by F. D. Soiron, after Morland, printed in colours, very fine and scarce. Large margin £50.

The Meet, Breaking Cover, Full Cry, The Death, a series of four coloured plates, by Charles Hunt, after Henry Alken, about 35in. by 24in. Fairly good, £2 10s.; good, £11 5s.

The Meet, Breaking Cover, Full Cry, The Death, the set of four oblong coloured plates, by T. Sutherland, after Henry Alken, 1824. The set. Good. £12.

The Meet of the Vine Hounds, by W. H. Simmons, after Calvert, published in 1844. Fine lettered impressions £2 5s.

Meeting at Cover, Breaking Cover, Full Cry, and The Death, after Alken, by Sutherland, a set of four, in colours. Fine. £21.

The Meeting of Her Majesty's Staghounds on Ascot Heath, by William Bromley, after F. Grant, published on Jan. 1st, 1839. Good. 18s.

The Meltonian, or the Pleasures of the Chase Developed, a set of 30 coloured plates, with dedication and frontispiece, by G. L. Jukes. Good, in four frames. £50.

"One of the Right Sort," and **"One of the Wrong Sort,"** by Henry Alken, about 12in. by 11in. Good. £2.

The Otter Hunt, after Sir E. Landseer, by C. G. Lewis, artist's proof, signed by the engraver £10. Again, signed by the painter, £21.

La Promenade du Matin, Départ pour la Chasse, and La Chasse au Cerf, after C. Vernet, by Levachez, three plates, in colours. Good. £2 5s.

The Quorn Hunt, after H. Alken, by F. C. Lewis, a set of eight, in colours, with original wrapper. Very fine £30.

The Quorn Hunt, after H. Alken, by F. C. Lewis, four plates, in colours. Good £7 17s. 6d.

The Stag at Bay, by Thomas Landseer, after Sir Edwin Landseer. £42 (artist's proof). £54 (*ibid.*)

Stag and Hare Hunting, a series of four prints, published without name of Painter, Engraver, or Publisher, but dated 1797. Fair. 14s

Stag Hunting by Moonlight, by Johann Jacobé, after Casanovo. Good, full margins. 17s

Sir M. M. Sykes' Hounds Breaking Cover, after H. B. Chalon, by Wolstenholme. Very fine. £11 11s

Curiously enough the principal figures in Chalon's painting, and consequently in the print, do not include Sir Mark Sykes. The man standing under the tree in the foreground is Foxton, the earth stopper, while the man on the brown horse under the broken tree represents Robert Bower, of Welham. William Carter, who hunted the hounds at the time, is the central figure, and his son Thomas Carter is seen jumping his horse out of cover. Sir Mark Sykes is on a white horse in a little group in the back-ground.

Tattersall's and Smithfield, a pair after S. Alken, in colours. Fair. 14s

Two Hacks, by G. T. Stubbs, after George Stubbs, in colours. Fair. £1 4s.

Treeing the Fox, and The Meeting Place, after Davis, both in colours. Good. £6 10s

The Unicorn Destroying a Huntsman, by Jean Juvet, ("The Master of the Unicorn") Fine impression. £12 12s; again, fair, £4

Unkennelling, after Alken, by Sutherland, proof, in colours. £2.

Unpleasant; The Scramble, &c., after H. Alken, a set of five, in colours. Good. £10.

View near Oakham, and A View near Melton Mowbray, after Alken, a pair, in colours. Very good impressions. £7 10s.

A Village Meet, proof before all letters, in colours Fair. £1 10s.

Weighing the Deer, after F. Tayler, by T. L. Atkinson, artist's proof. Good. £1.

Worcestershire, a set of four hunting subjects, by Fielding, after Woodward, in colours. Good. £12.

Yellowham Wood, and The Cock-Tails Done, after Hodges, by Alken and Reeve, a pair, in colours. Good. £7.

PORTRAITS OF SPORTING CELEBRITIES.

Portraits of Prizefighters; the series of 17 prints engraved by P. Roberts, from drawings by J. R. Cruikshank. Old and good impressions. £5 10s.

Francis Duckenfield Astley and His Harriers, after B. Marshall, by Woodman. Good. £2 15s.; again, £1 10s.

James Belcher, the Prizefighter, of Bristol, after Allingham, by E. Clint, printed in colours. Fine. £5 5s.

Thomas Belcher, the Prizefighter, after D. Guest, by C. Turner, proof. Fine. £7 7s.

Thomas Belcher, by Charles Turner, after B. Marshall, mezzotint, proof with full margins. £5.

Bendigo (William Thomson), the Prizefighter, by C. Hunt, in colours; William Neat, a Prize Fighter, after Rippingille, by J. F. Lewis. Both fair. £1 1s.

J. B. Blanchard, the Æronaut, by J. Newton, after R. Livesay. Good lettered impression. 7s.

John Broughton, a Prizefighter, mezzotint, published by W. Richardson; the same, whole length, after Hogarth, a lithograph. Both good impressions. £2 18s.

Buckhorse, a Prizefighter, mezzotint, proof before any letters. Good. £2 15s.

Deaf Burke, after Meyer, by C. Hunt; and Young Dutch Sam, after East, two Portraits of Prizefighters. Good. £1 3s.

Thomas Cribb, the Prizefighter, after D. Guest, by J. Young, proof, first state. Very fine. £10.

Tregonwell Frampton, Esq., Father of the Turf, after Wooton, mezzotint, by J. Jones. Good. £3 15s.

Thomas Futrell, a Prizefighter, of Warwickshire, after W. H. Kingsbury, in colours; and Thomas Winter (Spring), a Prize Fighter. Fair. 16s.

George III., full length portrait in the character of an Archer. Published in 1795, and dedicated to the Kentish Bowmen. Good. £3 12s. Geo III. was appointed Captain General of the Honourable Artillery Company in March, 1766.

John Gully, the Prizefighter, whole length in private dress, a mezzotint. Good. £2 10s.

John Gully, the Prizefighter, whole length, mezzotint, open letter proof. Fine. £7 7s.

John Gully, by Lopez. Good. £1 10s.

Johnny Hannan, Prizefighter, in colours; George Taylor, the Bruiser, after Hogarth. Both good £1 8s.

Joshua Hudson, a Prize Fighter, in colours; and Thomas Shelton, also a Prize Fighter. The pair, £1.

Richard Humphreys, mezzotint, by John Young, after Hoppner, proof, with full margins. Very fine. £17 17s. Again, proof with etched letters. £15 15s.

William Innes, "To the Society of Goffers at Blackheath," after Abbott. Very fine £21.

John Jackson, the Prizefighter, mezzotint, by Charles Turner, after B. Marshall, open letter proof. £5 5s.

William Long, Huntsman of the Duke of Beaufort, by Charles Hunt. Good. £1 1s.

Vincent Lunardi, the Æronaut, by Bartolozzi, after R. Cosway. Good lettered impression. 6s.

Daniel Mendoza, in fighting attitude, by H. Kingsbury, after T. Robineau, very rare. Good. £4 4s.

Daniel Mendoza, a Prizefighter, by Gillray, good impression of a scarce print, £1, again, earlier impression, £1 18s.

Molineux, a Prizefighter, by J. Young, after D. Guest, open letter proof, £4. Again, open letter proof. Fine. £7 7s.

Molineux, a Prizefighter, by Dighton. Fair. 6s.

Young Norley, a Prizefighter, after W. D., by C. Denn, in colours. Fair. 13s.

Thomas Oldaker, Huntsman to the Berkeley Hounds, after Marshall, by R. Woodman. Fine. £7 17s. 6d.

Philip Payne, the Duke of Beaufort's Huntsman, a mezzotint, by Charles Turner, after T. R. Davis, open letter proof. £5 5s.

Henry Pearce, a Prizefighter, by Lopez. Good. £1 10s.

Mr. Delme Radcliffe and his Harriers, 1833, in colours. Fair. £2 5s.

William Richmond, a Prizefighter, after Sharpels, by W. M. Fellows. Fair. 10s.

Dutch Sam, a Prizefighter, by and after P. Roberts, in colours. Fair. 5s.

James Sayer, a boy fishing, by Richard Houston, after Zoffany. £3 15s. (proof before letters, full margin).

Tom Sayers; Heenan, both in colours. Good. £2 10s.

George Wilson, the Pedestrian, accomplishing his task of walking 1,000 miles in 20 days, by Williams, in colours, 1815. 4to. 5s.

Mr. Tattersall, a mezzotint, by John Jones, after T. Beach. Good. £5 5s.

Johnny Walker, the Prizefighter, after A. S. Henning, by G. Hunt, printed in colours. Good. £2 5s. Again, fair, 15s.

James Ward, the Prizefighter, after Finnie, by T. Woolnoth, open letter proof. Good. £2.

James, Duke of York, as a Boy, Playing Tennis, line engraving, by ————, n d (cir 1665) 10s.

PORTRAITS OF RACEHORSES.

Portraits of Racehorses, a series of 40 portraits of 18th century racehorses, with descriptive letterpress beneath, 1753. 8vo. £3 18s (wrappers)

Portraits of Celebrated Racehorses, a series of mezzotints published by Laurie and Whittle; and a series of small line engravings published by Sayer. Sixteen prints. Fair. £1 2s.

Portraits of Racehorses, a set of 18 coloured prints of The Winners of the Derby and their Riders, from 1827 to 1845, inclusive, wanting that for 1840, after paintings by Herring, Hancock and Hall, engraved by Reeve, Hunt and Harris. All published by S and J Fuller, except that for 1842, which has Ackermann's name. Offered by Messrs. Robson and Co., of Coventry Street, at £35

Portraits of Racehorses, a set of 30 coloured prints of The Winners of the St. Leger and their Riders, from 1815 to 1845, inclusive, wanting that for 1833, after paintings by Herring, Ferneley, Hancock and Hall, engraved by Reeve, Sutherland, Hunt and others. Published by S and J. Fuller and R Ackermann. This series was recently on sale by Messrs. Robson and Co, of Coventry Street, W., for £52 10s.

Portraits of Racehorses, a series of six uncoloured plates, by Richard Houston, after Seymour and Spencer, mezzotints, with ornamental borders, full margins. Good. £3 10s.

Portraits of Celebrated Racehorses, with their Jockeys, a set of 12 plates, by Richard Houston, after Seymour, not coloured. Good. £6 10s.

Portraits of Racehorses, by Seymour and Spencer, engraved by R. Houston, 14in. by 12in., 1755-56. The horses were six in number, and comprised Chestnut Arabian, Bay Boston, Dormouse, Bald Charlotte, Cullen Arabian, and Sedbury. The set, £5 5s.

Portraits of Racehorses, 1755-56, from pictures by Seymour and Spencer, the series of 12 mezzotints engraved by R. Houston. Fine impressions with full margins, uniformly mounted in a portfolio. £12 5s.

Portraits of Racehorses, with their Pedigrees, Achievements, &c., 1740-53, a series of 33 line-engravings from pictures by T. Spencer and others. Very fine old impressions, bound with the original wrappers in a volume, oblong folio, smooth calf gilt. £20.

Portraits of Racehorses, with their Jockeys, viz., Othello, Basto, Carlisle, Second, Young Cartouch, Bonny Black, Bald Charlotte, Creeping Molly, Lamprie, Childers, Fearnought, Old Cartouch, Fox, Sedbury, Molly, and Bay Bolton, in all 16 plates, after James Seymour, with pedigrees and performances, T. Butler, 1753. Oblong 4to. £12 5s.

Portraits of Celebrated Racehorses, after Seymour and Spencer, by R. Houston, a set of six. Good. £3 18s.

Portraits of Celebrated Racehorses, with Jockeys up, after Spencer, printed in colours, with letterpress, a set of eight. Good. £7.

Portraits of Racehorses, coloured portraits of, by J. Rogers, size 23in. by 17in., published by McLean in 1826. About 10s. each. The series includes the portraits of "Cannon Ball," "George," "Selim," and others.

Portraits of Racehorses, a series of six coloured prints of racehorses, by Shayer and others, n.d. Folio. The subjects are "Van Tromp," "Kettledrum," "Alice Hawthorn," "Formosa," "Pero Gomez," and "The Baron." £5 (good impressions, full margins).

Portraits of Celebrated Racehorses, by G. T. Stubbs, after G. Stubbs, a series of eleven plates in colours. Good. £11 11s.

Portraits of Celebrated Horses, 13 oblong folio lithographic plates, proofs on India Paper, selected and retouched by James Ward, R.A., the artist. £20 (bound up in Russia). On another occasion, the same set, proofs and retouched as before, brought £2 15s only.

Antonio and Jerry, after J. F. Herring, by Sutherland, a pair, in colours. Good. £3 15s.

Barbarossa, after H. B. Chalon, by W. Ward; and Vandyke, after the same, by W. Say. Both good. £5 15s.

Bloomsbury and Grey Momus, after J. F. Herring, by C. Hunt, a pair, in colours. Good. £2 5s.

Bobtail, a celebrated Racer, by and after John Whessell, in colours. Good. 18s.

Brilliant and Tantrum, after Shaw and Sartorius, and A. Racehorse, after Seymour, by Burford, three plates. Good. £1 16s.

Bungay and Adonis, after B. Marshall, by C. T. Stubbs. Good. £2.

Copenhagen, by William Say, after Smyth, in colours. Good. £1. Again. Very fine. £2 5s.

Diamond, after B. Marshall; and Smolensko, after Sartorius, by W. Ward, proofs. Fine impressions. £9 19s 6d.

Diamond and Hambletonian, both by John Whessell, after Sartorius. Good. £1 8s.

Dick Andrews and Penelope, celebrated Racers, both by and after John Whessell, in colours. Good. £1 8s.

Dr. Syntax, after J. F. Herring, by C. Turner, touched proof. Fine. £6 15s.

Eclipse, by T. Burke, after G. Stubbs. Good. £2 12s.

Eclipse, after G. Stubbs, by T. Burke. Good. £3 3s.

Eclipse, mezzotint, by Thomas Burke, after George Stubbs, in colours. Fine. £4 4s.

Eclipse, by George Stubbs, after T. Burke, uncoloured. Very scarce. Fine impression. £4 10s.

Eleanor, by and after John Whessell, in colours. Good. 18s.

Eleanor and Parasol, by and after John Whessell, the pair, in colours. Good. £3 10s.

Firetail, mezzotint, published by Sayer and Bennett, uncoloured, very scarce. Good. £3 10s.

Grey Diomed and Smolensko, both after Sartorius. Good. £2 5s.

Gimcrack, after Sartorius; Eclipse, after Stubbs; Buzzard; and Skyscraper. Fair. £1 6s.

Gimcrack, after Stubbs, by G. T. Stubbs, open letter proof. Good. £1.

Godolphin, an Arabian, by James Scott, after Stubbs. Good. £1 1s.

Highflyer, after S. Gilpin, proof before all letters. £2.

Highflyer, after S. Gilpin, by F. Jukes, proof. Good. £2 2s.

Jupiter, by W. Ward after S. Gilpin, open letter proof with full margin. Good. £1 12s.

Jupiter, after S. Gilpin, by W. Ward, open letter proof. Fine. £3 13s 6d.

Little Driver, jockey up, by H. Roberts, after Spencer, pedigree of the horse at either side and list of prizes below, published August, 1751. Good. 12s.

Mambrino, by G. T. Stubbs, in colours. Fair. 11s.

Meteora and Parasol, both by and after John Whessell, in colours. Good. £1 15s.

Morel, with Jockey and Trainer, after H. B. Chalon, by W. Ward, proof before any letters. Very good impressions. £6 16s. 6d.

Orlando, winner of the Derby in 1844, by Charles Hunt, after J. F. Herring, in colours. Good. £1 8s.

Orville and his Trainer, with a list of his performances at Brighton, Newmarket, Doncaster, and York, by J. Scott, after Clifton Thompson. Fine proof with margins intact. £3 15s. The same, proof in colours. Very fine. £10 10s.

Pavilion, ridden by Chifney; and Violante, ridden by Buckle, after H. B. Chalon, by W. Ward, open letter proofs. Fine. £9 19s. 6d.

Pavilion, after H. B. Chalon, by W. Ward, proof before any letters. Fine. £6 6s.

Pavilion, rode by Chifney, by T. Burke, engraver's proof before any letters, touched by the artist. Very fine. £8 10s.

Phenomena, after Sartorius, by John Whessell; Tarrare, after Dolby; the latter a proof, both in colours. Good. £2 5s.

Pumpkin, after G. Stubbs, A.R.A., by G. Townley Stubbs, in colours. Good. £1 12s.

Quiz, by W. Ward, engraver's proof before any letters. Very fine. £11 5s.

Rosette, by W. Ward, engraver's proof before any letters, touched by the artist. Very fine. £7 15s. Again, the same in print state. Very fine. £4 18s.

Sir David, by W. Ward, after Chalon, engraver's proof before any letters, touched by the artist. Fine. £4 4s.

Sir Peter Teazle, after Gilpin, by W. Ward, proof; and Mambrino, after Stubbs, by C. Hodges. Good. £4 4s.

Tandem, after J. Pollard, by Gleadah, and Coventry, by and after Fellowes, a pair, in colours. Good £7 7s.

Trumpeter and Violante, celebrated Racers, both by and after John Whessell, in colours. Good £1 16s.

Violante, rode by Buckle, by T. Burke, engraver's proof before any letters, touched by the artist. Very fine. £4 15s.

Violante, by and after John Whessel, in colours. Good. £2.

Volunteer, by G. T. Stubbs, in colours. Fair. 11s.

RACING.

Ascot: Returning from Ascot Races, by Edward Duncan, after Henderson. Good coloured impression. £3 3s.

Ascot: His Majesty's Gold Plate, after J. Pollard, in colours. Good. £4 4s.

Ascot: The Oatlands Sweepstakes, after Sartorius, by Edy, in colours. Fine. £5.

Aylesbury Grand Steeplechase, ran in February, 1866, by C. Bentley, after Alken, in colours. Good. £5 5s.

Aylesbury Grand Steeplechase, a set of four plates, in colours, by Harris, after Pollard. Very good. £18 18s.

Bramham Moor Hunt Races, the set of six coloured plates, after H. Watkins Wild. Fair. £1 5s.

The Breeding and Training of Racehorses, the series of six engravings by W. Elliott, from pictures by T. Smith, a fine uniform set. £13.

Chantilly Races, 1841, engraved by C. Hunt, a set of four aquatints. Good. £3 5s.

Chantilly Races, 1841, after Campion and Herring, two proofs in colours. Good. £11.

A Country Race Course: Preparing to Start; Horses Running, both by Jenkins, after Mason, in colours. Indifferent. £1.

A Country Race Course, after W. Mason, by Jukes and Jenkins, a very fine uncoloured impression. £7.

Mr. Coventry's Sacripant Winning at Epsom, in colours. Good. £4 5s.

Derby Pets, a series of four plates, in colours, after Pollard. Fair. £1 5s.

Derby Stakes, 1820, after H. Alken; Racing, by the same; others after S. Alken, Stubbs, etc., all old coloured impressions. Seven plates. Good. £6 15s.

The Derby Stakes of 1828 and 1829; and The Ascot Gold Cup, 1829, after J. Pollard, a set of three, in colours. Good. £10.

The Derby of 1839, after Pollard; and the Derby of 1820, after Alken, both in colours. Fair. £2 2s.

The Derby of 1848, after Charles Hunt, in colours. Fair. 8s.

The Derby: Panoramic View of the Derby, four strips, about 5 feet long by 5 inches wide, coloured, in a black and gilt frame. Very rare. £21.

The Derby: a pair of coloured plates, after J. F. Turner, engraved by Charles Hunt; Start for the Derby, Coming in for the Derby (40¼in. by 27¼in.), 1870. Inferior. 15s.

The Derby: Coming in for the Derby, after J. F. Turner, by Charles Hunt, in colours. Good. £2 14s.

The Derby; Going to the Derby; the Settlement at the Corner, four long strips, coloured, in a black and gold frame. Very rare. £25 10s.

Doncaster Races, by Harris, after Pollard, a series of four plates in colours. Good. £3 10s.

Doncaster Races: The St Leger of 1836, after Pollard, by Harris, a set of three, in colours. Good. £9.

Doncaster Races, after Pollard; and the St. Leger of 1839, after J. F. Herring, both in colours. Good. £6 6s.

Doncaster Great St. Leger, 1859; and Grand Stand, Ascot, 1859, by J. F. Herring, a pair, coloured. Fair. 14s.

Epsom, after J. Pollard, by C. Hunt, a set of six, in colours. Very fine. £31.

Epsom Races, by J. Pollard, in colours. Very fine. £12 10s.

Epsom Races (the Derby), by J. Pollard, in colours. Very fine. £15.

Epsom Races, by Sutherland, after Alken, a pair, in colours. Good. £4 10s.

Epsom Races, after Pollard, by Smart and Hunt, a set of three, in colours. Very fine. £31.

Epsom: The Great Derby Stakes, after J. Pollard, in colours. Good. £4 4s.

Epsom, Goodwood, and Ascot Races, after Pollard, by Pyall, a set of three, in colours. Fine. £18 10s.

Epsom (The Derby); Ascot (The Oatlands Sweepstakes), both by J. Edy, after Sartorius. Good. £5 5s. *See* **Ascot,** *supra*.

Epsom Downs, 1848: The Grand Stand; The Stewards' Stand; and The Winning Post, after Alken, a series of three coloured lithographs. Good. £2 10s.

Epsom Grand Stand; and Goodwood Grand Stand, after Pollard, by Reeve, both in colours. Good. £6.

Epsom National Derby Day, open to all Nations, 1851; a folding coloured print, by Henry Alken, opening to about 8 feet, published by Ackermann, n d (1851). £3 3s. (pictorial bds.) *See* **Race and The Road, The.** *Post*

The Field and the Road, both by Charles Hunt, after J. F. Turner, in colours. Good. £2 12s.

Goodwood: The Grand Stand at Goodwood, by C. Hunt, in colours. Good. £4 15s.

The High Mettled Racer, by Thomas Sutherland, after Alken, a series of six plates, in colours. Good. £5 15s.

The Last Horse Race run before Charles II., by Francis Barlow, a very rar and curious plate. Good. £12 10s.

The Leamington Grand Steeplechase, a set of four plates, in colours, by C. Hunt, after Turner. Fair. £3 5s.

Life and Death of a Racehorse, a series of six plates, in aquatint, by and after Gooch, 1792. Fine. £9 9s. Again, £1 6s. (inferior).

The Liverpool Great National Steeplechase, 1839, after Harris, plates 1 and 4, in colours. Fair. £1 10s.

Match between Flying Dutchman and Voltigeur for £1,000, Run at York on May 13th, 1851, by Charles Hunt, after Harry Hall, in colours. Good. £5 5s. The same, very fine, £14 14s.; the same, uncoloured, good, £1.

A Match for One Thousand Pounds, after Pollard, in colours. Fair. £1 12s.

Newton Races, 1831, after C. Towne, by Hunt, in colours. Good. £5 5s.

The Punchestown Races, view of the Grand Stand with the Prince of Wales on a White Horse, by T. L. Sayer, after Barraud. 34in. by 17in. £2 15s (artist's proof, good).

Mr. Osbaldeston's Match against Time, by Harris, after H. Alken, in colours. Fair. 16s.

Race and The Road, The, Epsom 1851, a folding coloured print, by Henry Alken, opening to about 8 feet, describing scenes on the road to Epsom and the race for the Derby Stakes, published by Ackermann, n.d. (1851). £3 3s. (pictorial bds.) *See* **Epsom National Derby Day.** *Supra.*

Race for the Great St. Leger Stakes, 1836, by John Harris, after Pollard, in colours. Fine. £3 10s.

Race for the Great St. Leger Stakes, by Charles Hunt, in colours. Good. £2 5s.

Race between Bay Malton and Gimcrack, by Richard Houston, after Sartorius, uncoloured, a very scarce print. Good £3 10s.

Race: Bay Melton beating King Herod and the Field, by R. How, uncoloured. Scarce. Good. £3 10s.

Racing Incidents, a set of six coloured plates, by Thomas Rowlandson, scarce. Good. £7.

Racing Subjects, a set of eight plates, each about 18in. by 12in. lengthways, in colours, by S. Alken, jun., an extremely rare set. £99 15s. (in old, common frames, tolerably good impressions).

Five Racers Preparing to Start, after C. Vernet, by Deboucourt. Very fine. £8 18s 6d.

St. Alban's Steeplechase, a set of four plates by Reeves and Hunt, after Pollard, with the "Key." Good. £4 4s.

The St. Leger, 1812; and Start for the St. Leger, 1816, after Clifton Thomson, both in colours. Fair. £3 15s.

Scenes on the Road, or a Trip to Epsom and back, by John Harris, after James Pollard, a series of four plates in colours. £2 8s. (fair); £16 (very fine); £24 3s. (*ibid.*)

Start for the Derby, and Coming in for the Derby, after F. C. Turner, a pair, coloured. Fair. £1 1s.

The Steeple Chase, a set of six 4to coloured plates, by Henry Alken. Good. £5 5s.

Steeple Chase Scenes, a set of six folio coloured plates, after Henry Alken. Good. £7 7s.

A Steeplechase, after H. Alken, a pair, in colours. Good £3 10s.

The First Steeplechase on Record, a series of four coloured plates, by John Harris, after Henry Alken. £2 18s. (good). £7 7s. (fine set). This well-known series has been reprinted more than once. The reprints are frequently offered for sale at about 30s. the set.

Chances of the Steeplechase, a set of seven coloured plates, all after J. Pollard. Fairly good set. £10.

The Trademan's Plate, Chester, 1839, by John Harris, after T. C. Turner, in colours. £1 4s. (good).

Training, Starting, Running, After Running, a set of four coloured plates, by Hunt, after Pollard. Good. £10.

The Walk, Starting, The Race, Rubbing Down, a set of four coloured plates, by Sutherland, after Alken. Very fine, £22.

The Wolverhampton Stakes, 1839, after F C Turner, in colours. Fair. 10s.

Worcester Race Course, after Ziegler, and St Albans Tally-ho Stakes, after Pollard, both in colours. Fine £9 10s

SHOOTING (including SPORTING DOGS).

Ball, painted and engraved by C. Turner, old impression in colours; and Dogs Fighting, by the same. Good. £1 18s.

The Beagles, by Thomas Reeve, after Wolstenholme, in colours. Good. £1 16s.

Cover Shooting, a pair, by Thomas Reeve, after Wolstenholme, in colours. Good £3 10s.

Crib and Rosa, by J Scott, after A. Cooper, open letter proof; and the same, a modern impression. £1 6s

Crib and Rosa, after A Cooper, by J Scott, Jem Burns' four pets, after Clater, both open letter proofs Very fine £6 6s.

Dash, a pointer in the possession of Colonel Thornton, by Robert Pollard, in colours. Good £2 15s.

Deer Stalking, a series of six plates by Ansdell, viz, Shot, Chase, Examining Ground, Deer Disturbed, Waiting for Help, Returning Home. £1. Fair

Duck, Snipe, Woodcock, Pheasant, Partridge, and Grouse Shooting, a series of six plates by Charles Hunt, after Turner, in colours. Good £6.

Duck Shooting, by Charles Catton, after Morland, in colours. Good. £4 10s.

A Famous Setter, after H. B. Chalon, by W. Ward, proof before any letters. Good £1 1s

A Famous Newfoundland Dog, after H. B. Chalon, by C. Turner, open letter proof. Very fine £2 10s.

The First of September, Morning and Evening, by William Ward, after Morland. £30 (very fine pair, in colours); £16 (*ibid.*); £5 10s. (fair, in colours), £1 12s. (uncoloured, good)

The First of September, after D. Wolstenholme, by Reeve, a pair, in colours. £2 15s.

Going to the Moors, Going to Cover, a pair, after S. Alken, in colours Fair. 14s.

Grouse, Partridge, Pheasant, and Wild Fowl Shooting, a set of four plates, by Thomas Sutherland, after Wolstenholme. £5 10s. (uncoloured, good); £6 6s (coloured, good). Again, fine, coloured, £15 10s.

Grouse Shooting, Wild Fowl Shooting, Snipe Shooting, &c., after H. Alken, all old coloured impressions, eight plates Good. £3 3s

Hare Shooting; Pheasant Shooting, a pair, by James Ward, after Morland, in colours. Fine. £8 5s.

Lucy, a Bull Bitch by Pyall, after Smith. £1 5s. Good.

Morning; Partridge Shooting; Pheasant Shooting; Snipe Shooting; Duck Shooting; **Evening,** a set of six large oblong folio plates, chiefly etched by Rowlandson, aquatinta by S. Alken, after George Morland. Published in 1792. £28 (fine original coloured impressions, in a wrapper), £1 19s. (the same, uncoloured, fair impressions).

Partridge, Pheasant, Woodcock, and other Shooting, after S. Alken, all old coloured impressions, six plates. £4 15s.

Partridge Shooting, by Charles Catton, after Morland, plain. Fine impression. £2.

Pheasant and Woodcock Shooting, the series of four plates, old coloured impressions, by Thomas Sutherland, after Wolstenholme. Fair. £4 18s., £14 14s. (fine impressions).

Pheasant, Partridge, Grouse, and Wild Fowl Shooting, a series of four plates, in colours, after Henry Alken. Inferior. £1 2s.

Pheasant Shooting; Woodcock Shooting, both by Robert Dodd, after J. Ibbetson, in colours. Good. £1 15s.

Setters, by R. Laurie, after F. Sartorius, proof before any letters. £2 15s.

Shooting; Coursing, a pair, by Robert Pollard, proofs before letters, plain. Good. £2 2s.

Shooting, Eight representations of Shooting, engraved by Woodman and Turner, after R. Frankland, coloured. Cambridge, 1813. Oblong 4to. £4 4s. (orig. covers).

Shooting, by William Woollett, after George Stubbs. Fair. 5s.

Shooting Prints, a set of seven coloured plates (10in. by 8in.), by Henry Alken (about 1847). The subjects are, In the Woods, In the Open, In the Fens, On the Downs, In the Covers, On the Moors, and Rest and Refreshments. Good. £3 5s.

Snipe Shooting, by Charles Catton, after Morland, in colours. Good. £2 4s.

The Spanish Pointer, by W. Woollett, after G. Stubbs. Rare. £6 5s.

Sporting Dogs, by S. Phillips, in colours. Good. £2 2s.

Sporting Dogs, Fox-hounds, Stag-hounds, Beagles, Spaniels, &c., six plates, after H. Alken, old coloured impressions. £2.

Sportsmen at the Door of an Inn, by Christian Friedrich Boetius, engraved about 1760. Good. 8s.

Sportsman's Return, The, by William Ward, after Morland, in colours. Fine. £15. £8 8s. (a good impression); £23 (very fine).

Wasp, Child, and Billy, after H. B. Chalon, by W. Ward, open letter proof. Very fine. £22 1s.

VARIOUS.

Archery Competition, by J. Heath, proof before letters. Good. £1 16s.

Boys Skating, by E. Scott, after George Morland, printed in colours. Fine. £6 6s.

Children's Sports, a series of 12 plates from copper, comprising scenes of Cricket, Leap Frog, Spell and Knurr, &c., 1818. 16s.

Cricketer, The, a Song, with Music, by W. J. Bullock, n.d. (1857) Large folio 3s (sewed) This is, in fact, "a piece of music," but mentioned here because pieces of that kind relating to the subject are rarely seen.

Easter Monday in Epping Forest, after J. Pollard, a pair, in colours. £13 13s. (good impressions, but no margins).

Gambado, a series of 20 coloured plates on 5 sheets, illustrating the life of Geoffrey Gambado, folio, published without date (but about 1810). £1 10s. (as issued).

Game of Quoits, The, coloured print measuring about 14in. by 4in., n.d. (cir. 1815). 10s.

Jorrocks' Sporting Lecture, two engravings in folio, illustrating 10 phases of Jorrocks' Life, by T. J. Rawlins, n.d. (1850), Ackermann. 10s. (as issued).

Mezzotints of Various Sporting Subjects, published by Bowles and Carver, mostly with full margins. 17 plates £10

Panorama of Human Life, a series of 31 coloured etchings, by Henry Alken, illustrating various episodes of life, inclusive of Duelling, Gaming, Prize-fighting, Ratting, &c., &c. Etchings on a long roll, 15ft 4in. long. Published by Fuller, n.d. (but 1820). £7 15s. (in a cylinder).

Poaching, after S. Alken, a set of four coloured plates. Good. £2 5s.

Six Scenes in the Life of James Green, Esq., a Special Constable, sketched by a "Special" (William Heath), n d. (ca 1848) Large 8vo 5s. (orig. wrappers).

The Sporting Education of "Master George," old coloured impressions. Five plates by H. Alken Good. £3 10s.

Sporting Medallions, by H Alken, the set of four plates, with six small engravings of various sports on each, fine old coloured impressions; and the title to "British Sports," by the same. Five plates. Fine. £12 5s.

Sporting Miseries, or Six Red-Letter Days in the Country, a series of six coloured engravings and title by Seymour, n d (1830), Fores. £1 12s.

Sporting Miseries, or Six Red Letter Days in the Country, a series of seven coloured plates and engraved title, 1st issue, 1836. Oblong 4to Laird. £3 12s. (hf mor. with label)

Sports and Pastimes, the series of 10 large coloured plates, by John Leech, 1865. Atlas folio. £9 15s (original covers).

Winter, a Skating Scene on the Serpentine, by V. M Picot, after De Loutherbourg, proof before letters. £1 1s

Winter Amusement, a View in Hyde Park from the Moated House; a View in Hyde Park from the Sluice at the East End, by Eyde, after Ibbetson, a pair, in aquatint. Good. £3 3s

Works by the Same Author.

Library Manual, The. A Guide to the Formation of a Library, and the Values of Rare and Standard Books. Third Edition. Revised and Greatly Enlarged. *In cloth gilt, price 7s. 6d. nett; by post, 7s. 10d.*

Engravings and their Value. Containing a Dictionary of all the Greatest Engravers and their Works. New Edition, Revised and brought up to date, with latest Prices at Auction. *In cloth gilt, price 15s. nett, by post, 15s. 5d.*

Other Works for Collectors.

Painters and their Works. A Work of the Greatest Value to Collectors and such as are interested in the Art, as it gives, besides Biographical Sketches of all the Artists of Repute (not now living) from the 13th Century to the present date, the Market Value of the Principal Works Painted by Them, with Full Descriptions of Same. *In 3 vols., cloth gilt, price 15s. nett per vol., by post 15s. 5d.; or 37s. 6d. nett the set of 3, by post 38s. 3d.*

Autograph Collecting. A Practical Manual for Amateurs and Historical Students, containing ample information on the Selection and Arrangement of Autographs, the Detection of Forged Specimens, &c., &c., to which are added numerous Facsimiles for Study and Reference, and an extensive Valuation Table of Autographs worth Collecting. By HENRY T. SCOTT, M.D., L.R.C.P., &c. *In leatherette gilt, price 7s. 6d. nett, by post 7s. 10d.*

London: L. UPCOTT GILL, 170, Strand, W.C.

INDEX.

A.

Accomplish'd Lady's Delight, The, 140
Adams, John, 4
"Aesop," 114
Aflalo, F. G., 41, 141, 149
Akerman, J. Y., 120
Aldam, W. H., 94
Alexander, Sir J. E., 102
Alfred, H. J., 147
Aiken, Henry, Books Illustrated by—
    Aiken's Sketches, 3
    Analysis of the Hunting Field, 4
    Angling Sports, 8
    Annals of Sporting, 9
    Beauties, &c., of the Horse, 17
    Book of Sports, 19
    British Proverbs, 23
    Chase, the Turf, and the Road, 24, 119
    Cock Fighting, &c., 26
    Cockney's Shooting Season, 26
    Collection of Sporting Designs, 27
    Cracks of the Day, 33
    Down the Road, 39
    Driving Discoveries, 39
    Fashion and Folly, 46
    Few Ideas, A, 47
    Gretna Green, 56
    High Mettled Racer, 58
    How to Qualify, 62
    Hunting, 63
    Hunting Reminiscences, 64
    Hunting Sketches, 64
    Jorrocks's Jaunts and Jollities, 67
    Landscape Scenery, 65
    Life of John Mytton, 77
    Melange of Humour, 77
    Moments of Fancy, 79
    National Sports, 81
    New Scrap Book, 82
    New Sketch Book, 83
    Notitia Venatica, 85
    Popular Songs, 66
    Qualified Horses, 94
    Scraps from the Sketch Book, 105
    Shooting, 107
    Sketch Book, 108
    Sketches, 109
    Specimens of Riding, 110
    Sporting Notions, 114
    Sporting Repository, 114
    Sporting Review, 114
    Sporting Satirist, 115
    Sporting Scenes, 115
    Sporting Scrap Book, 115
    Sporting Sketches, 115
    Steeple Chase, The, 121
    Symptoms, 122
    Touch at the Fine Arts, 125
    Tutor's Assistant, 133
    SEE also Appendix under subject required.
Aiken S., 36
Allen, Jno., 93
Allom, S. R., 134
Almanac of Twelve Sports, 3, 140
"Amateur Sportsman," An, 112
Anderson, E. L., 79
Andrewes, Geo., 37
Angelo, H., 103

Angelo, junr., 131
Angler's Hand Book, The, 141
Angler's Library, The, 141
Apperley, C. J., 9, 24, 61, 64, 74, 77, 98, 112
Arber, Edw., 105
"Archer, W. N.," SEE Neade, William
Armiger, Chas, 120
Armstrong, W., 15
Arrianus, 34
Ascham, R., 127
Aspin, Jehoshaphat, 89
Astley, P., 79, 122
Atkinson, G. F., 34, 67
Atkinson, J. A., 108
Auldjo, Jno, 81
Ayrton, W., 140

B

Badcock, J., 109
Baddeley, Jno., 75
Badminton Library, The, 14
Badminton Magazine, The, 142
Bainbridge, G. C., 49
Baker, Sir S. W., 99
Baldwin, W. C., 3
Ball, John, 3
Bannatyne, Richd., 88
Barker, Thos., 10, 16, 140
Barlow, Francis, 106
Barnard, M R., 111
Barrett, 95
Barrier, G., 44
Barry, M., 14
Bateman, C. S. L., 48
Bates, H W., 128
Bauchope, C R., 55
Beard, Jno., 37
Beaufort, Duke of, 14, 60
Beaumont, A., 129
Beckford, P., 123
Bedingfield, Thos., 13
"Bee, John" SEE Badock, J.
Beerbohm, Julius, 135
Belamy, J. C., 131
Bennett, Chas., 19
"Ben Tally Ho," 113, 133

Berenger, Baron de, 88
Berenger, Lieut., 57
Berenger, R., 59
Beresford, Jas., 91
Berkeley, C G F, 42, 79, 80, 98, 119
Berlepsch, H., 4
Berners, Juliana, 18, 54, 58
Bert, Edm, 9
Best, J. J., 44
Best, Thos, 32
Bewick, Thos., 24
"Bickerdyke (John)," 15, 20, 137
Binnell, R, 37
Bisset, J. J., 111
Blacker, Wm, 10
"Blackmantle Bernard," SEE Westmacott, W.
Blackwell, Hy, 42, 55
Blaine, D P., 41
Blakey, R, 6, 141
Blane, W, 34, 43
Blew, W. C. A., 21, 84, 85, 94
Blome, R, 54
Blundeville, Thos., 13, 50, 83
Bol, Hans, 134
Boner, Chas., 23
Bonney, T G., 4, 17, 87, 88, 134
Boosey, T., 90
Bowers, G., 45, 64, 71, 75, 80, 84, 145, 148
Bowlker, R and C., 10
Bradley, C, 98
Bradley, R, 53
Bradley, T, 86
Bradwood, Wat, 145
Brassey, Annie, 135
Brindley, C., 64, 91, 92, 113, 116, 119, 120, 121, 130
Broadfoot, W, 15
Brockedon, W, 65
Brodrick, W., 45
Brookes, R., 10
"Brooksby," SEE Elmhirst, E P.
Brown, J M., 91, 121
Browne, H K., Books Illustrated by:
    Derby Carnival, The, 36
    Hawbuck Grange, 57

How Pippins enjoyed a Day, 62
Hunting Bits, 63
Hunting Songs, 65
Jorrocks's Jaunts and Jollities, 69
Racing and Chasing, 95
Romford's Hounds, 80
Run with the—Stag Hounds, 100
SEE also Appendix under subject required
Browne, Moses, 8, 28, 148
Bryden, H A., 56
Buckland, F. T, 48, 75
Bunbury, H. W., 1, 8, 93
Burnaby, Elizabeth A F., 58
Burnand, F. C., 146
Burrows, Ed., 94
Burton, Alfred, SEE Mitford, John
Burton, Sir R. F, 45, 142
Bury, Viscount, 15
Buxton, E. N., 107

C.

Cairnie, 42
Campbell, Jas, 129
Campbell, W, 86
Campion, J. S, 86
"Careless, John," 86
Carey, David, 73
Carleton, J W, 97, 115
Carnegie, A, 4
Carnegie, W., 92, 93
Carpenter, P, 61
Carroll, W., 7
Cartwright, W., 95
Castle, Egerton, 104
Catlow, A. and M. E., 109
"Cecil," SEE Tongue, C.
Chapman, A, 48
"Charfy, Guiniad," 30
Charlton, Jno., 133
Chatto, W A, 7, 102
Cheetham, Jas., 7
Cheever, Geo. B., 136
Chitty, E, 49
Cholmondeley-Pennell, H., 15
Churchill, G. C., 38

Clark, J. H., 50
Clark, R., 55
Clarke, Chas., 33
Clarmorgan, J, 24
"Clericus," SEE Cartwright, W.
Clias, P. H., 40
Cockaine, Sir T., 108
Cole, Ralph, 139
Coleman, E. T., 103
Collyns, C P, 85
Colquhoun, Jno, 79, 102
Combe, Wm., 35, 41, 60, 74, 122, 126
Conway, Sir W. M., 4, 25
Cook, C. H., SEE "Bickerdyke, John"
Cook, John, 85
Cooper, J W., 52
Cooper, Jno., 136
Corbet, H., 122
Corbett, E., 86
Corte, Claudio, 13
"Cosmopolite," A, 117, 119
Cowper, Frank, 101
Cowper, W., 139
Cox, Harding, 15
Cox, N, 54
"Crafty," 110
Crawhall, Jos, 26, 31, 143
"Craven," 114
Crawfurd, Oswald, 139
Crealock, H. H, 4, 36, 138
Crignelle, H. de, 71
Crowquill, A, 106, 109
Cruikshank, Isaac, 50
Cruikshank, Geo., Books Illustrated by
    Annals of Gallantry, 8
    Annals of Sporting and Fancy Gazette, 9
    Dictionary of Slang, 37
    Eccentric Song Book, 40
    Epping Hunt, The, 42
    Helps to Protect Life, &c., 57
    Humourist, The, 62
    Life in London, 72
    Life in Paris, 73
    Lover's Panorama, The, 147
    Midnight Merriment, 77

Particulars of the Stadium, 88
Philosophy in Sport, 89
Progress of a Midshipman, 93
Scourge, The, 105
Tales of Humour, 122
SEE also Appendix

Cruikshank, J. R., Books Illustrated by:
Corinthian Parodies, 32
Devil among the Fancy, The, 37
Life of Samuel D. Hayward, 146
Tom and Jerry, 125
SEE also Appendix.

Cruikshank, R., Books Illustrated by:
Doings in London, 38
English Spy, The, 42
Fashion and Folly, 46
Finish to Life in London, 47
High Mettled Racer, The, 58
Lovel's Panorama, The, 147
Treadmill, The, 129
SEE also Appendix.

Cumming, R. Gordon, 48, 137
Cunningham, C D., 90
Custance, Hy., 99

D.

Dagley, R., 36, 122
Dalziel, Hugh, 144
Dance, Chas., 146
Daniel, W. B., 101
Dansey, W., 34
Darvill, R., 130
Davenport, W. B., 111
Davies, G. C., 149
Davy, Sir H., 102
Davy, J., 5
Day, Wm., 94
De Fonvielle W., 2
Demidov, A., 145
Dennys, Jno., 105
Dent, Clinton, 1
Dent, C. T., 15
Dewar, G. A. B., 20
Dewar, J C., 135
Dibdin, Chas., 58
Digby, Sir Everard, 13, 31, 107

"Diomed," 114
Dixon, H. H., 92, 101, 105, 108
Dixon, Wilmot, 70, 77, 146
Dobson, William, 70
Dodge, R. I., 64
Donato, Prince de, SEE Demidov, A.
Donnelly, Edwd., 106
Doyle, R., 34, 40
D'Oyly, Sir C., 67, 125
Drayson, A. W., 115
"Druid," The, SEE Dixon, H. H.
Drummond, W. H., 70
Dunlop, R H. W., 64

E

Edie, Geo., 12
Edwards, E B., 134
Egan, Pierce, Works by
Boxiana, 21
Every Gentleman's Manual, 44
Finish to Life in London, 47
Lecture on the Art of Self-Defence, 71
Life in London, 72
Life of an Actor, 74
Life of Samuel D. Hayward, 146
Pierce Egan's Anecdotes, 90
Pierce Egan's Book of Sports, 90
Real Life in Ireland, 95
Real Life in London, 96
Show Folks, The, 108
Sporting Anecdotes, 113

Egerton, D T., 81
Elmhirst, E. Pennell, 17, 33, 51
Encyclopædia of Sport, 41, 144
English, H. G., 130
English-man's Mentor, The, 144
"Ephemera," SEE Fitzgibbon, Edw.

F.

F. (G.), 39
Fahey, J., 100
Fairbairn, 45
Fairfax, Thos., 32
Faithorne, Wm., 90
Faliscus, Gratius, 34

Fellows, Sir C., 81
Fewtrell, Thomas, 21
Fisher, A L, 52
"Fisher, Paul," SEE Chatto, W. A.
Fisherman's Magazine and Review, The, 144
Fitzgerald, E A., 25
Fitzgerald, R. A, 63
Fitzgibbon, Edw, 20, 29, 41, 56, 80, 132
Fletcher, Phineas, 148
"Fly, A," SEE Fitzgibbon, Edw
Folkard, H. C., 137
Forbes, J D., 84, 127, 129
Fores, 60
"Forester, Frank," SEE Herbert, H W.
Forsyth, Jas, 115
Forsyth, Capt. J., 58
Forsyth, J S, 12
Fortescue, J W, 97
Foster, Birket, 55
Foster, David, 104
Fowler, J. K., 97
Foxe Road Scrapings, 99
Francis, Francis, 20, 83, 115
Frankland, R, 17, 36, 48, 103
Freeman, G E., 92
Freshfield, D W., 146
Frost, Jno., 104

G

Gale, Fredk, 78
Gallini, G A., 130
Gallwey, Sir R Payne, 16, 19, 37, 50, 72
Gambado, Geoffrey, SEE Bunbury, H W.
Gardner, Alan, 99
George, H. B., 3, 85
Gerstaecker, F., 138
Gheyn, Jakob de, 44
Gilbert, J., 38
Gillmore, P., 35, 63, 93
Glaisher, J. G, 129
Gooch, Thos., 72
Goodlake, T, 33
Gordon, A., 130

Gosden, T., 66
Goubaux, A, 44
Grace, W. G, 33
Grassi, Giacomo di, 132
Gray, Thos De La, 31
Greener, W W, 56, 78, 104
Greenwood, Geo., 59
Greenwood, Thos, 72
Griffiths, R, 37
Griffiths, W., 93
Grimble, A, 36, 58, 63, 107
Grisone, F, 83
Grohman, W A B, 111, 133
Grove, Lily, 15
Guérinière, R. de la, 40

H.

H (R), 103
Hale, Capt, 62
Halford, F. M, 39, 48
Hall, H. B, 58
Hallam, Isaac, 26
Hamilton, E, 96
Hamilton, J. P, 98
Hamilton, Lt.-Col, 97
Hanbury, Mrs, 87
Hanger, Col. George, 27, 124
Hansard, G. A., 131
Harcourt, E. V, 113
Hardy, Campbell, 112
"Harewood, Harry," 37
Hargrove, E and A E, 5
Harper, A P., 90
Harris, S, 26, 85
Harris, Sir W. C, 92, 138
Harting, J E., 9, 17
Hawker, Col. P, 37, 68
Hawkes, —, 77
Hawkins, Sir John 28, 147
Haworth, M. E, 99
Head, F. B., 61
Heath, Hy., 121
Heath, Wm, 43, 46, 73, 74, 112
Heathcote, C G, 16
Heathcote, J M., 16
Henderson, C C, 99
Henderson, Wm., 84

Henry, Wm., 16
Herbert, H. W., 47, 51
Hewes, R., 100
"Hieover, Harry," SEE Brindley, C
Hillier, G. L, 15
Hinchliff, T. W, 121
Hissey, J. J., 2, 39, 61, 86, 125
Hodgson, R. L., 86
Hofland, T C., 22
Holdsworth, E. W. H, 36
Hood, Tom, 42
Hooker, Sir J D, 59
Hope, Wm, 29, 31, 82, 104, 135, 148
Hore, J. P., 60
Horlock, K. W, 62, 75, 76, 96
Howitt, Saml, 22, 23, 49, 87
Howitt, Wm., 101
Howlet, R, 7
Hudson, F., 149
Hughes, Wm, 92
Hughes, W. E., 143
Humphrey, R. J, 66
Hunt, Chas, 3, 136
Hunt, W. S., 23
Hurstone, J. P., 89
Hutchinson, H G., 15, 22, 45
Hutton, Alfred, 26

J

Jackson, J, 92
Jackson, Wm., 82
Jackson ("Fly and Fly Hooks"), 129
Jalland, G H., 112
Jardine, Alfred, 141
Jeans, Thos., 125
Jefferies, Richd, 52
Jerrold, D, 57
Jesse, Capt, 71
Johnson, D, 109
Johnson, C., 30, 53
"Johnson, T. B.," 52, 64, 106, 118
Jones, Capt., 130
Jones, H., 97
Jones, J., 56
Jones, O. Glynne, 100

K

Karr, H. W. Seton, 17
Kellie, Sir T, 88
Kemp, Dixon, 139
Kennedy, W. R, 112
Kent, Jno, 95
Killmister, A K, 85
King, S. W., 69
King, W. R., 117
Kinloch, A. A., 71
Kirby, F. V., 67
Knapp and Baldwin, 82
Knox, A E., 14, 52

L

L'Abbat, M, 12
Lacy, R., 79
"Lady Pioneer," A, 146
Lafosse, 32
La Guérinière, R de, 40
Landseer, E and C., 11, 19, 22, 35, 117
Lang, And, 8, 45
Lascelles, Hon G., 15
Lascelles, R, 7
Lascelles, Sir C., 14
Latham, S, 71
Lathy, T. P, 5
Lawrence, John, SEE "Scott, Wm. Henry"
Lawrence, R., 32
Leech, John. Works Illustrated by
  Ask Mamma, 14
  Encyclopædia of Rural Sports, 41
  Flyers of the Hunt, 49
  Handley Cross, 57
  Plain or Ringlets, 91
  Romford's Hounds, 80
  Sponge's Sporting Tour, 110
  Sports and Pastimes
  SEE also Appendix
Lemon, Mark, 125
Lemoine, H, 79
Lennox, Lord, 89, 97
Leveson, H A., 50, 64, 138
Liebault, Jno., 75
Life of a Nobleman, 146

Lillywhite, W., 65
Lloyd, F., 150
Lloyd, L., 47, 52, 102
Locke, Jas., 133
Lockwood, Sir F., 64
Longman, C. J., 15
Lucas, C., 123
Lydekker, Richd., 143
Lyttleton, R. H., 15

M.

McArthur, J., 9
McBane, D., 44
"McCringer, Joel," 27
Mackintosh, A., 39
Maclaren, A., 128
Mahon, A., 12
Major, J., 28
Malbie, N., 91
Malet, H. E., 9
Manley, J. J., 148
Mannering, G. E., 138
March, J., 69
Markham, F., 107
Markham, Gervase, Works by:
    Cavalerice, 23
    Cheape and Good Husbandry, 24
    Compleat Husbandman, 143
    Country Contentments, 32
    Gentleman's Academie, The, 54
    How to Chuse Horses, 145
    Hunger's Prevention, 63
    Maison Rustique, 75-6
    Perfect Horseman, The, 148
    Way to Get Wealth, A, 136
    Young Sportsman's Instructor, 139
"Markwell, Marmaduke," 2
Marryat, F., 80
Marsh, J., SEE March, J.
Marston, Ed., 35, 86
Marston, R. B., 29
Martelli, C., 66
"Martingale," SEE White
Mascall, L., 142
Mason, G. Finch, 32, 47, 49, 50, 63, 114, 115, 124

Mason, R. O., 93
Mathews, C. E., 147
Mathewson, T., 46
Maudsley, A., 59
Maxwell, Sir H. E., 11, 36, 119, 141
Maxwell, W. H., 47, 135, 138
Mayer, A. M., 112
Mayer, John, 118
Medwin, Thos., 6
Melville, Whyte, 55, 95, 99
Middleton, Chr., 107
Miles, H. D., 19, 94
Millais, J. G., 21, 22, 52, 142
Millais, Sir J. E., 21, 52
Miller, Capt., 129
Miller, Thos., 116
Mills, Jno., 37, 49, 73, 119, 120
Mitchell, E. B., 15
Mitford, John, 2
Moore, A., 8
Moore, A. W., 4
Moore, T., 69
Morgan, Geo., 38, 82
Morland, T. H., 52
Morris, Beverley R., 22
Morris, M. O'Connor, 58, 131
Morris, Mowbray, 15
Moseley, W. M., 42
Mountague, J., 85
Muir, J. B., 95
Mummery, A. F., 80
Murphy, J. M., 112
Myers, A. B. R., 74

N.

N'Zau, Bula, 128
Napier, E. H. D. E., 103, 137
Neade, William, 39
Newall, J. T., 40, 61
Newcastle, Duke of, 53, 148
Newgate Calendar, The, 82
Newhouse, C., 103, 109
Newhouse, S., 128
Newland, H. G., 42
"Newtonensis," 57
Nicholson, W., 3, 140
"Nimrod," SEE Apperley, C. J.

"Nimrod," 83
Nobbes, R., 32, 143
North, Roger, 38, 143

O

Oakleigh, Thomas, SEE Killmister, A. K.
O'Bradley, A., 56
O'Connor, R., 68
"Old Bushman," The, 115
"Old Shekarry," The, SEE Leveson, H. A.
"Olio Rigmaroll," 3
"Oliver, Stephen," SEE Chatto, W. A.
Olivier, J., 46
Orme, Edw., 87
Osbaldiston, W. A., 23
"Otter," SEE Alfred, H. J.

P.

Palliser, Jno., 110
Paris, J. A., 89
Parkyns, Sir T., 67
"Pasquin, Peter," 35
Paterson, M., 80
Paul, J. B., 60
Peacham, H., 30
Pease, A. E., 25, 64
Peek, H., 15, 41
Peel, E. L., 58
Pelham, Camden, 25
Penn, Richd., 147
Pennell, H. C., 79, 113, 144
Percy, Wm., 31
Percival, W. S., 70
Perry, A. W., 150
Persius, Chas., 100
Peters, J. G., 129
Phillips, H., 132
"Phiz," SEE Browne, H. K.
"Piscator," SEE Lathy, T. P.
"Piscator," SEE Hughes, Wm.
Pitman, C. B., 60, 95
Pluvinel, A. de, 67
Pocock, George, 3
Pollock, A. J. O., 113
Pollock, W. H., 15
Pollok, F. T., 66
Pope, A., 134
Porter, John, 70
Powell, Major, 48
Pownall, T., 59
"Priam," 18
Price, Luke, 122
Pritt, T. E., 20, 139
"Prosody Dr.," 125
Pye, H. T., 118

Q.

"Quid," SEE Fitzgerald, R. A.
"Quiz," Peter, 46
"Quizem, Caleb," 8

R.

Radcliffe, F. P. Delmé, 84
Rambler's Magazine, The, 149
Ramsay, John, 2
Randall, John, 86
Ranjitsinhji, Prince, 70
Ranking, John, 59
"Rapier," SEE Watson, A. E. T.
Rarey, J. S., 68
Rawlins, J. T., 52
Rawstorne, L., 52
Raymond, 87
Reed, W., 125
Revnardson, Birch, 3, 116
Ribblesdale, Lord, 94
Rice, Jas., 60
Rice, Wm., 67, 124
Richardson, Capt. M., 62
Roberts, J. and H., 120
Roberts, Sir R., 55
Roberts, Saml., 121
Roberts, T., 41
Robinson, J. R., 86
Roland, Geo., 130
Roland, Jos., 4
Rolando, Guzman, 12
Ronald, Geo., 69
Ronalds, A., 49
Roosevelt, Theodore, 65, 95, 137
Ross, Chas. H., 139

Roth, A., 38
Rowlandson, Thos., Books Illustrated by or in his style:
    Advice to Sportsmen, 2
    Annals of Sporting, 8-9
    Comforts of Bath, 27
    Dance of Life, The, 35
    Doctor Comicus, 38
    English Dance of Death, 41
    Horse Accomplishments, 61
    Hungarian Broad Sword, 63
    Humourist, The, 63
    Ingeniously Tormenting, 43
    Johnny Quæ Genus, 66
    Matrimonial Comforts, 76
    Military Adventures of Johnny Newcome, 78
    Old English Squire, 86
    Pleasures of Human Life, 91
    Qui Hi? in Hindustan, 55
    Sketches of the Lower Orders, 21
    Syntax in Paris, 122
    Tom Raw, the Griffin, 125
    Tour of Dr. Syntax, 126
    Treatise on Education, 27
    Utility of Fencing, 131
Roworth, C., 11
Russell, Rev. Jno., 77

S.

S. (J.), 132
St. John, C. W. G., 107, 125
St. John, C., 81
St. John, H. C., 84
Salgado, J., 66
Saltau, G. W., 132
Salter, R., 78
Salter, T. F., 6, 141
Salvin, F. H., 45
Sandeman, J., 8, 23
Sanderson, Geo. P., 123
San Donato, Prince de, SEE Demidor, A.
Satchell, T., 142
Saunders, Jas., 30
Saumer, G. de, 145
Saviolo, V., 59

Scarlett, G. M., 55
Schlegel and Wulverhorst, 123
Schreiner, W. H., 104
Scott, J., 60, 120
Scott, S., 142
"Scott, William Henry," 22, 80
Scrope, Wm., 11, 35, 119
"Scrutator," SEE Horlock, K. W.
Sebright, Sir J. S., 85
Segar, Sir W., 21, 61
Selkirk, G. H., 56
Selous, F. C., 128, 145
Seymour, Richd., 30
Seymour, Robert, 43, 75, 109, 147
"Shadow," 78
Shakespear, Hy., 138
Sharp, Henry, 93
Shearman, M., 15
Shields, G. O., 33
Shipley, Wm., 132
Shirley, E. P., 110
Shirley, Thomas, 141
Sidney, Samuel, 20
Silver, Geo., 88
Simeon, C., 121
Sinclair, Captain, 34
Sinclair, A., 16
Sinigaglia, L., 23
Sketchley, W., 26
Smeeton, Geo., 38
Smith, Alex., 30
Smith, Albert, 121
Smith, C. L., 109
Smith, Horace, 47
Smith, J. T., 134
Smith, Thomas, 45, 73, 119
Smith, Tom, 114
"Snaffle," 56
Solleysell, Jacques de, 31, 148
Somerville, Wm., 24, 34, 60
"South, Theophilus," SEE Chitty, E.
Speedy, Thos., 111
Spiller, T., 23
"Sportsman, A," 130
Springfield, Rollo, 61
Steedman, Chas., 76
Steel, A. G., 15
Stevens, Chas., 75

Stevenson, Matthew, 133
Steward, Chas., 81
Stewart, W. C., 92
Stocqueler, J. H., 17
Stoddart, T., 6
Stoddart, T. T., 8, 11
Stone, S. J., 66
"Stonehenge," SEE Walsh, J. H.
Stradanus, J., 134
Strutt, Jos., 116
Stuart, Chas. Edw., 71
Stuart, John, 19
Stuart, John Sobieski, 71
Stubbs, Geo., 5
Sturgess, Jno., 17, 33, 51, 85, 86, 94
Suffolk, Earl of, 16, 41
Sullivan, Sir E., 16
Surtees, R. S., 4, 14, 57, 59, 69, 80, 91, 110
Swayne, H. G. C., 106
Swetnam, Joseph, 103
Swiflet, R., 76
Swift, Owen, 57
Syntax, Dr., SEE Combe, Wm.
"Syntax," Dr., 127, 136

T

Taplin, Wm., 113
Tartaglia, N., 123
Tattersall, Geo., 33, 89, 113
Taunton, T., 46
Taunton, T. H., 91
Taylor, Jas., 34
Theakston, M., 147
Thevenot, M., 13
Thibault, G., 1
Thom, Walter, 89
"Thomas, B.," SEE Johnson, T. B.
Thomas, H. S., 100
Thompson, R. F. M., 149
Thormanby, SEE Dixon, Wilmot
Thornhill, R. B., 107
Thornton, A., 38
Thornton, Col. Thos., 116, 119
Tolfrey, F., 56, 117
Tomlinson, K., 11
Tongue, C., 65, 97, 120, 121

"Touchstone, S. F.," 60
Tristram, W. O., 26
Turberville, Geo., 21, 83
Turner, Sir James, 88
Turnor, C. H., 14
"Twenty-Bore," 149
Twici, Wm., 12
Tyndall, Jno., 55, 62, 80

U

Umlauft, F., 140
Underhill, G. F., 124

V.

Valdin, M., 12
"Vates," 87, 114
Venables, Col. R., 44
"Venator," SEE Cooper, John
"Veteran Traveller, A," SEE Wilson, W. R.
Vyner, R. T., 85

W.

Wade, H., 100
Walker, C. E., 148
Walker, Dr., 143
Walker, Donald, 104
Walker's Hunting Atlas, 51
Wallwork, Jas., 78, 147
Walrond, Col. H., 15
Walsh, J. H., 56, 62, 76, 108
Walsingham, Lord, 16
Walton, Elijah, 88
Walton, Isaac, 27
"Wanderer," 2, 14, 45, 75
Warburton, R. E. E., 65, 124
Ward, R., 41, 96, 119
Wase, Chr., 84
Watson, A. E. T., 14, 94, 109, 133, 149
Watt, W., 97
Webber, Byron, 70
Webster, David, 5
Weir, Harrison, 76
Westmacott, W., 42
Wheeley, C. H., 141

Whitaker, Jas, 36
White, Jas, 66
White, J. C., 60
White ("Martingale"), 70, 115
"Whitefeather, Capt. Barabbas," SEE Jerrold, D
Whitehead, C. E., 23
Whymper, Ed., 14, 105, 128
Wildrake (The Artist), 59, 64
"Wildrake," SEE Tattersall, Geo.
"Wildfowler," 107
Wilkinson, G. T., 82
Williams, C., 2, 75, 127
Williamson, A., 111
Williamson, Jno., 21
Williamson, T., 31, 87
Wills, A., 39, 135
Wilmot, Sir J. E., 98

Wilson, H. S., 3
Wilson, Jas., 100
Wilson W. R., 84
Wolley, C. Phillipps, 16
Wood, Wm., 41
Woodgate, W. B., 15
Woodward, G. M., 9, 40, 43, 61, 76
Wylde, Z., 144

X.
Xenophon, 34, 59

Y.
Young, J. H. L., 105

Z.
Zouch, Thos, 146

BIBLIOLIFE

Old Books Deserve a New Life
www.bibliolife.com

Did you know that you can get most of our titles in our trademark **EasyScript**™ print format? **EasyScript**™ provides readers with a larger than average typeface, for a reading experience that's easier on the eyes.

Did you know that we have an ever-growing collection of books in many languages?

Order online:
www.bibliolife.com/store

Or to exclusively browse our **EasyScript**™ collection:
www.bibliogrande.com

At BiblioLife, we aim to make knowledge more accessible by making thousands of titles available to you – quickly and affordably.

Contact us:
BiblioLife
PO Box 21206
Charleston, SC 29413

Printed in Great Britain by
Amazon.co.uk, Ltd.,
Marston Gate.